LEARNING BEYOND THE CLASSROOM

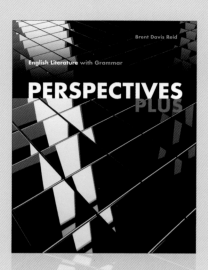

 COMPANION **web+** ™

D1316021

Go to the *Perspectives Plus Companion Website Plus* for

- supplementary readings for literary analysis;
- additional vocabulary and revision exercises to reinforce your writing skills;
- the Grammar and Style Guide eText, including links to over 100 exercises;
- instant feedback and automatic grading for all exercises;
- a grade book for teachers to track students' progress.

STUDENT ACCESS CODE

❶ Go to the Companion Website Plus address: ▶ **http://cw.pearsonelt.ca/perspectivesplus**

❷ Click on "Register" and then follow the onscreen instructions.

This access code is valid for **five months** from the date of registration.

Access code ▶

WARNING! This book CANNOT BE RETURNED if the sticker has been removed and the code, uncovered.

In need of assistance? Go to: ▶ http://247pearsoned.custhelp.com

TEACHER ACCESS CODE

To obtain a username and password for access to the Teacher Section of the Companion Website Plus, please contact your Pearson ELT consultant.

W134593 (A46900)

Brent Davis Reid

English Literature with Grammar

PERSPECTIVES PLUS

PEARSON

Montréal

Managing Editor
Patricia Hynes

Project Editor
Tessa Hearn

Proofreader
Stacey Berman

Coordinator, Rights and Permissions
Pierre Richard Bernier

Rights and Permissions
Marie-Chantal Masson

Art Director
Hélène Cousineau

Graphic Design Coordinator
Lyse LeBlanc

Book and Cover Design / Layout
Claire Senneville

Acknowledgements

I would like to thank those who helped make *Perspectives Plus* the best it can be: Julie Hough, Patricia Hynes and Tessa Hearn for miraculously transforming a manuscript into a manual; and Christian Giguère and Corinne Mäder for generously sharing their expertise.

I would also like to thank the following colleagues for kindly providing feedback: Jennifer Caylor, Cégep de Rimouski; Mira Facchin, Cégep de Saint-Hyacinthe; Stewart Johnson, Cégep régional de Lanaudière (Collège de L'Assomption); Nancie Kahan, Cégep de Saint-Jérôme; Sherry Kent, Cégep Saint-Jean-sur-Richelieu; Sandra Koop, Cégep Marie-Victorin; Sophie Nadon, Collège Ahuntsic; Denise Peter, Collège François-Xavier-Garneau; Rachel Tunnicliffe, Collège Mérici.

For Éric, whose personal narrative continues to inspire

Introduction

Perspectives Plus: English Literature with Grammar is the second in a series of two college-level textbooks designed for advanced students of English. The first volume, *Perspectives: English Skills with Grammar*, is a high-intermediate textbook focusing on English language and culture; *Perspectives Plus: English Literature with Grammar* is an advanced textbook focusing on English language and literature.

In *Perspectives Plus*, students are presented with a variety of literary works, both fictional (short poems, short stories) and non-fictional (memoirs). Through careful reading, guiding questions and the study of four key literary elements (theme, character and characterization, setting and narrative point of view) and of literary techniques (alliteration, foreshadowing, irony, metaphor, simile, etc.), students are led to interpret an interesting array of contemporary Canadian writings.

Perspectives Plus features the following components:
• Seven theme-based units
• A comprehensive grammar and style guide
• Three appendices, covering the formal analytical essay, the formal analytical speech and researching, referencing and revising
• A literary handbook
• A Companion Website Plus

The first unit is recommended for all students as it presents the underlying concept of the *Perspectives* series: each person formulates opinions from a different perspective, and these perspectives demand understanding and respect if everyone is to participate fully and authentically in society. The remaining six units deal with the universal topics of solitude, survival, the future, the nature of evil, lost youth and leaving; these units can be dealt with in any order, in part or in whole. In all seven units, words in **bold** are literary terms defined in the *Literary Handbook*. Each unit focuses on one of four literary elements: Unit 1, on theme; Units 2 and 5, on character and characterization; Units 3 and 6, on setting; and Units 4 and 7, on narrative point of view. It is necessary to examine all four literary elements before reading and analyzing any of the fourteen fictional literary works in *Perspectives Plus*, and it is advisable to examine the appendices before preparing a formal analytical essay or speech.

An important part of the *Perspectives* series is the Grammar and Style Guide, also available as an eText on the Companion Website. As students review grammar notions and writing style in their books, they are reminded to practise their skills on the website, which contains more than 100 grammar and style exercises. The website also offers exercises to reinforce vocabulary and practise revision skills.

As a whole, *Perspectives Plus* invites students to dialogue with other intelligences—authors, classmates and the teacher—giving students the opportunity to hear or experience something outside of their usual way of thinking. In other words, *Perspectives Plus* invites students to learn something that, it is hoped, will enrich their education and their lives.

Brent Davis Reid

Highlights

The **Preview** section offers background for the topic explored in the unit.

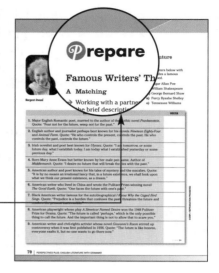

The **Prepare** section contains a warm-up activity on the unit topic.

The **Ponder** section usually opens with a short poem and related vocabulary, comprehension and discussion questions. Two longer readings follow; they are either short stories or memoirs and are developed more fully than the introductory readings.

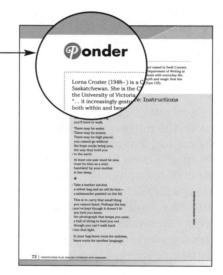

After reading fictional works, students analyze them for one of four **literary elements**: theme, character and characterization, setting or narrative point of view. In-depth **discussion questions** encourage further critical thinking.

Vocabulary exercises are integrated in the reading activities. Further practice is provided on the Companion Website.

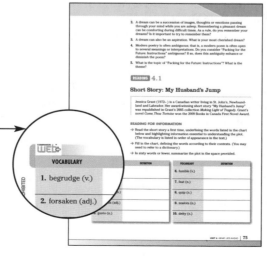

In the **Post** section, students are asked to produce various types of texts, from paragraphs to essays.

The **Present** section provides topics for one short speaking activity and one longer formal speech.

The **Participate** section presents a joint writing or speaking project that fosters collaborative learning.

Suggestions of works for further study of the unit topic are listed in the **Pursue** section.

Three **appendices** contain guidelines for writing an analytical essay, preparing an analytical speech, and researching, referencing and revising.

The **Grammar and Style Guide**, also available as an eText on the Companion Website, reviews essential grammar notions and covers basic elements of good writing style. Extensive practice is provided on the Companion Website.

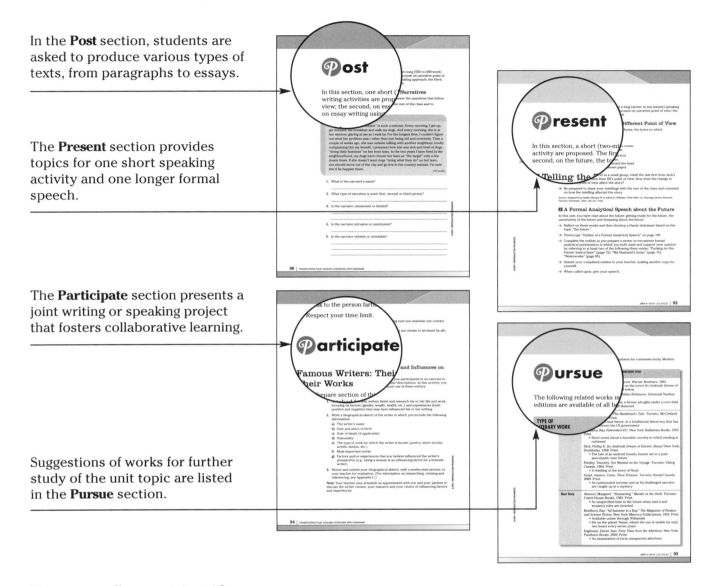

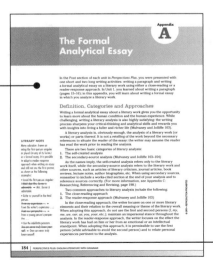

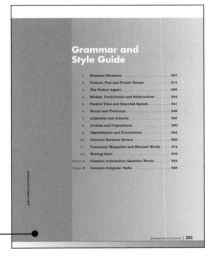

Scope and Sequence

	UNIT 1 Understanding Perspectives ... and More	UNIT 2 Solitary Lives	UNIT 3 Surviving and Thriving
Reading	• Identify factors influencing opinion • Demonstrate reading comprehension • Identify topic and theme • Read a short story and a novel	• Demonstrate reading comprehension • Identify topics and themes • Read a poem and two short stories	• Demonstrate reading comprehension • Identify topics and themes • Read a short story and a memoir
Writing	• Write a 60-word plot summary • Write a 100- to 150-word paragraph • Write a 550- to 600-word essay on theme or on questions about perspective • Write a report on a novel	• Write two 60-word plot summaries • Write a 100- to 150-word paragraph about first impressions • Write a 550- to 600-word essay on character and characterization or on solitude/loneliness	• Write a 60-word plot summary • Write a 100- to 150-word paragraph about a memorable moment • Write a 550- to 600-word essay on setting or on questions about survival/thriving
Listening	• Demonstrate understanding of / respect for others' opinions	• Demonstrate understanding of / respect for others' opinions	• Listen to a story and sequence events • Demonstrate understanding of/respect for others' opinions
Speaking	• Share opinions about topics presented in the textbook • Express agreement/ disagreement • Discuss a short story • Adopt a different opinion/ perspective • Brainstorm ideas • Examine the effect of detail on theme in art • Present a 7- to 10-minute formal analytical speech about influences on perspective • Discuss a novel	• Distinguish loneliness from solitude • Discuss and support opinions • Adopt a different opinion/perspective • Interpret character traits from works of art • Present a 7- to 10-minute formal analytical speech about loneliness • Apply a personality test to a character studied and discuss the results	• Take and discuss a survival quiz • Discuss and support opinions • Discuss a story in the oral tradition, a short story and a memoir • Adopt a different opinion/ perspective • Discuss the influences of setting on plot • Present a 7- to 10-minute formal analytical speech about survival • Tell a survival story
Vocabulary	• Define words from context • Find synonyms	• Define words from context • Find synonyms	• Define words from context • Find synonyms • Find defined words
Critical Thinking	• Analyze theme • Analyze a paragraph • Interpret a short story • Consider influences on opinions • Identify, explain and interpret literary techniques: irony and simile	• Analyze character and characterization • Interpret a poem and two short stories • Identify, explain and interpret literary techniques: symbolism, irony, alliteration, simile and onomatopoeia	• Analyze dramatic structure (plot) • Analyze setting • Interpret a short story • Identify, explain and interpret literary techniques: simile, foreshadowing, image, symbolism and juxtaposition

UNIT 4 What Lies Ahead	UNIT 5 What Lies Beneath	UNIT 6 Childhood Revisited	UNIT 7 Leaving
• Demonstrate reading comprehension • Identify topics and themes • Read a poem, a short story and a memoir	• Demonstrate reading comprehension • Identify topics and themes • Read three short stories	• Demonstrate reading comprehension • Identify topics and themes • Read a poem, a short story and a memoir	• Demonstrate reading comprehension • Identify topics and themes • Read a poem, a short story and a memoir
• Write a 60-word plot summary • Write a 100- to 150-word narrative in the first or third person • Write a 550- to 600-word essay on narrative point of view or on questions about the future • Write a biographical sketch of a famous writer	• Write two 60-word plot summaries • Write a 100- to 150-word paragraph for an in-role writing assignment • Write a 550- to 600-word essay on character and characterization or on questions about misbehaviour • Write a film character analysis	• Write a 60-word plot summary • Write a 100- to 150-word introductory paragraph to a short story, clearly establishing setting • Write a 550- to 600-word essay on setting or on questions about childhood • Write a report about establishing "where and when" (setting) in visual works	• Write a 60-word plot summary • Write a 100- to 150-word paragraph from a point of view that differs from the narrator's • Write a 550- to 600-word essay on narrative point of view or on questions about leaving • Write a short short story
• Demonstrate understanding of / respect for others' opinions	• Demonstrate understanding of / respect for others' opinions	• Demonstrate understanding of / respect for others' opinions	• Demonstrate understanding of / respect for others' opinions
• Match famous writers with famous quotations about the future and discuss • Discuss and support opinions • Adopt a different opinion/perspective • Tell a nursery rhyme from different points of view • Present a 7- to 10-minute formal analytical speech about the future	• Qualify and discuss bad behaviour • Discuss and support opinions • Adopt a different opinion/perspective • Participate in a "hot seat" discussion • Present a 7- to 10-minute formal analytical speech about malice	• Support opinions • Discuss and support opinions • Adopt a different opinion/perspective • Participate in an improvisation • Discuss the impact of setting on plot • Present a 7- to 10-minute formal analytical speech about childhood	• Support opinions • Discuss and support opinions • Adopt a different opinion/perspective • Participate in the retelling of a short story from a point of view that differs from the narrator's • Present a 7- to 10-minute formal analytical speech about leaving
• Define words from context • Find synonyms • Find defined words	• Define words from context • Find synonyms	• Define words from context • Find synonyms • Find defined words	• Define words from context • Find synonyms • Find defined words
• Analyze narrative point of view • Interpret a poem and a short story • Identify, explain and interpret literary techniques: simile, symbolism, personification, repetition, allusion, metaphor, irony and allegory	• Analyze character and characterization • Interpret three short stories • Identify, explain and interpret literary techniques: irony, foreshadowing, simile, epiphany, allusion and metaphor	• Analyze setting • Interpret a poem and a short story • Identify, explain and interpret literary techniques: repetition, simile, synecdoche, onomatopoeia, allusion, metonymy, hyperbole, metaphor and sarcasm	• Analyze narrative point of view • Interpret a poem and a short story • Identify, explain and interpret literary techniques: personification, allusion, foreshadowing, irony, simile and symbolism

Table of Contents

Understanding Perspectives ... and More

People descending
a spiral staircase

review

Have you ever wondered what other people think of you? Do you think they all have the same opinion of you, or do opinions differ? Do your parents think of you in the same way that your grandparents do? What about your friends and your enemies? Your teachers and your classmates? As you probably already know, no two people share the exact same opinion of you—or of anyone or anything else for that matter. Opinions differ. Now why should this be so? Well, it's all a matter of perspective.

Each person formulates opinions from a different perspective, one shaped by factors (age, gender, health, wealth, race, sexual orientation, etc.) and experiences (both positive and negative) that are uniquely his or her own. *Who we are* and *what we have experienced* influence our opinions: they influence our perspectives.

In this introductory unit, you will read a short story about an elderly Canadian woman who is viewed by different characters in a variety of ways. Few of these viewpoints would please her very much were she to become aware of them. The story was selected for the introductory unit of *Perspectives Plus* because it serves as a **metaphor** for the unifying theme of the textbook: a person, object or concept can be viewed in completely different ways depending on individual perspectives—and each of these individual perspectives deserves to be understood, if not necessarily adopted.

You will be reading a number of literary works in this textbook. As you read, please bear the following in mind: "… Once [you've] understood an author's perspective, [you] may choose to resist it. But whether [you] accept, adapt or resist an author's perspective, [you] must first understand it" (Smith, quoted in Smith and Wilhelm 121).

Enjoy the stories!

What Do You Think?

Below is a list of statements based on subjects covered in this textbook.

→ In the spaces provided, indicate your level of disagreement or agreement with each of the statements.

→ Be prepared to discuss your answers.

1	2	3	4	5
Strongly disagree	Disagree	Undecided	Agree	Strongly agree

STATEMENTS

LEVEL OF AGREEMENT

1. A person's true wealth is better measured by the number of stories she or he has to tell than by the amount of money she or he has to spend. _____

2. Everyone has a valuable story to tell. _____

3. Getting to know literary characters can be a life-changing experience. _____

4. No perspective has a monopoly on the truth. _____

5. Stories from the past merit present-day consideration. _____

6. The *where* and *when* of your life influence what you do. _____

7. The teller affects the tale. _____

8. You have to put yourself in someone else's shoes before you can truly understand that person. _____

9. We all think alike. _____

10. You can never truly see yourself. _____

onder

Short Story: Mrs. Turner Cutting the Grass

Carol Shields (1935–2003) was born in Illinois. She married Donald Hugh Shields, a Canadian with whom she had five children. She became a Canadian citizen in 1971 and received an MA in English from the University of Ottawa. She was appointed chancellor of the University of Winnipeg in 1996 and was made a Companion of the Order of Canada in 2002, a year before she died of breast cancer. She is known mostly as an author of novels and short stories, two of which are listed in the Pursue section of this unit. The story reprinted here, "Mrs. Turner Cutting the Grass," first appeared in the short-story collection *Various Miracles* (Toye 575–577).

READING FOR INFORMATION

→ Read the short story a first time, underlining the words listed in the chart below and highlighting information essential to understanding the plot. (The vocabulary is listed in order of appearance in the text.)

→ Fill in the chart, defining the words according to their contexts. (You may need to refer to a dictionary.)

→ In sixty words or fewer, summarize the plot in the space provided.

COMPANION
web+

VOCABULARY	DEFINITION	VOCABULARY	DEFINITION
1. queasy (adj.)		**6.** gnarled (adj.)	
2. lad (n.)		**7.** paltry (adj.)	
3. wretched (adj.)		**8.** cluttered (adj.)	
4. foundling (n.)		**9.** avuncular (adj.)	
5. mottled (adj.)		**10.** relish (v.)	

Mrs. Turner Cutting the Grass

by Carol Shields

Oh, Mrs. Turner is a sight cutting the grass on a hot afternoon in June! She climbs into an ancient pair of shorts and ties on her halter top and wedges her feet into crepe-soled sandals and covers her red-grey frizz with Gord's old golf cap—Gord is dead now, ten years ago, a seizure on a Saturday night
5 while winding the mantel clock.

The grass flies up around Mrs. Turner's knees. Why doesn't she use a catcher, the Saschers next door wonder. Everyone knows that leaving the clippings like that is bad for the lawn. Each fallen blade of grass throws a minute shadow that impedes growth and repair. The Saschers themselves
10 use their clippings to make compost, which they hope one day will be as ripe as the good manure that Sally Sascher's father used to spread on his fields down near Emerson Township.

Mrs. Turner's carelessness over the clippings plucks away at Sally, but her husband, Roy, is far more concerned about the Killex that Mrs. Turner
15 dumps on her dandelions. It's true that in Winnipeg the dandelion roots go right to the middle of the earth, but Roy is patient and persistent in pulling them out, knowing exactly how to grasp the coarse leaves in his hand and how much pressure to apply. Mostly they come up like corks with their roots intact. And he and Sally are experimenting with new ways to cook
20 dandelion greens, believing as they do that the components of nature are arranged for a specific purpose—if only that purpose can be divined.

In the early summer Mrs. Turner is out every morning by ten with her sprinkling can of chemical killer, and Roy, watching from his front porch, imagines how this poison will enter the ecosystem and move by quick
25 capillary surges into his fenced vegetable plot, newly seeded now with green beans and lettuce. His children, his two little girls aged two and four—that they should be touched by such poison makes him morose and

angry. But he and Sally so far have said nothing to Mrs. Turner about her abuse of the planet because they're hoping she'll go into an old-folks home
30 soon or maybe die, and then all will proceed as it should.

High school girls on their way home in the afternoon see Mrs. Turner cutting her grass and are mildly, momentarily repelled by the lapped, striated flesh on her upper thighs. At her age. Doesn't she realize? Every last one of them is intimate with the vocabulary of skin care and knows that
35 what has claimed Mrs. Turner's thighs is the enemy called cellulite, but they can't understand why she doesn't take the trouble to hide it. It makes them queasy; it makes them fear for the future.

The things Mrs. Turner doesn't know would fill the Saschers' new compost pit, would sink a ship, would set off a tidal wave, would make her want to
40 kill herself. Back and forth, back and forth she goes with the electric lawn mower, the grass flying out sideways like whiskers. Oh, the things she doesn't know! She has never heard, for example, of the folk-rock recording star Neil Young, though the high school just around the corner from her house happens to be the very school Neil Young attended as a lad. His initials can
45 actually be seen carved on one of the desks, and a few of the teachers say they remember him, a quiet fellow of neat appearance and always very polite in class. The desk with the initials N.Y. is kept in a corner of Mr. Pring's homeroom, and it's considered lucky—despite the fact that the renowned singer wasn't a great scholar—to touch the incised letters just before an
50 exam. Since it's exam time now, the second week of June, the girls walking past Mrs. Turner's front yard (and shuddering over her display of cellulite) are carrying on their fingertips the spiritual scent, the essence, the fragrance, the aura of Neil Young, but Mrs. Turner is as ignorant of that fact as the girls are that she, Mrs. Turner, possesses a first name—which is Geraldine.

55 Not that she's ever been called Geraldine. Where she grew up in Boissevain, Manitoba, she was known always—the Lord knows why—as Girlie Fergus, the youngest of the three Fergus girls and the one who got herself in hot water. Her sister Em went to normal school and her sister Muriel went to Brandon to work at Eaton's, but Girlie got caught one night—she was nineteen—in a
60 Boissevain hotel room with a local farmer, married, named Gus MacGregor. It was her father who got wind of where she might be and came banging on the door, shouting and weeping. "Girlie, Girlie, what have you done to me?"

Girlie had been working in the Boissevain Dairy since she'd left school at sixteen and had a bit of money saved up, and so, a week after the
65 humiliation in the local hotel, she wrote a farewell note to the family, crept out of the house at midnight and caught the bus to Winnipeg. From there she got another bus down to Minneapolis, then to Chicago and finally New York City. The journey was endless and wretched, and on the way across Indiana and Ohio and Pennsylvania she saw hundreds and hundreds of
70 towns whose unpaved streets and narrow blinded houses made her fear some conspiratorial, punishing power had carried her back to Boissevain. Her father's soppy-stern voice sang and sang in her ears as the wooden bus rattled its way eastward. It was summer, 1930.

CULTURAL NOTE

Neil Young is a Canadian rock singer-songwriter born in Toronto in 1945 and raised in Ontario and Manitoba. He formed his first band as a student at Earl Grey Junior High School in Fort Rouge, Winnipeg. He has won Juno and Grammy awards and has been inducted into the Canadian Music Hall of Fame and the Rock and Roll Hall of Fame. He was made an Officer of the Order of Canada in 2009.

New York, 1930

New York was immense and wonderful, dirty, perilous and puzzling. She found herself longing for a sight of real earth, which she assumed must lie somewhere beneath the tough pavement. On the other hand, the brown flat-roofed factories with their little windows tilted skyward pumped her full of happiness, as did the dusty trees, when she finally discovered them, lining the long avenues. Every last person in the world seemed to be outside, walking around, filling the streets, and every corner breezed with noise and sunlight. She had to pinch herself to believe this was the same sunlight that filtered its way into the rooms of the house back in Boissevain, fading the curtains but nourishing her mother's ferns. She sent postcards to Em and Muriel that said, "Don't worry about me. I've got a job in the theatre business."

It was true. For eight and a half months she was an usherette in the Lamar Movie Palace in Brooklyn. She loved her perky maroon uniform, the way it fit on her shoulders, the way the strips of crinkly gold braid outlined her figure. With a little flashlight in hand she was able to send streams of light across the furry darkness of the theatre and onto the plum-coloured aisle carpet. The voices from the screen talked on and on. She felt after a time that their resonant declarations and tender replies belonged to her.

She met a man named Kiki her first month in New York and moved in with him. His skin was as black as ebony. *As black as ebony*—that was the phrase that hung like a ribbon on the end of his name, and it's also the phrase she uses, infrequently, when she wants to call up his memory, though she's more than a little doubtful about what *ebony* is. It may be a kind of stone, she thinks, something round and polished that comes out of a deep mine.

Kiki was a good-hearted man, though she didn't like the beer he drank, and he stayed with her, willingly, for several months after she had to stop working because of the baby. It was the baby itself that frightened him off, the way it cried, probably. Leaving fifty dollars on the table, he slipped out one July afternoon when Girlie was shopping, and went back to Troy, New York, where he'd been raised.

Her first thought was to take the baby and get on a bus and go find him, but there wasn't enough money, and the thought of the baby crying all the way on the hot bus made her feel tired. She was worried about the rent and about the little red sores in the baby's ears—it was a boy, rather sweetly formed, with wonderful smooth feet and hands. On a murderously hot night, a night when the humidity was especially bad, she wrapped him in a clean piece of sheeting and carried him all the way to Brooklyn Heights, where the houses were large and solid and surrounded by grass. There was a house on a corner she particularly liked because it had a wide front porch (like those in Boissevain) with a curved railing—and parked on the porch, its brake on, was a beautiful wicker baby carriage. It was here that she placed her baby, giving one last look to his sleeping face, as round and calm as the moon.

She walked home, taking her time, swinging her legs. If she had known the word *foundling*—which she didn't—she would have bounded along on its rhythmic back, so airy and wide did the world seem that night.

Most of these secrets she keeps locked away inside her mottled thighs or
125 in the curled pinkness of her genital flesh. She has no idea what happened to Kiki, whether he ever went off to Alaska as he wanted to or whether he fell down a flight of stone steps in the silverware factory in Troy, New York, and died of head injuries before his thirtieth birthday. Or what happened to her son—whether he was bitten that night in the baby carriage by a rabid
130 neighbourhood cat or whether he was discovered the next morning and adopted by the large, loving family who lived in the house. As a rule, Girlie tries not to think about the things she can't even guess at. All she thinks is that she did the best she could under the circumstances.

In a year she saved enough money to take the train home to Boissevain.
135 She took with her all her belongings, and also gifts for Em and Muriel, boxes of hose, bottles of apple-blossom cologne, phonograph records. For her mother she took an embroidered apron and for her father a pipe made of curious gnarled wood. "Girlie, my Girlie," her father said, embracing her at the Boissevain station. Then he said, "Don't ever leave us again," in a way
140 that frightened her and made her resolve to leave as quickly as possible.

But she didn't go so far the second time around. She and Gordon Turner—he was, for all his life, a tongue-tied man, though he did manage a proper proposal—settled down in Winnipeg, first in St. Boniface, where the rents were cheap, and then Fort Rouge and finally the little house in River
145 Heights just around the corner from the high school. It was her husband, Gord, who planted the grass that Mrs. Turner now shaves in the summertime. It was Gord who trimmed and shaped the caragana hedge and Gord who painted the little shutters with the cut-out hearts. He was a man who loved every inch of his house, the wide wooden steps, the oak door with its
150 glass inset, the radiators and the baseboards and the snug sash windows. And he loved every inch of his wife, Girlie, too, saying to her once and only once that he knew about her past (meaning Gus MacGregor and the incident in the Boissevain Hotel), and that as far as he was concerned the slate had been wiped clean. Once he came home with a little package in his
155 pocket; inside was a diamond ring, delicate and glittering. Once he took Girlie on a picnic all the way up to Steep Rock, and in the woods he took off her dress and underthings and kissed every part of her body.

After he died, Girlie began to travel. She was far from rich, as she liked to say, but with care she could manage one trip every spring.

160 She has never known such ease. She and Em and Muriel have been to Disneyland as well as Disneyworld. They've been to Europe, taking a sixteen-day trip through seven countries. The three of them have visited the south and seen the famous antebellum houses of Georgia, Alabama and Mississippi, after which they spent a week in the city of New Orleans. They went to
165 Mexico one year and took pictures of Mayan ruins and queer shadowy gods cut squarely from stone. And three years ago they did what they swore they'd never have the nerve to do: they got on an airplane and went to Japan.

The package tour started in Tokyo, where Mrs. Turner ate, on her first night there, a chrysanthemum fried in hot oil. She saw a village where everyone earned a living by making dolls and another village where everyone made pottery. Members of the tour group, each holding up a green flag so their tour leader could keep track of them, climbed on a little train, zoomed off to Osaka, where they visited an electronics factory, and then went to a restaurant to eat uncooked fish. They visited more temples and shrines than Mrs. Turner could keep track of. Once they stayed the night in a Japanese hotel, where she and Em and Muriel bedded down on floor mats and little pillows stuffed with cracked wheat, and woke up, laughing, with backaches and shooting pains in their legs.

That was the same day they visited the Golden Pavilion in Kyoto. The three-storied temple was made of wood and had a roof like a set of wings and was painted a soft old flaky gold. Everybody in the group took pictures —Em took a whole roll—and bought postcards; everybody, that is, except a single tour member, the one they all referred to as the Professor.

The Professor travelled without a camera, but jotted notes almost continuously into a little pocket scribbler. He was bald, had a trim body and wore Bermuda shorts, sandals and black nylon socks. Those who asked him learned that he really was a professor, a teacher of English poetry in a small college in Massachusetts. He was also a poet who, at the time of the Japanese trip, had published two small chapbooks[1] based mainly on the breakdown of his marriage. The poems, sadly, had not caused much stir.

It grieved him to think of that paltry, guarded, nut-like thing that was his artistic reputation. His domestic life had been too cluttered; there had been too many professional demands; the political situation in America had drained him of energy—these were the thoughts that buzzed in his skull as he scribbled and scribbled, like a man with a fever, in the back seat of a tour bus travelling through Japan.

Here in this crowded, confused country he discovered simplicity and order and something spiritual too, which he recognized as being authentic. He felt as though a flower, something like a lily, only smaller and tougher, had unfurled in his hand and was nudging along his fountain pen. He wrote and wrote, shaken by catharsis, but lulled into a new sense of his powers.

Not surprisingly, a solid little book of poems came out of his experience. It was published soon afterward by a well-thought-of Boston publisher who, as soon as possible, sent him around the United States to give poetry readings.

---

1. small book of poetry

The Professor read his poems mostly in universities and colleges where his book was already listed on the Contemporary Poetry course. He read in 215 faculty clubs, student centres, classrooms, gymnasiums and auditoriums, and usually, partway through a reading, someone or other would call from the back of the room, "Give us your Golden Pavilion poem."

He would have preferred to read his Fuji meditation or the tone poem on the Inner Sea, but he was happy to oblige his audiences, though he felt 220 "A Day at the Golden Pavilion" was a somewhat light piece, even what is sometimes known on the circuit as a "crowd pleaser." People (admittedly they were mostly undergraduates) laughed out loud when they heard it; he read it well too, in a moist, avuncular amateur actor's voice, reminding himself to pause frequently, to look upward and raise an ironic eyebrow.

225 The poem was not really about the Golden Pavilion at all, but about three midwestern lady tourists who, while viewing the temple and madly snapping photos, had talked incessantly and in loud, flat-bottomed voices about knitting patterns, indigestion, sore feet, breast lumps, the cost of plastic raincoats and a previous trip they'd made together to Mexico. They had 230 wondered, these three—noisily, repeatedly—who back home in Manitoba should receive a postcard, what they'd give for an honest cup of tea, if there was an easy way to remove stains from an electric coffee maker, and where they would go the following year—Hawaii? They were the three furies, the three witches, who for vulgarity and tastelessness formed a shattering 235 counterpoint to the Professor's own state of transcendence. He had been affronted, angered, half-crazed.

LITERARY NOTE

The Furies are spirits of punishment from Greek mythology, often represented as three goddesses: Allecto, Megaera and Tisiphone.

William-Adolphe Bouguereau, *Orestes Pursued by the Furies,* circa 1862

One of the sisters, a little pug of a woman, particularly stirred his contempt, she of the pink pantsuit, the red toe-nails, the grapefruity buttocks, the overly bright souvenirs, 240 the garish Mexican straw bag containing Dentyne chewing gum, aspirin, breath mints, sun goggles, envelopes of saccharin, and photos of her dead husband standing in front of a squat, ugly house in Winnipeg. This defilement she had spread before the ancient and exquisitely 245 proportioned Golden Pavilion of Kyoto, proving—and here the Professor's tone became grave—proving that sublime beauty can be brought to the very doorway of human eyes, ears and lips and remain unperceived.

When he comes to the end of "A Day at the Golden 250 Pavilion" there is generally a thoughtful half second of silence, then laughter and applause. Students turn in their seats and exchange looks with their fellows. They have seen such unspeakable tourists themselves. There was old Auntie Marigold or Auntie Flossie. There was that tacky Mrs. Shannon with her rouge and her jewellery. They know— 255 despite their youth they know—the irreconcilable distance between taste and banality. Or perhaps that's too harsh; perhaps it's only the difference between those who know about the world and those who don't.

It's true that Mrs. Turner remembers little about her travels. She's never had much of a head for history or dates; she never did learn, for instance, the difference between a Buddhist temple and a Shinto shrine. She gets on a tour bus and goes and goes, and that's all there is to it. She doesn't know if she's going north or south or east or west. What does it matter? She's having a grand time. And she's reassured, always, by the sameness of the world. She's never heard the word *commonality*, but is nevertheless fused with its sense. In Japan she was made as happy to see carrots and lettuce growing in the fields as she was to see sunlight, years earlier, pouring into the streets of New York City. Everywhere she's been she's seen people eating and sleeping and working and making things with their hands and urging things to grow. There have been cats and dogs, fences and bicycles and telephone poles, and objects to buy and take care of; it is amazing, she thinks, that she can understand so much of the world and that it comes to her as easily as bars of music floating out of a radio.

Her sisters have long forgotten about her wild days. Now the three of them love to sit on tour buses and chatter away about old friends and family members, their stern father and their mother who never once took their part against him. Muriel carries on about her children (a son in California and a daughter in Toronto), and she brings along snaps of her grandchildren to pass round. Em has retired from school teaching and is a volunteer in the Boissevain Local History Museum, to which she has donated several family mementos: her father's old carved pipe and her mother's wedding veil and, in a separate case, for all the world to see, a white cotton garment labelled "Girlie Fergus's Underdrawers, handmade, trimmed with lace, circa 1918." If Mrs. Turner knew the word *irony* she would relish this. Even without knowing the word *irony*, she relishes it.

The professor from Massachusetts has won an important international award for his book of poems; translation rights have been sold to a number of foreign publishers; and recently his picture appeared in the *New York Times*, along with a lengthy quotation from "A Day at the Golden Pavilion." How providential, some will think, that Mrs. Turner doesn't read the *New York Times* or attend poetry readings, for it might injure her deeply to know how she appears in certain people's eyes, but then there are so many things she doesn't know.

In the summer, as she cuts the grass, to and fro, to and fro, she waves to everyone she sees. She waves to the high school girls, who timidly wave back. She hollers hello to Sally and Roy Sascher and asks them how their garden is coming on. She cannot imagine that anyone would wish her harm. All she's done is live her life. The green grass flies up in the air, a buoyant cloud swirling about her head. Oh, what a sight is Mrs. Turner cutting her grass, and how, like an ornament, she shines.

(3633 words)

Source: Shields, Carol. "Mrs. Turner Cutting the Grass." From *The Collected Stories of Carol Shields*. Toronto: Random House, 2004. 29–39. Print.

READING FOR MEANING

→ Read the questions below.

→ Read the short story a second and a third time (or more), answering the questions as you do so.

1. Describe Mrs. (Geraldine) Turner as she goes back and forth, cutting the grass. What does this description tell us about Mrs. Turner?

   _____

   _____

   _____

   _____

2. What does Mrs. Turner do that causes her neighbours, Sally and Roy Sascher, to hope she might be sent to an old-folks home soon or die? What does this shared hope tell us about their characters? And what does their decision not to confront Mrs. Turner about her actions tell us about them?

   _____

   _____

   _____

   _____

3. What is it about Mrs. Turner that repels the high school girls? What does this repulsion suggest about the girls?

   _____

   _____

4. In the summer of 1930, why does Mrs. Turner, at the time known as "Girlie Fergus," leave her hometown of Boissevain, Manitoba and move to New York City? What does her departure tell us about her character?

   _____

   _____

5. While living in New York City in the 1930s, Mrs. Turner—presumably a white woman, since her hair is described as a "red-grey frizz" (line 3)— meets and moves in with a Kiki, a black man. What does this relationship tell us about Mrs. Turner?

   _____

   _____

6. After Mrs. Turner gives birth to Kiki's baby son, Kiki leaves her and the baby. Worried about money and the baby's health, she abandons her baby to people living in what appears to be a nice home. What does the abandonment of her child tell us about Mrs. Turner?

   _____

   _____

7. Mrs. Turner abandons her son on "a murderously hot night" (line 113). Explain the significance of this description.

_____

_____

_____

8. As indicated in the previous question, it is "a murderously hot night" when Mrs. Turner abandons her baby. After the abandonment, the world seems "airy and wide" to Mrs. Turner. How is this change in setting significant?

_____

_____

_____

9. How does Gord feel about the house he and Mrs. Turner shared? How does the Professor feel about the house? Why do their feelings about the same house differ so?

_____

_____

_____

_____

_____

10. Where does the story take place? When does the story take place?

_____

_____

_____

_____

11. Compare and contrast the first and last sentences of the short story. What is implied in the first? What is implied in the last?

_____

_____

_____

_____

_____

LITERARY NOTE

Rhetoric is the study of the effective use of language. As a discipline, rhetoric teaches how language works, encouraging writers to apply what they have learned to their own writing and speaking (Burton). Rhetoric includes literary techniques such as **irony** and **simile**.

READING FOR RHETORIC

→ Throughout "Mrs. Turner Cutting the Grass," you will find examples of two common literary techniques: **irony** and **simile**. Answer the following questions, which deal with these two aspects of rhetoric.

1. Explain the **irony** of Gord's death.

_____

_____

2. Why is it **ironic** that Girlie Fergus's underdrawers are on exhibit at the Boissevain Local History Museum?

_____

_____

_____

_____

3. The Professor is contemptuous of Mrs. Turner's appearance, referring to her as a "pug of a woman" and mocking her for her "pink pantsuit, … red toenails, … grapefruity buttocks … and … garish Mexican straw bag." How are the Professor's contemptuousness and mockery **ironic**? What do his contempt and mockery reveal about his character?

_____

_____

_____

_____

4. In "Mrs. Turner Cutting the Grass," Carol Shields uses several **similes**. Fill in the chart below, indicating the enhanced meaning each **simile** brings to the work. The first one has been done for you as an example.

	LINES	SIMILE	ENHANCED MEANING
a)	98–101	"_As black as ebony_—that was the phrase that hung <u>like</u> a ribbon on the end of his name, and it's also the phrase she uses, infrequently, when she wants to call up his memory, though she's more than a little doubtful about what _ebony_ is."	• "_As black as ebony_ …": Ebony is a black, hard wood. Definite reference to Kiki's skin colour and possibly an allusion to his character: hard. (He abandoned Mrs. Turner and his baby.) • "… the phrase that hung like a ribbon on the end of his name …": The phrase helps Mrs. Turner to "pull out" Kiki's memory much in the same way a ribbon attached to an object allows you to pull that object out of something else.
b)	119–120	"It was here that she placed her baby, giving one last look to his sleeping face, <u>as</u> round and calm <u>as</u> the moon."	...........➤

	LINES	SIMILE	ENHANCED MEANING
c)	180–183	"The three-storied temple was made of wood and had a roof <u>like</u> a set of wings and was painted a soft old flaky gold."	
d)	200–204	"His domestic life had been too cluttered; there had been too many professional demands; the political situation in America had drained him of energy— these were the thoughts that buzzed in his skull as he scribbled and scribbled, <u>like</u> a man with a fever, in the back seat of a tour bus travelling through Japan."	
e)	298–299	"Oh, what a sight is Mrs. Turner cutting her grass, and how, <u>like</u> an ornament, she shines."	

EXAMINING AN ELEMENT: Theme

Working with a partner, examine the theme of "Mrs. Turner Cutting the Grass." Turn to pages 2–3 and 6–7 in the *Literary Handbook* for an explanation of topic and theme and a worksheet on theme. Complete a copy of the worksheet, applying it to the short story. Be prepared to discuss your completed worksheet with the rest of the class.

DISCUSSION

→ Discuss each of the questions below in small groups.

→ Be prepared to share your answers with the rest of the class and to explain them.

1. Do you abhor or admire Mrs. Turner?

2. Could a man have written "Mrs. Turner Cutting the Grass"?

3. Change is an inherent part of learning. Did you learn anything from reading "Mrs. Turner Cutting the Grass?" Did reading the story change you in any way?

4. Did you like the story?

5. Explain the significance of the title.

ost

In this section, one short (100- to 150-word) and two long (550- to 600-word) writing activities are proposed. The first activity focuses on paragraph writing; the second, on essay writing using a close-reading approach; the third, on essay writing using a reader-response approach.

1A Analyzing a Paragraph

The short story "Mrs. Turner Cutting the Grass" is made up of thirty-three units of writing, more commonly referred to as *paragraphs*. A paragraph deals with one particular idea. In non-fiction writing especially, the main idea of a paragraph is often referred to as the "controlling idea," and the controlling idea is always accompanied by supporting details (or evidence). A paragraph typically moves from the general to the specific in order to advance a particular point of view.

The Paragraph

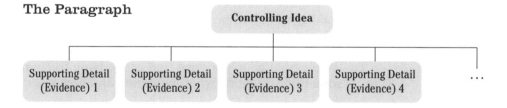

Example Paragraph

Some people see the glass as half empty and others, as half full. A few years ago, my friends Bob and Linda Peters both lost their jobs at the local car plant. Bob was devastated: he figured he'd never get another job due to his age and felt he was far too old to learn another craft. He convinced himself that "you can't teach an old dog new tricks," parked his behind on the sofa and picked up the remote control—content to spend his golden years in front of a flickering screen. Linda, on the other hand, was not so easily defeated. She was upset about losing her job but felt she was far too young to be put out to pasture. She had put a bit of money aside, so she decided to go to business school and do something she'd always dreamed of doing: opening an upscale restaurant. It's been a few months now, and Linda's trendy new bistro is, like its owner, doing very well. As for Bob, he's no longer parking himself on the sofa; he's working for Linda as a valet, parking cars.

EXERCISE

→ Referring to the example paragraph, answer the questions below.

1. What is the controlling idea? _____

_____

2. What details support the controlling idea? _____

_____

_____

_____

3. True or false? The paragraph moves from the general to the specific.

_____

1B Writing a Paragraph

→ Write a paragraph of 100 to 150 words in response to one of the questions below.

→ Begin your paragraph by presenting your opinion and then support it with pertinent details, moving from the general to the specific.

1. Do you see the glass as half empty or half full; that is, are you an optimist or a pessimist?

2. What is the most important thing others should know about you?

3. "The apple doesn't fall far from the tree" is a proverb that means that a child grows up to be like his or her parents. Are you like your parents?

4. Is studying literature an enriching experience or a waste of time?

5. Write about an experience that caused you to change your mind about something. Indicate what happened and how your opinion changed.

2 Essay Using a Close-Reading Approach: Theme

LITERARY NOTE

In a close-reading approach, you examine a literary work by focusing on relevant literary elements and techniques, tracing their occurrence throughout the text to determine meaning.

→ Using a close-reading approach, write a formal analytical essay of approximately 550 words in response to the following question:

What is the theme of "Mrs. Turner Cutting the Grass"?

→ In the Ponder section of this unit, you answered questions on the short story and applied Worksheet 1: Examining Theme to it (see pages 11–14). Before determining your thesis (your opinion), review your answers and completed worksheet.

→ If you are working alone, write a four- or five-paragraph essay.

→ If you are working with a partner, write a four-paragraph essay in which you co-write the introductory and concluding paragraphs and you each write one paragraph of the development alone.

→ If you are working in a group of three, write a five-paragraph essay in which you co-write the introductory and concluding paragraphs and you each write one paragraph of the development alone.

→ Double space your work and revise it before submitting it. You can find information about researching, referencing and revising in Appendix C (page 198).

LITERARY NOTE

In a reader-response approach, you are asked to respond emotionally or intellectually to a literary work, making connections between the work and experiences you have had and agreeing or disagreeing with important ideas presented in the work.

3 Essay Using a Reader-Response Approach

→ Using a reader-response approach, write a formal analytical essay of approximately 550 words in response to one of the following questions:

1. Is beauty in the eye of the beholder?

2. Is it possible to be a good person and still do bad things?

3. Do you need others in order to know yourself?

4. Are people and things pretty much the same wherever you go?

5. Is perfection a requisite of beauty?

→ Justify your answer by referring directly to "Mrs. Turner Cutting the Grass."

→ Before determining your thesis (your opinion), review your answers to the questions about the story in the Ponder section of this unit (pages 11–14).

→ Follow your teacher's instructions as to whether or not you may use the first-person singular when writing an essay using a reader-response approach.

→ Double space your work and revise it before submitting it. You can find information about researching, referencing and revising in Appendix C (page 198).

Present

In this section, a short (two-minute) and a long (seven- to ten-minute) speaking activity are proposed. The first activity focuses on theme; the second, on personal perspective, the topic of this unit.

1 A Brief Presentation: Variations on a Theme

Below, you will find three paintings. Painting A is "American Gothic" by American artist Grant Wood. Paintings B and C are variations on this painting.

→ Working with a partner or in a small group, determine the topic of each painting.

→ Determine the theme of each painting by examining details and patterns that connect these details.

Source: Smith, Michael W. & Jeffrey D. Wilhelm. *Fresh Takes on Teaching Literary Elements*. Toronto: Scholastic, 2010. 174. Print.

◪ A Formal Analytical Speech about Personal Perspective

As mentioned in the introduction to this unit, personal perspectives are influenced by factors (age, gender, wealth, etc.) and experiences.

→ Reflect on how you or one character from "Mrs. Turner Cutting the Grass" views the main character, Mrs. Turner, and think about the factors and experiences that may have influenced the perspective selected.

→ Photocopy "Outline of a Formal Analytical Speech" on page 196.

→ Complete the outline as you prepare a seven- to ten-minute formal analytical speech in which you both present the perspective and explain the influencing factors and experiences.

→ Submit your completed outline to your teacher, making another copy for yourself.

→ When called upon, give your speech.

→ If you are working alone, give the entire speech.

→ If you are working with a partner, one of you gives the introduction and presents one (or two) main points while the other presents the remaining main point(s) and gives the conclusion.

→ If you are working in a group of three, one of you gives the introduction, another, the development and another, the conclusion.

Important tips

→ Do not read or recite your speech.

→ Refer to your outline appropriately, making sure you maintain eye contact with audience members.

→ Speak to the person farthest from you (so you are certain to be heard by all).

→ Respect your time limit.

⑨articipate

There are two parts to this project. In part A, you are asked to work alone, reading a novel and writing up a brief report. In part B, you are asked to work with others, preparing and participating in a group discussion in which you share your perspective on the novel. Teachers often assign a novel at the start of the academic session in order to allow you sufficient time to read the novel, write up a report and get ready to participate fully in a discussion; typically, reports are submitted and discussions take place at some point after the midsession.

◪ Reading the Novel and Writing a Report

→ Read the English-language novel assigned by your teacher.

→ Write a three-paragraph report.

The first paragraph is the introduction. In the introduction, indicate the title of the book, the author's name and the publishing details; present the main idea(s).

The second paragraph is a summary. In the summary, indicate the main parts of the book, relating the important points of each part; explain how these parts are related to the main idea(s).

The third paragraph is the conclusion. In the conclusion, give your appreciation of the book, referring to elements discussed in the introduction and summary.

→ Submit your report to your teacher for evaluation.

B Preparing for and Participating in a Discussion

Discuss the novel in a small group of four or five students, following the procedure outlined below.

Procedure

1. Working alone, write a list of ten discussion questions about the novel.

2. Working together, create a common list of twenty discussion questions, working from your individual lists; eliminate redundant questions and keep those the group finds interesting; proofread the list and submit it to your teacher for evaluation.

3. Working together, discuss the novel, using the twenty questions as the basis of your discussion. Your teacher may evaluate your discussion.

The following related works may be of interest for continued study. Modern editions are available of all books listed.

TYPE OF LITERARY WORK	ANNOTATED TITLES
Film	*Citizen Kane*. Dir. Orson Welles. RKO Pictures, 1941. • Examination of the life and legacy of Charles Foster Kane, a fictional character based on newspaper magnate William Randolph Hearst, as seen through the eyes of those who knew him *I'm Not There*. Dir. Todd Haynes. The Weinstein Company, 2007. • Biographical musical film about the life of Bob Dylan—different facets of the singer-songwriter's life as depicted by six actors *Vantage Point*. Dir. Pete Travis. Columbia Pictures, 2008. • The attempted assassination of a US president as told from several different perspectives

TYPE OF LITERARY WORK	ANNOTATED TITLES
Novel	Faulkner, William. *As I Lay Dying*. New York: Jonathan Cape, 1930. Print. • A multiple-**narrative** story considered one of the best novels of the twentieth century Picoult, Jodi. *My Sister's Keeper: A Novel*. New York: Atria–Simon & Schuster, 2003. Print. • A multiple-**narrative** story about a family in crisis Shields, Carol. *Swann*. Toronto: Stoddart, 1987. Print. • A "literary mystery" about the murder of a rural Canadian poet by her husband Shields, Carol. *Unless*. Toronto: HarperCollins, 2002. Print. • A woman's life is upset when her daughter drops out of university and moves onto a downtown street, sitting in silence and wearing a sign that says "Goodness."
Personal Essay	Katz, Jon. "Why I Shot My Lamb." *Slate*. 4 May 2007. Web. 15 June 2011. • Two very different perspectives on sick animals
Short Story	Atwood, Margaret. "The Victory Burlesk." *Murder in the Dark*. Toronto: Coach House Press, 1983. Print. • A change of perspective related to age McLean, Stuart. "The Key." *The Vinyl Cafe Notebooks*. Toronto: Viking–Penguin Canada, 2010. Print. • An oral **narrative** about a man falsely accused, as related by a master storyteller

Solitary Lives

Chimera, Notre Dame
Cathedral, Paris

 **review**

In this unit, you will read two **narratives** that take place in the recent past and one that takes place in the distant past: first, a poem set in recent years, about a solitary moment in a person's life; then, a short story set in the 1930s, about collective loneliness; finally, a short story set in the 1970s about a couple leading separate lives. All three works have much to teach us about solitude, loneliness and separation.

The distant-past story in this unit, "1933," is set in Montreal, near Parc Lafontaine (known in the 1800s as Logan's Park). Once or twice a week, I walk my dogs in Parc Lafontaine, and every time, I am awed by the majestic trees and the connection they give me to the past: I try to determine when the trees were planted, I wonder who planted them, and I am amazed at the fact they are still here. Are stories written in or about the past relevant to the present? Does it matter that the trees in Parc Lafontaine still stand? The answer to both of the questions is a resounding "yes," for we stand on the shoulders of those who came before us.

℗repare

Lonely or Simply Alone?

Solitude is the state of being or living alone. It can be a lonely experience, or it can be an experience in which you are simply alone: the former is a sad place; the latter, a peaceful place.

→ For each of the following pictures, write A or L on the line to indicate whether, in your view, the main character pictured is lonely or simply alone.

→ Be prepared to explain your choices.

1 _____

2 _____

3 _____

4 _____

5 _____

6 _____

℗onder

Evelyn Lau (1971–) is an award-winning Vancouver author who grew up in a Chinese immigrant family. Her bestselling memoir *Runaway: Diary of a Street Kid* documents her drug use, suicide attempts and prostitution (Toye 358–9). An annotated reference to her memoir, which was made into a CBC-TV movie, can be found in the Pursue section of this unit on page 43.

Swimming Lessons

by Evelyn Lau

The white doves flew in
and out of the trees below our balcony.
In our room we were fighting.
It was nothing, you said, *just a silly crack,*
5 *it meant less than nothing—*
a crack through which one moment slid
into another, swift as the sunset
in Honolulu. One moment the green Pacific
at our feet and then night,
10 sea and sky a thick blanket
thrown over the homes around Diamond Head.
The next afternoon the wave that knocked us both over
at Waikiki Beach stole my Fendi sunglasses—
and for a moment I wished
15 it had been a person instead, drowned
and swept away by the undercurrent, even someone
I knew but liked only a little, not like
I loved those glasses. The wave closed over
and over my head, I swallowed salt water
20 like medicine for a sore throat,
the sky suddenly miles above
and my body locked inside this watery room,
thrashing in a blue and airless bed.
So this was what it was like,
25 no time for remorse or reflection,
only an animal dying,
all helpless instinct and fear.
I struggled back to shore
where you stood, hand held over
30 your eyes, looking in every direction
but this one.

(369 words)

Diamond Head,
Honolulu, Oahu,
Hawaii

Source: Lau, Evelyn. "Swimming
Lessons." *The Best Canadian Poetry
in English 2010*. Ed. Lorna Crozier.
Toronto: Tightrope Books, 2010. Print.

VOCABULARY AND COMPREHENSION

→ You may wish to work with a partner as you answer the questions below.

1. What do "white doves" (line 1) **symbolize**?

   _____

2. Explain the **irony** of line 3 with reference to lines 1 and 2.

   _____

   _____

3. In lines 4–6, the word *crack* is used twice, each time with a different meaning. What does the word mean the first time? The second time?

   _____

   _____

4. What does "night" (line 9) **symbolize**?

   _____

   _____

5. Whose demise does the narrator wish for (lines 12–18)? Explain.

   _____

   _____

   _____

6. In line 24, what does the word *this* refer to?

   _____

7. Explain the significance of the last sentence (lines 28–31).

   _____

   _____

8. Copy down one example of **alliteration** from the poem.

   _____

DISCUSSION

→ Discuss each of the questions below in small groups.

→ Be prepared to share your answers with the rest of the class and to explain them.

1. Whom is the narrator addressing in the poem?

2. Who do you feel more empathy for, the narrator or her partner?

3. A wave steals an expensive pair of glasses from the narrator, who momentarily wishes the wave had taken a person instead. What does this momentary wish reveal about the narrator?

4. What is the significance of the title?

5. What is the topic of "Swimming Lessons"? What is the theme?

Short Story: 1933

Mavis Gallant (1922–) is a Montreal-born writer living in Paris. She is a long-time contributor to *The New Yorker*, a Companion of the Order of Canada and the 2006 winner of the Prix Athanase-David for literary excellence—the first English-language author to be so honoured. Her short story "1933" first appeared in her volume of stories *Across the Bridge*.

READING FOR INFORMATION

→ Read the short story a first time, underlining the words listed in the chart below and highlighting information essential to understanding the plot. (The vocabulary is listed in order of appearance in the text.)

→ Fill in the chart, defining the words according to their contexts. (You may need to refer to a dictionary.)

→ In sixty words or fewer, summarize the plot in the space provided.

VOCABULARY	DEFINITION	VOCABULARY	DEFINITION
1. flat (n.)		**6.** withered (adj.)	
2. tarpaulin (n.)		**7.** mourning (n.)	
3. squat (adj.)		**8.** bolt (v.)	
4. patronize (v.)		**9.** wailed (v.)	
5. gilt (adj.)		**10.** calamity (n.)	

PLOT SUMMARY

1933

by Mavis Gallant

About a year after the death of M. Carette, his three survivors—Berthe and her little sister, Marie, and their mother—had to leave the comfortable flat over the furniture store in Rue Saint-Denis and move to a smaller place. They were not destitute: There was the insurance and the money from the
5 sale of the store, but the man who had bought the store from the estate had not yet paid and they had to be careful.

Some of the lamps and end tables and upholstered chairs were sent to relatives, to be returned when the little girls grew up and got married. The rest of their things were carried by two small, bent men to the second floor
10 of a stone house in Rue Cherrier near the Institute for the Deaf and Dumb. The men used an old horse and an open cart for the removal. They told Mme. Carette that they had never worked outside that quarter; they knew only some forty streets of Montreal but knew them thoroughly. On moving day, soft snow, like greying lace, fell. A patched tarpaulin protected the
15 Carettes' wine-red sofa with its border of silk fringe, the children's brass bedstead, their mother's walnut bed with the carved scallop shells, and the round oak table, smaller than the old one, at which they would now eat their meals. Mme. Carette told Berthe that her days of entertaining and cooking for guests were over. She was just twenty-seven.

20 They waited for the moving men in their new home, in scrubbed, empty rooms. They had already spread sheets of *La Presse* over the floors, in case the men tracked in snow. The curtains were hung, the cream-coloured blinds pulled halfway down the sash windows. Coal had been delivered and was piled in the lean-to shed behind the kitchen. The range and the squat, round
25 heater in the dining room issued tidal waves of dense metallic warmth.

The old place was at no distance. Parc Lafontaine, where the children had often been taken to play, was just along the street. By walking an extra few minutes, Mme. Carette could patronize the same butcher and grocer as
30 before. The same horse-drawn sleighs would bring bread, milk, and coal to the door. Still, the quiet stone houses, the absence of heavy traffic and shops made Rue Cherrier seem like
35 a foreign country.

Change, death, absence—the adult mysteries—kept the children awake. From their new bedroom they heard the clang of the first streetcar at
40 dawn—a thrilling chord, metal on metal, that faded slowly. They would have jumped up and dressed at once,

Parc Lafontaine, Montreal, circa 1933

but to their mother this was still the middle of the night. Presently, a new, continuous sound moved in the waking streets, like a murmur of leaves.
45 From the confused rustle broke distinct impressions: an alarm clock, a man speaking, someone's radio. Marie wanted to talk and sing. Berthe had to invent stories to keep her quiet. Once she had placed her hand over Marie's mouth and been cruelly bitten.

They slept on a horsehair mattress, which had a summer and a winter
50 side, and was turned twice a year. The beautiful stitching at the edge of the sheets and pillows was their mother's work. She had begun to sew her trousseau at the age of eleven; her early life was spent in preparation for a wedding. Above the girls' bed hung a gilt crucifix with a withered spray of box hedge that passed for the Easter palms of Jerusalem.

55 Marie was afraid to go to the bathroom alone after dark. Berthe asked if she expected to see their father's ghost, but Marie could not say: She did not yet know whether a ghost and the dark meant the same thing. Berthe was obliged to get up at night and accompany her along the passage. The hall light shone out of a blue glass tulip set upon a column painted to
60 look like marble. Berthe could just reach it on tiptoe; Marie not at all.

Marie would have left the bathroom door open for company, but Berthe knew that such intimacy was improper. Although her First Communion was being delayed because Mme. Carette wanted the two sisters to come to the altar together, she had been to practice confession. Unfortunately,
65 she had soon run out of invented sins. Her confessor seemed to think there should be more: He asked if she and her little sister had ever been in a bathroom with the door shut, and warned her of grievous fault.

On their way back to bed, Berthe unhooked a calendar on which was a picture of a family of rabbits riding a toboggan. She pretended to read
70 stories about the rabbits and presently both she and Marie fell asleep.

They never saw their mother wearing a bathrobe. As soon as Mme. Carette got up, she dressed herself in clothes that were in the colours of half mourning—mauve, dove grey. Her fair hair was brushed straight and subdued under a net. She took a brush to everything—hair, floors, the
75 children's elbows, the kitchen chairs. Her scent was of Baby's Own soap and Florida Water. When she bent to kiss the children, a cameo dangled from a chain. She trained the girls not to lie, or point, or gobble their food, or show their legs above the knee, or leave fingerprints on windowpanes, or handle the parlour curtains—the slightest touch could crease the lace.
80 They learned to say in English, "I don't understand" and "I don't know" and "No, thank you." That was all the English anyone needed between Rue Saint-Denis and Parc Lafontaine.

In the dining room, where she kept her sewing machine, Mme. Carette held the treadle still, rested a hand on the stopped wheel. "What are you
85 doing in the parlour?" she called. "Are you touching the curtains?" Marie had been spitting on the window and drawing her finger through the spit. Berthe, trying to clean the mess with her flannelette petticoat, said, "Marie's just been standing here saying 'Saint Marguerite, pray for us.'"

Downstairs lived M. Grosjean, the landlord, with his Irish wife and an
90 Airedale named Arno. Arno understood English and French; Mme. Grosjean
could only speak English. She loved Arno and was afraid he would run
away: He was a restless dog who liked to be doing something all the time.
Sometimes M. Grosjean took him to Parc Lafontaine and they played at
retrieving a collapsed and bitten tennis ball. Arno was trained to obey both
95 "*Cherchez!*" and "*Go fetch it!*" but he paid attention to neither. He ran with
the ball and Mme. Grosjean had to chase him.

Mme. Grosjean stood outside the house on the back step, just under the
Carettes' kitchen window, holding Arno's supper. She wailed, "Arno, where
have you got to?" M. Grosjean had probably taken Arno for a walk. He made
100 it a point never to say where he was going: He did not think it a good thing
to let women know much.

Mme. Grosjean and Mme. Carette were the same age, but they never
became friends. Mme. Carette would say no more than a few negative things
in English ("No, thank you" and "I don't know" and "I don't understand")
105 and Mme. Grosjean could not work up the conversation. Mme. Carette had
a word with Berthe about Irish marriages: An Irish marriage, while not to be
sought, need not be scorned. The Irish were not English. God had sent
them to Canada to keep people from marrying Protestants.

That winter the girls wore white leggings and mittens, knitted by their
110 mother, and coats and hats of white rabbit fur. Each of them carried a
rabbit muff. Marie cried when Berthe had to go to school. On Sunday after-
noons they played with Arno and M. Grosjean. He tried to take their picture
but it wasn't easy. The girls stood on the front steps, hand in hand, mitten
to mitten, while Arno was harnessed to a sled with curved runners. The red
115 harness had once been worn by another Airedale, Ruby, who was smarter
even than Arno.

M. Grosjean wanted Marie to sit down on the sled, hold the reins, and
look sideways at the camera. Marie clung to Berthe's coat. She was afraid
that Arno would bolt into the Rue Saint-Denis, where there were streetcars.
120 M. Grosjean lifted her off the sled and tried the picture a different way, with
Berthe pretending to drive and Marie standing face-to-face with Arno.
As soon as he set Marie on her feet, she began to scream. Her feet were cold.
She wanted to be carried. Her nose ran; she felt humiliated. He got out his
handkerchief, checked green and white, and wiped her whole face rather hard.

125 Just then his wife came to the front door with a dish of macaroni and cut-
up sausages for Arno. She had thrown a sweater over her cotton housecoat;
she was someone who never felt the cold. A gust of wind lifted her loose
hair. M. Grosjean told her that the kid was no picnic. Berthe, picking up
English fast, could not have repeated his exact words, but she knew what
130 they meant.

Mme. Carette was still waiting for the money from the sale of the store.
A brother-in-law helped with the rent, sending every month a generous
postal order from Fall River. It was Mme. Carette's belief that God would

work a miracle, allowing her to pay it all back. In the meantime, she did
135 fine sewing. Once she was hired to sew a trousseau, working all day in the
home of the bride-to-be. As the date of the wedding drew near she had to
stay overnight.

Mme. Grosjean looked after the children. They sat in her front parlour,
eating fried-egg sandwiches and drinking cream soda (it did not matter if
140 they dropped crumbs) while she played a record of a man singing, "Dear
one, the world is waiting for the sunrise."

Berthe asked, in French, "What is he saying?" Mme. Grosjean answered
in English, "A well-known Irish tenor."

When Mme. Carette came home the next day, she gave the girls a hot
145 bath, in case Mme. Grosjean had neglected their elbows and heels. She took
Berthe in her arms and said she must never tell anyone their mother had
left the house to sew for strangers. When she grew up, she must not refer to
her mother as a seamstress, but say instead, "My mother was clever with
her hands."

150 That night, when they were all three having supper in the kitchen, she
looked at Berthe and said, "You have beautiful hair." She sounded so tired
and stern that Marie, eating mashed potatoes and gravy, with a napkin
under her chin, thought Berthe must be getting a scolding. She opened her
mouth wide and started to howl. Mme. Carette just said, "Marie, don't cry
155 with your mouth full."

Downstairs, Mme. Grosjean set up her evening chant, calling for Arno.
"Oh, where have you got to?" she wailed to the empty backyard.

"The dog is the only thing keeping those two together," said Mme. Carette.
"But a dog isn't the same as a child. A dog doesn't look after its masters in
160 their old age. We shall see what happens to the marriage after Arno dies."
No sooner had she said this than she covered her mouth and spoke through
her fingers: "God forgive my unkind thoughts." She propped her arms on
each side of her plate, as the girls were forbidden to do, and let her face
slide into her hands.

165 Berthe took this to mean that Arno was doomed. Only a calamity about
to engulf them all could explain her mother's elbows on the table. She got
down from her chair and tried to pull her mother's hands apart, and kiss
her face. Her own tears ran into her long hair, down onto her starched
piqué collar. She felt tears along her nose and inside her ears. Even while
170 she sobbed out words of hope and comfort (Arno would never die) and
promises of reassuring behaviour (she and Marie would always be good)
she wondered how tears could flow in so many directions at once.

Of course, M. Grosjean did not know that all the female creatures in his
house were frightened and lonely, calling and weeping. He was in Parc
175 Lafontaine with Arno, trying to play go-fetch-it in the dark.

(2079 words)

Source: Gallant, Mavis. "1933." *The Collected Short Stories of Mavis Gallant*. Toronto: McClelland & Stewart, 1996. Print.

READING FOR MEANING

→ Read the questions below.

→ Read the short story a second and a third time (or more), answering the questions as you do so.

1. Who has bought Mme. Carette's store? Who helps with Mme. Carette's rent? Who doesn't know that all the "female creatures" in his house are "frightened and lonely, calling and weeping" (line 174)? What do all three have in common?

_____

_____

2. Explain the significance of the following: "Mme. Carette told Berthe that her days of entertaining and cooking for guests were over. She was just twenty-seven" (lines 18–19).

_____

_____

_____

3. Explain the significance of the following: "She had begun to sew her trousseau at the age of eleven; her early life was spent in preparation for a wedding" (lines 51–53).

_____

_____

_____

_____

4. Why is it significant that Mme. Carette dresses "in the colours of half mourning" (lines 72–73)?

_____

_____

_____

_____

5. What is implied in the following: "Arno understood English and French; Mme. Grosjean could only speak English" (lines 90–91)?

_____

_____

_____

_____

6. In your opinion, what are Mme. Carette's "unkind thoughts" (line 162)?

_____

_____

_____

7. In "1933," death separates Mme. Carette from her husband. Other factors separate and isolate characters in the story. Complete the chart below, explaining how each of the factors listed separates and isolates one (or more) of the characters from one (or more) of the other characters. Refer to the short story directly (quote) or indirectly (paraphrase) to support your point; in both cases, indicate the appropriate line number(s) from the story. The first one has been done for you as an example.

FACTOR	WHO IS ISOLATED	SUPPORT FROM WHOM
a) Age	Berthe and Marie / adults	• Berthe and Marie don't fully understand "the adult mysteries" of change, death and absence (lines 36–37). • Marie mistakes her mother's fatigue for a reprimand directed at Berthe, a mistake that ironically elicits from her mother a reprimand directed at her (lines 151–155). • Berthe misunderstands her mother's actions in lines 162–164: "Berthe took this to mean that Arno was doomed" (line 165). • We know the first names of the children (and the dog), but not of the adults; the author is more formal in her treatment of the adults.
b) Gender		
c) Geography		
d) Language		
e) Religion		

8. While Marie is howling and Berthe is sobbing and Mrs. Grosjean is wailing and Mme. Carette is sitting dejectedly at the small round oak table, what is M. Grosjean doing? When is he doing it, and how is the timing significant?

_____

_____

_____

_____

READING FOR RHETORIC

→ Answer the following questions.

LITERARY NOTE

Using **similes** and **onomatopoeic** terms enriches a text by appealing to a reader's senses.

1. Copy out the **simile** in paragraph 2 (lines 7–19).

_____

2. In paragraph 5 (lines 36–48), three **onomatopoeic** words are used. What are they?

_____

3. Copy out the **simile** (which includes **onomatopoeic** language) in paragraph 5 (lines 36–48).

_____

_____

_____

EXAMINING AN ELEMENT: Character and Characterization

Working with a partner, examine character and characterization in "1933." Turn to pages 3 and 8–9 in the *Literary Handbook* for an explanation of character and characterization and a worksheet on it. Complete a copy of the worksheet, applying it to the short story. Be prepared to discuss your completed worksheet with the rest of the class.

DISCUSSION

→ Discuss each of the questions below in small groups.

→ Be prepared to share your answers with the rest of the class and to explain them.

1. Do you agree or disagree with the following statement: "North Americans in the 1930s lived their lives locally, not globally; North Americans today live their lives globally, not locally"?

2. Are **narratives** written in or about the past relevant to today's world? To the world in the future?

3. Is it still a man's world?

4. In general, is it an advantage or a disadvantage to be in a romantic relationship with a person whose first language is different from your own?

5. What is the topic of "1933"? What is the theme?

A Question of PERSPECTIVE If you were a widow with just enough money to take care of yourself and your two young children in modern-day Montreal, would you get a full-time job to supplement your income and allow yourself some of life's luxuries? Would you have done the same in the Montreal of the 1930s?

READING 2.2

Short Story: The Black Queen

Barry Callaghan (1937–) has worn many hats: literary editor, television host, documentary producer, filmmaker and English professor. He is also the founder of *Exile*, a Canadian literary magazine, and a writer of short stories, essays and novels. The short story "The Black Queen" was originally published in a collection of the same name. He is the son of Morley Callaghan, a celebrated Canadian author (Toye 86–7).

READING FOR INFORMATION

→ Read the short story a first time, underlining the words listed in the chart below and highlighting information essential to understanding the plot. (The vocabulary is listed in order of appearance in the text.)

→ Fill in the chart, defining the words according to their contexts. (You may need to refer to a dictionary.)

→ In sixty words or fewer, summarize the plot in the space provided.

COMPANION
web+

VOCABULARY	DEFINITION	VOCABULARY	DEFINITION
1. fastidious (adj.)		**6.** nettled away (v.)	
2. tattered (adj.)		**7.** unsullied (adj.)	
3. aloofness (n.)		**8.** weeds (n.)	
4. slyly (adv.)		**9.** smirked (v.)	
5. sulked (v.)		**10.** squabble (n.)	

PLOT SUMMARY

The Black Queen

by Barry Callaghan

Hughes and McCrae were fastidious men who took pride in their old colonial house, the clean simple lines and stucco walls and the painted pale blue picket fence. They were surrounded by houses converted into small ware-houses, trucking yards where houses had been torn down, and along the
5 street, a school filled with foreign children, but they didn't mind. It gave them an embattled sense of holding on to something important, a tattered remnant of good taste in an area of waste overrun by rootless olive-skinned children.

McCrae wore his hair a little too long now that he was going grey, and while Hughes with his clipped moustache seemed to be a serious man
10 intent only on his work, which was costume design, McCrae wore Cuban heels and lacquered his nails. When they'd met ten years ago Hughes had said, "You keep walking around like that and you'll need a body to keep you from getting poked in the eye." McCrae did all the cooking and drove the car.

But they were not getting along these days. Hughes blamed his bursitis
15 but they were both silently unsettled by how old they had suddenly become, how loose in the thighs, and their feet, when they were showering in the morning, seemed bonier, the toes longer, the nails yellow and hard, and what they wanted was tenderness, to be able to yield almost tearfully, full of a pity for themselves that would not be belittled or laughed at, and when
20 they stood alone in their separate bedrooms they wanted that tenderness from each other, but when they were having their bedtime tea in the kitchen, as they had done for years using lovely green and white Limoges cups, if one touched the other's hand then suddenly they both withdrew into an unspoken, smiling aloofness, as if some line of privacy had been
25 crossed. Neither could bear their thinning wrists and the little pouches of darkening flesh under the chin. They spoke of being with younger people and even joked slyly about bringing a young man home, but that seemed

such a betrayal of everything that they had believed had set them apart
from others, everything they believed had kept them together, that they
30 sulked and nettled away at each other, and though nothing had apparently
changed in their lives, they were always on edge, Hughes more than McCrae.

One of their pleasures was collecting stamps, rare and mint-perfect, with
no creases or smudges on the gum. Their collection, carefully mounted in
a leatherbound blue book with seven little plastic windows per page, was
35 worth several thousand dollars. They had passed many pleasant evenings
together on the Directoire settee arranging the old ochre- and carmine-
coloured stamps. They agreed there was something almost sensual about
holding a perfectly preserved piece of the past, unsullied, as if everything
didn't have to change, didn't have to end up swamped by decline and
40 decay. They disapproved of the new stamps and dismissed them as crude
and wouldn't have them in their book. The pages for the recent years
remained empty and they liked that; the emptiness was their statement
about themselves and their values, and Hughes, holding a stamp into the
light between his tweezers, would say, "None of that rough trade for us."

45 One afternoon they went down to the philatelic shops around Adelaide
and Richmond streets and saw a stamp they had been after for a long time,
a large and elegant black stamp of Queen Victoria in her widow's weeds.
It was rare and expensive, a dead-letter stamp from the turn of the century.
They stood side by side over the glass counter-case, admiring it, their hands
50 spread on the glass, but when McCrae, the overhead fluorescent light

catching his lacquered nails, said, "Well, I
certainly would like that little black sweet-
heart," the owner, who had sold stamps to
them for several years, looked up and smirked,
55 and Hughes suddenly snorted, "You old queen,
I mean why don't you just quit wearing those
goddamn Cuban heels, eh? I mean why not?"
He walked out leaving McCrae embarrassed
and hurt and when the owner said, "So what
60 was wrong?" McCrae cried, "Screw you," and
strutted out.

Through the rest of the week they were deferential around the house,
offering each other every consideration, trying to avoid any squabble
before Mother's Day at the end of the week when they were going to hold
65 their annual supper for friends, three other male couples. Over the years
it had always been an elegant, slightly mocking evening that often ended
bittersweetly and left them feeling close, comforting each other.

McCrae, wearing a white linen shirt with starch in the cuffs and mother-
of-pearl cuff links, worked all Sunday afternoon in the kitchen and through
70 the window he could see the crabapple tree in bloom and he thought how
in previous years he would have begun planning to put down some jelly in
the old pressed glass jars they kept in the cellar, but instead, head down, he
went on stuffing and tying the pork loin roast. Then in the early evening he
heard Hughes at the door, and there was laughter from the front room and

75 someone cried out, "What do you do with an elephant who has three balls on him ... you don't know, silly, well you walk him and pitch to the giraffe," and there were howls of laughter and the clinking of glasses. It had been the same every year, eight men sitting down to a fine supper with expensive wines, the table set with their best silver under the antique carved wooden
80 candelabra.

Having prepared all the raw vegetables, the cauliflower and carrots, the avocados and finger-sized miniature corns-on-the-cob, and placed porcelain bowls of homemade dip in the centre of a pewter tray, McCrae stared at his reflection for a moment in the window over the kitchen sink and then he
85 took a plastic slipcase out of the knives and forks drawer. The case contained the dead-letter stamp. He licked it all over and pasted it on his forehead and then slipped on the jacket of his charcoal-brown crushed velvet suit, took hold of the tray, and stepped out into the front room.

The other men, sitting in a circle around the coffee table, looked up and
90 one of them giggled. Hughes cried, "Oh my God." McCrae, as if nothing was the matter, said, "My dears, time for the crudités." He was in his silk stocking feet, and as he passed the tray he winked at Hughes who sat staring at the black queen.

(1100 words)

Source: Callaghan, Barry. "The Black Queen." *The Oxford Book of Canadian Short Stories in English*. Selected by Margaret Atwood and Robert Weaver. Toronto: Oxford University Press, 1986. Print.

READING FOR MEANING

→ Read the questions below.

→ Read the short story a second and a third time (or more), answering the questions as you do so.

1. Describe the house in which Hughes and McCrae live. Describe the neighbourhood and the neighbours. Explain the significance of the description of the house as it relates to the description of the neighbourhood and the neighbours.

_____

_____

_____

_____

_____

2. Describe McCrae's physical appearance. Describe Hughes's physical appearance. How are these descriptions significant?

_____

_____

_____

_____

3. Why does Hughes think McCrae needs to be protected?

_____

_____

_____

_____

4. Why are Hughes and McCrae not getting along?

_____

_____

_____

_____

_____

5. Why is it significant that Hughes and McCrae collect only old stamps in perfect condition and that they refuse to collect new stamps?

_____

_____

_____

_____

6. What is a "dead-letter" stamp?

_____

_____

7. What instigated Hughes's outburst in the philatelic shop?

_____

_____

8. Explain the significance of the following: "… through the window he [McCrae] could see the crabapple tree in bloom and he thought how in previous years he would have begun planning to put down some jelly …" (lines 69–71).

_____

_____

_____

9. Explain the significance of McCrae pasting the "black queen" stamp to his forehead and then serving Hughes and their guests.

_____

_____

_____

READING FOR RHETORIC

→ Answer the following questions.

1. What does a white picket fence **symbolize**? Why is it significant that the picket fence is painted pale blue (lines 2–3)?

_____

_____

_____

_____

2. What do the stamps Hugh and McCrae collect **symbolize**?

_____

_____

_____

_____

3. Explain the **irony** of Hughes's outburst in the philatelic shop.

_____

_____

_____

_____

4. Explain the **irony** of the following quotation: "Over the years it had always been an elegant, slightly mocking evening that often ended bittersweetly and left them [Hughes and McCrae] feeling close, comforting each other" (lines 65–67).

_____

_____

EXAMINING AN ELEMENT: Character and Characterization

Working with a partner, examine character and characterization in "The Black Queen." Turn to pages 3 and 8–9 in the *Literary Handbook* for an explanation of character and characterization and a worksheet on it. Complete a copy of the worksheet, applying it to the short story. Be prepared to discuss your completed worksheet with the rest of the class.

DISCUSSION

→ Discuss each of the questions below in small groups.

→ Be prepared to share your answers with the rest of the class and to explain them.

1. In general, is society accepting or unaccepting of nonconformists?

2. What sustains society: dissent or conformity?

3. Distinguish "tolerating differences" from "accepting differences."

4. Do most people embrace or resist change?

5. What is the topic of "The Black Queen"? What is the theme?

A Question of PERSPECTIVE

Pretend you are McCrae. Would you leave Hughes because he mocked you?

 **Post**

In this section, one short (100- to 150-word) and two long (550- to 600-word) writing activities are proposed. The first activity focuses on character and characterization; the second, on essay writing using a close-reading approach; the third, on essay writing using a reader-response approach.

❶ A Paragraph about First Impressions

First impressions can be deceiving. They can also be accurate. Whether accurate or inaccurate, they are always very powerful—so much so that it is often difficult to move beyond them. This is why it is important to verify first impressions when determining character—in life and literature (Smith and Wilhelm 22).

→ Write a 100- to 150-word paragraph in the first-person singular describing one of the following:

1. How your first impressions of your teacher were either confirmed or disproved. (Note: If your current impressions aren't entirely positive, you may wish to select another topic!)

2. How people typically first see you and why their first impressions are either right or wrong.

3. Your first and final impressions of Mme. Carette, the main character from "1933" (page 26); McCrae, the main character from "The Black Queen" (page 34); or any other main character from a short story assigned by your teacher.

❷ Essay Using a Close-Reading Approach: Character and Characterization

→ Using a close-reading approach, write a formal analytical essay of approximately 550 words on one of the following subjects:

1. Short Story: "1933"

Defend or disprove the following thesis: Mme. Carette is partly responsible for her loneliness.

2. Short Story: "The Black Queen"

McCrae's attachment to the past renders him incapable of fully living in the present. Discuss.

→ In the Ponder section of this unit, you answered questions on the short stories and applied Worksheet 2: Examining Character and Characterization to each of them (see pages 30–39). Before determining your thesis (your opinion), review your answers and completed worksheet for the story you have chosen.

→ Double space your work and revise it before submitting it. You can find information about researching, referencing and revising in Appendix C (page 198).

❸ Essay Using a Reader-Response Approach

→ Using a reader-response approach, write a formal analytical essay of approximately 550 words in response to one of the following questions:

1. Why are some people lonely when they are not alone?

2. How is the short story "1933" relevant to your life today?

3. What lessons can you glean from Hughes and McCrae's relationship in "The Black Queen"?

4. Is loneliness surmountable?

5. Is a romantic relationship a safeguard against loneliness?

→ Justify your answer by referring directly to one or more of the following works: "Swimming Lessons"; "1933"; "The Black Queen."

→ Before determining your thesis (your opinion), review your answers to the questions about the literary work(s) in the Ponder section of this unit (pages 24–39).

→ Follow your teacher's instructions as to whether or not you may use the first-person singular when writing an essay using a reader-response approach.

→ Double space your work and revise it before submitting it. You can find information about researching, referencing and revising in Appendix C (page 198).

℗resent

In this section, a short (two-minute) and a long (seven- to ten-minute) speaking activity are proposed. The first activity focuses on character and characterization; the second, on loneliness, the topic of this unit.

1 Can You See What They're Like?

Authors help you infer character traits by showing you a character's words, actions and thoughts; similarly, portrait artists help you infer character traits by showing you a subject in a certain way. The painting, then, is a visual text from which character traits can be inferred (Smith and Wilhelm 34). Below, you will find four portraits painted by four different Canadian artists. For each person portrayed, infer three to five character traits. Be prepared to justify your inferences.

Portrait 1: Marie Francoise Globensky (nee Brousseau dit Lafleur) by Jean-Baptiste Roy-Audy (1778–1848)

Portrait 2: John H. R. Molson by Robert Harris (1849–1919)

Portrait 3: Wah-Pus by Paul Kane (1810–1871)

Portrait 4: "Demasduit, 1819" by Lady Henrietta Martha Hamilton (1780–1857)

Source: Adapted from Smith, Michael W. and Jeffrey D. Wilhelm. *Fresh Takes on Teaching Literary Elements*. Toronto: Scholastic, 2010. 34. Print.

❷ A Formal Analytical Speech about Loneliness

In this unit, you have read about loneliness: a poem about a woman's lonely moment, a short story about female isolation and a short story about a couple's separation.

→ Reflect on these works and then develop a thesis statement based on the topic "loneliness."

→ Photocopy "Outline of a Formal Analytical Speech" on page 196.

→ Complete the outline as you prepare a seven- to ten-minute formal analytical presentation in which you both state and support your opinion by referring to at least two of the following three works: "Swimming Lessons" (page 23); "1933" (page 26); "The Black Queen" (page 34).

→ Submit your completed outline to your teacher, making another copy for yourself.

→ When called upon, give your speech.

Important tips

→ Do not read or recite your speech.

→ Refer to your outline appropriately, making sure you maintain eye contact with audience members.

→ Speak to the person farthest from you (so you are certain to be heard by all).

→ Respect your time limit.

Taking a Personality Test

The Myers-Briggs Type Indicator (MBTI) is a well-known psychometric test that assesses personality by establishing preferences across four dichotomies:

1. Extroversion (E) – (I) Introversion
2. Sensing (S) – (N) Intuition
3. Thinking (T) – (F) Feeling
4. Judgment (J) – (P) Perception

Once these preferences are established, a person is typed into one of sixteen categories: ESTJ, INFP, ENFJ and so on.

In this activity, you and a partner are asked to determine your personality types and the type of one of the following characters: Mme. Carette from "1933" (page 26), McCrae from "The Black Queen" (page 34) or any other main character from a short story assigned by your teacher. Then, you will be asked to share your findings with others in the class.

Source: Adapted from Smith, Michael W. & Jeffrey D. Wilhelm. *Fresh Takes on Teaching Literary Elements.* Toronto: Scholastic, 2010. 32–33. Print.

Procedure

A Working Alone

1. Go to www.humanmetrics.com/cgi-win/JTypes1.htm[1] and take the test, responding to all seventy-two questions.

2. Print out your individual results: your MBTI type and your type as described by J. Butt and M. M. Heiss.

3. Validate the results: in your opinion, were you "typed" correctly and does the description ring true for you?

B Working Together

1. Select one of the literary characters mentioned on the previous page and take the test again, this time answering the questions as if you were the literary character.

2. Print out your character's results: his or her MBTI type and his or her type as described by J. Butt and M. M. Heiss.

3. Validate the results: in your opinion, was the character "typed" correctly and does the description of the character ring true to two of you?

C Working as a Class

1. Form groups based on the character selected, joining other students who selected the same character. As a group, come to a consensus as to the character's type and description.

2. Present your findings to the other groups in the class.

The following related works may be of interest for continued study. Modern editions are available of all books listed.

TYPE OF LITERARY WORK	ANNOTATED TITLES
Film	*Cast Away*. Dir. Robert Zemeckis. 20th Century Fox, 2000. • A man is stranded on an uninhabited island after his plane crashes *Into the Wild*. Dir. Sean Penn. Paramount Vantage / River Road Entertainment, 2007. • Recounts the story of Christopher McCandless, a young man who sacrifices everything in search of solitude *Lost in Translation*. Dir. Sofia Coppola. Focus Features, 2003. • Exploration of loneliness, alienation and culture shock set in Japan ....➤

1. Read the disclaimer at the bottom of the page.

TYPE OF LITERARY WORK	ANNOTATED TITLES
Memoir	Lau, Evelyn. *Runaway: Diary of a Street Kid*. Toronto: Harper-Collins, 1989. Print. • Memoir of the author of "Swimming Lessons," the lyric poem reprinted on page 23 of this textbook
Novel / Novella	Moore, Brian. *The Lonely Passion of Judith Hearne*. Toronto: McClelland & Stewart, 2010. Print. (First published as *Judith Hearne*. London: Andre Deutsch. 1955.) • A plain and lonely woman turns to alcohol for comfort Munro, Alice. "The Bear Came Over the Mountain." *Hateship, Loveship, Courtship, Marriage*. Toronto: McClelland & Stewart, 2001. Print. • Alzheimer's separates an older couple • Made into a film: *Away from Her* (2006)
Short Story	Callaghan, Morley. "Rigmarole." *Canadian Short Stories*. Eds. Russell Brown and Donna Bennett. Toronto: Pearson Longman, 2005. 77–82. Print. (First published in *Morley Callaghan's Stories*. Toronto: Macmillan, 1959.) • Story of a young couple whose relationship is at times quite distant and at other times, quite close Chopin, Kate. "Story of an Hour." • Story of a woman who mistakenly believes her husband has died • Available online in print and audio at Wikisource Faulkner, William. "A Rose for Emily." • A lonely Mississippi woman's resistance to change has deadly consequences • First published in 1931 and available online through *Wikipedia* Perkins Gilman, Charlotte. "The Yellow Wallpaper." • A woman confined to her room slowly loses her mind • First published in 1892 and available online at the Project Gutenberg

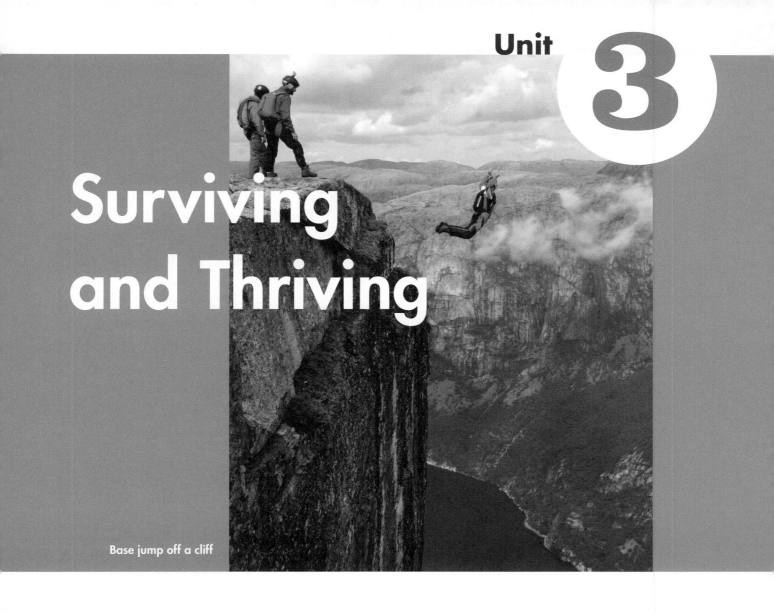

Surviving and Thriving

Base jump off a cliff

Unit 3

𝒫review

What does it take to survive? What does it take to thrive? These are two of many questions you will examine in this unit.

You'll begin by listening to a riveting account of a young boy's descent over Niagara Falls. You will then read a short story about a young life cut short and finally a moving memoir written by a child of Holocaust survivors.

In each work, either physical or emotional survival or both are threatened, and each work offers a lesson about surviving and thriving.

repare

Survival Quiz

How much do you know about survival? Take the quiz below to find out. Give yourself one mark for each correctly answered question. There are ten questions: the higher your score, the better your odds of survival in a variety of life-threatening situations!

1. Fill in each blank with a number from one to ten. In extreme survival situations, the average person cannot survive more than

   a) _____ minutes without air;

   b) _____ hours without shelter;

   c) _____ days without water;

   d) _____ weeks without food; or

   e) _____ months without hope.

2. Fill in the blank.
   To avoid dehydration under wilderness conditions, a person must drink _____ litres of water per day.

3. What is the most common error people make when constructing a temporary shelter for protection from the cold?

   _____

   _____

4. Circle the correct answer.
   When constructing a shelter for protection from the cold, it is essential to place insulating materials such as leaves on the floor because you can lose as much as _____ percent of your body heat to the ground.

   a) eighty   **b)** sixty   **c)** forty   **d)** twenty

5. After unbuckling your seat belt, what is the first thing you must do to survive in a sinking car?

   _____

6. Circle the correct answer.
   In a burning house, you must always check closed doors for heat before opening them. Which part of the door should you check?

   a) the doorknob   **b)** the bottom of the door   **c)** the top of the door

7. Fill in the blank.
   In a lightning storm, if you can't count more than _____ seconds between lightning and thunder, you're in danger and need to find shelter.

8. During a lightning storm, it's safer not to talk on a land-line phone.
   ☐ True   ☐ False

9. If you're caught in an open field during a lightning storm, you should lie down to avoid getting hit.

☐ True ☐ False

10. Circle the correct answer.
If you're caught outside during a tornado,

a) get in a car.

b) lie down flat in a ditch or other low spot on the ground.

c) seek shelter among trees.

℗onder

 **LISTENING**

Roger Woodward and Niagara Falls

Stuart McLean (1948–) is a Canadian radio broadcaster, humorist and host of the popular CBC radio program the *Vinyl Cafe*. McLean's *Vinyl Cafe* stories have been published in a collection of entertaining and (often) moving books, for which McLean has thrice been awarded the Stephen Leacock Memorial Medal for Humour.

Roger Woodward and Niagara Falls
by Stuart McLean

On April 24, 2004, Stuart McLean broadcast the *Vinyl Cafe* from Goderich, Ontario, a small town located on the eastern shore of Lake Huron, about 300 km from Niagara Falls. During the broadcast, McLean told the story of Roger Woodward, a seven-year-old boy who, on July 9, 1960, survived a trip over the falls. Listening to the story that day was fifty-one-year-old Roger Woodward, who concludes the broadcast segment by commenting on his miraculous experience and McLean's gripping rendition of it.

BEFORE LISTENING

→ Read the quotations below, taken directly from the segment.

→ Rewrite the words in *italics* and write the definition for each in the chart below. You may wish to use a dictionary. The first one has been done for you as an example.

1. "Every time I stand on the observation deck … and I watch the hypnotically and impossibly black water roaring over the *escarpment*, I wonder about him and what it could possibly have been like to be in that water."

2. "Deanne was in the front seat; her brother Roger behind her. Jim was in the *stern*. And there were two life jackets on board. Roger wore one of them."

3. "The little fishing boat he was in hit the *shoal*."

4. "… because the current was picking up and the boat was starting to *drift* … down the river, toward the falls."

5. "His head was *throbbing* …"

6. "… later, doctors would tell him he had a *concussion*."

7. "His head was slammed against the rocks, and he was sucked under the *churning* water and shot back out again like he was being blown out of a whale's blowhole."

8. "John had seen the capsized fishing boat *whisk* by him."

9. "What Roger saw was that he was moving swiftly toward the edge of an *abyss*."

10. "He just knew he was approaching a *void* …"

WORDS IN ITALICS	DEFINITIONS
1. *escarpment*	(long and steep) cliff
2.	
3.	
4.	
5.	
6.	
7.	
8.	
9.	
10.	

WHILE LISTENING

Stories have a beginning and a middle, plus an end that differs from the beginning because something *happens* in the middle. In other words, stories have a plot.

German dramatist and novelist Gustav Freytag (1816–1895) considered plot a dramatic structure that can be divided into five parts:

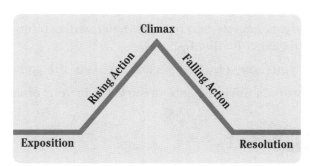

Exposition: setting, introduction of main character(s) and basic conflict

Rising Action: complications or secondary conflicts arise, creating tension

Climax: turning point, marking a change for the better or for the worse

Falling Action: tying up loose ends

Resolution: conflict(s) resolved

The story "Roger Woodward and Niagara Falls" fits Freytag's dramatic structure. As you are listening, apply this structure to the story. Sequence the events of the story and indicate whether each is part of the exposition (E), the rising action (RA), the climax (C), the falling action (FA) or the resolution (R).

SEQUENCE	THE STORY "ROGER WOODWARD AND NIAGARA FALLS"	PART
	The current quickens, and the boat begins to drift.	
1	A boy, his sister and a family friend decide to go for a boat ride.	E
	The boy returns to the falls ten years later and is not as terrified.	
	The boat hits a shoal, and the propeller stops working.	
	The boy arrives at the edge of the falls (and is at peace) and begins his drop.	
	The boat is hit by waves, and the boat flips.	
	The boy approaches the falls.	
	The boy is cared for in the hospital.	
	The boy floats in a cloud of mist.	
	The boy returns to the falls a few weeks later and is terrified.	
	The boy is saved by the captain of the *Maid of the Mist*.	
	The sister is saved by bystanders.	

AFTER LISTENING

→ Discuss each of the questions below as a class.

1. What makes the story riveting?

2. Of all the bystanders watching the story unfold, why did only two step forward to help the victims?

3. Roger gets angry when he sees the crowd watching him yet doing nothing. Was his anger justified?

4. Were you moved by Roger's comments at the end of the segment? Explain.

5. The story is obviously about survival. In your opinion, what is the theme?

READING 3.1

Short Story: Sociology

Katherine Govier (1948–) is an educator, editor, novelist and short-story writer living in Toronto. She is a winner of the Toronto Book Award (1992) and the Marian Engel Award (1997).

READING FOR INFORMATION

→ Read the short story a first time, underlining the words listed in the chart below and highlighting information essential to understanding the plot. (The vocabulary is listed in order of appearance in the text.)

→ Fill in the chart, defining the words according to their contexts. (You may need to refer to a dictionary.)

→ In sixty words or fewer, summarize the plot in the space provided.

VOCABULARY	DEFINITION	VOCABULARY	DEFINITION
1. drawling (adj.)		6. spared (v.)	
2. morbidly (adv.)		7. callousness (n.)	
3. divined (v.)		8. gloated (v.)	
4. carriage (n.)		9. put a damper on (something) (exp.)	
5. perilous (adj.)		10. startled (adj.)	

PLOT SUMMARY

Sociology

by Katherine Govier

On the porch Ellen stood without looking behind her, like a pack horse at a crossing where she'd stopped many times before. Alec came up the steps: she heard the clinking as his hands sorted the keys from the change in his pocket. Then she heard a low, drawling voice.

5   "You folks stay right where you are, and this gun ain't going off. You keep right on looking at that door."

She supposed it was time this happened. Their house was in what you called a transition area: you couldn't afford to buy there any more, but you weren't supposed to live there yet. Ellen enjoyed living there, however.
10 She was morbidly fascinated by the differences in circumstances between themselves and the next-door neighbour who sat on his steps after dark and raised Newfoundland fishing songs to the sky. It fit with her view of the world, which was that as close as your hand were people who were not as lucky as you and therefore would like to kill you.

15   The man with the gun came up the stairs. He found Alec's wallet and took it. He took Ellen's purse. He asked for Alec's watch. The watch was gold with a gold band; it had been his father's, awarded for forty years' work in the factory in Quebec. Having died two months after retirement, his father had never worn it. When Alec reached 21 without a cigarette, his mother
20 added the gold band and gave it to her only son. Wordlessly, Alec snapped it off his wrist and handed it over. Ellen groaned. Then the gunman got greedy.

   "Your jewellery too," he said. He took a handful of Ellen's hair and pulled it back to see if she was wearing earrings. She wasn't. She had only a couple of rings, her wedding band and one other, which was a pearl she'd gotten
25 for her sixteenth birthday. Earlier that month the pearl had become tight, and she had switched it to a smaller finger. Now she pulled and got it off. The wedding ring was hopeless.

"I can't get it off," she said to the mugger. "My fingers are swollen because I'm pregnant."

30 She looked him in the eye as she said the word pregnant. She felt she had never been in such danger; she had to enunciate the point of greatest risk. She was testing. It had been her fantasy during these last months that she would run into one of those maniacs who shot pregnant women in the belly or cut them open with a knife.

35 But the mugger looked back at her with a disinterested rage. Perhaps he would shoot her finger off and get the ring that way. It was still early in the evening, however, and a man was walking by only fifteen feet away, so the mugger just snarled and ran off.

Ellen and Alec attended prenatal classes in a boys' club gymnasium in
40 Cabbagetown. Alongside nine other pregnant women Ellen lay on the gym floor on a blanket brought from home and practised breathing patterns to prepare herself for labour. Her head on the pink and blue flowered pillow-case from their bedroom, she raised her hips and lowered them again; the water balloon that was her stomach went up and down. Then she got
45 on hands and knees and Alec rolled tennis balls on her back as she humped it up and down like a dog trying to vomit. The idea was to make the birth natural.

They kept this up for six consecutive Thursdays. On the whole Ellen was disappointed in the classes. It was not the material so much as the other
50 people. She'd thought their common predicament would promote instant friendship, but it had not. This was not for lack of effort on the part of the instructor, Riva, who used the word "share" frequently. By the end they would develop a limited closeness, like that of people stuck together in a train which is liable to go off the tracks. But where they came from, where
55 they would go afterward would not be mentioned.

Ellen tried to pin down some information. She learned that Gloria and Ted were born-agains. She divined that Miriam was at least forty and was not married to the man she came with. She explained them to Alec, who disapproved of her curiosity. The only ones she could not explain were
60 Robert and June.

June was tall with blonde hair and moved hesitantly, but gracefully. Her eyes were cloudy blue. Sometimes the irises darted back and forth as if panicked, but Ellen did not believe she saw anything at all, not even light and shadow, because of the way she held her head. The way she held her
65 head was the best part about her. Her carriage was like that of a large and elegant bird, her head alert and still as if she were listening for an alarm. Her seeing-eye dog lay at her feet, so devoted that he made the husband look like a redundancy. Robert was thickset, pimply, and sullen, and he watched June all the time.

70 June gave what the rest withheld; she laughed, she talked her fear. Ellen remembered best the day she sat on her metal stacking chair like an oracle, transparent eyelids showing the darting of sightless eyes. "I can't believe it's me who's pregnant," she said. "I suppose because I've never seen myself."

But isn't that what it's like, Ellen thought.

75 On the last night of class they watched a film of natural childbirth. Someone had brought popcorn, and they stared at the screen, silently passing the bucket. In the dark room Ellen could hear Robert's nasal voice very softly telling June what was being shown. "The baby is coming out of the mother's body," he said. Ellen and Alec both cried. Ellen thought that most of the
80 other people in the class did too. She didn't know for sure though because when the lights went up, she didn't want to look too closely at their faces.

Riva packed the projector, and the women and their supporters made ready to leave. Swollen feet pushed back into bulging shoes, knees poked out to ten and two o'clock as legs strained to lift the immobile trunks.
85 Stomachs first, they walked; the hard, heavy egg shapes pushing flesh away from the centre up to chest, arms, puffing the cheeks. Eyes red from strain, the ten making each other seem more grotesque than ever, the women made ready to go alone into the perilous future.

In the hospital, Ellen forgot all about her childbirth training and began
90 screaming for an anaesthetic. The baby was two weeks late and labour was being induced with a drug. "This baby must like you a lot," said the doctor, turning up the dose again. "He doesn't want to be born." When he came, he wasn't breathing, so the nurse grabbed him and ran down the hall. "My mother always said the cord around the neck meant they're lucky,"
95 said Alec. Ellen lay draped in green sheets, being stitched up by the doctor. She felt robbed, raped, aching, and empty. She told Alec it was just like being mugged, and they both began to laugh.

"Tell that to Riva," he said.

"But I don't feel bad. I feel—purified."

CULTURAL NOTE

Inspired by the gods, an oracle (derived from the Latin verb *orare* "to speak") was a priest or priestess in classical antiquity who gave counsel or made prophetic predictions.

"Anyone who feels purified after a mugging has a bad case," said Alec.

In two hours they brought Alain back, cleaned up and swathed in a little white flannel blanket with a toque on his head to keep in the heat. Ellen began to think of the others in the class and how it would be for them. "I wonder what the odds are in ten births," she said, holding her son.

105 The party was at their place. There had been an RSVP on the invitation, but by the evening before, Ellen had only heard from seven of the ten couples. They were bringing potluck, and she wanted to know how many paper plates to get. She found the class list with the telephone numbers.

The first thing she discovered was that Miriam's phone had been discon-
110 nected. Ellen began to feel superstitious. The idea of losing track of one of the group, of not knowing about one of Alain's peers, startled her. She called information and found Miriam's new listing. When she reached it, it turned out she had a new baby boy, and everything was perfectly all right.

Ellen's confidence returned. She decided to call the others she hadn't
115 heard from. The Uruguayan woman had a girl, but Ellen didn't understand any of the details because of the language problem. She hung up and dialed June. The telephone rang seven times, and no one answered.

That was odd; there was always someone home when you have a new baby. She waited until after dinner and then tried again. This time Robert
120 answered. Ellen felt irritated by the sound of his voice; that was when she realized how much she wanted to speak with June. But she said who she was to Robert and asked if they were coming to the party.

Robert cleared a rasp from his throat. Then he sucked in air. "I might as well be straight with you," he said. "We lost our baby."

125 "Oh my God," said Ellen. "I'm so sorry. I'm so sorry to intrude."

"We got the invitation," he said, continuing as if she hadn't spoken, "and we thought about coming. June wanted to, but I didn't."

Ellen was silent. "But anyway," he said, "it's kind of you to call."

"Oh no, no I shouldn't have. I had no idea."

130 "June didn't want to tell people. She wanted them just to find out," he said, "naturally." Oh of course it would be natural, thought Ellen, and at whose expense? She was ready to cry with embarrassment. She was dying to know what happened too, but she couldn't ask. "I am very sorry to intrude," she said again, more firmly. "It's a terrible thing."

135 "Yes," said Robert.

Then no one said anything. Robert started the conversation again with greater energy. "But that doesn't stop me from asking about your baby."

"We had a little boy," Ellen said, "and he's just fine." She didn't tell Robert about the fright they'd had when Alain didn't breathe. It didn't seem proper
140 to have complaints when you had a live son.

"Congratulations," said Robert. "Your baby will bring you a lifetime of happiness." His tone was mean, humble but punishing. Ellen wanted to tell him that their lifetimes would never be so exclusive as he imagined, especially not now, but she didn't.

145 It was only as she told Alec that Ellen got mad. "Riva knew; she could have spared me that call; why didn't she tell me?"

"Maybe sparing you wasn't her concern," said Alec. He had not been in favour of holding this reunion. The incident only confirmed his belief that coming too close to strangers was asking for trouble. But he was 150 sympathetic. He stood in the kitchen, holding Alain very tightly against his chest, and comforted his wife.

At noon the next day the new parents began to come up the narrow sidewalk. It was funny how nine babies looked like a mob. The oldest was three months, the youngest three weeks. Two of them had great swirls of black 155 hair, but most were bald like Alain. One baby, born by Caesarian to the born-agains, had an angelic, calm face, but most were pinched and worried, unused to life on the outside. All through the house babies bounced on shoulders, slept on laps, sat propped in their infant seats. Now that it was all over, the parents could talk. They told birth stories about the heroism 160 of wives, the callousness of physicians. Those whose babies slept through the night gloated over those whose babies didn't. It turned out one man was a lawyer like Alec and even had an office in the same block. One couple had a live-in already, and about half the women were going back to work.

Ellen got the sociology she wanted all along, and she was happy. Word 165 had gone around about June, and everyone agreed it was better she hadn't come because it would have put such a damper on the party. The story was that she'd been two weeks overdue and had to go in for tests. At her second test the doctor told her the baby was dead. The worst part, all agreed, must have been having to carry the dead baby for another week. Finally 170 June went through a difficult labour. There was nothing wrong with the baby that anyone could see.

When they told the story the women's eyes connected and their lips pressed down. It was as if a train had crashed and the person in the next seat had been crushed. They could not help but feel relief, lucky to have been 175 missed. But with luck came fear that luck would not last, and the long, hard oval of dread that had quickened in Ellen along with her offspring was born.

Ellen wanted a picture of the babies together. They put Alain out first, in the corner of the couch, propped on his blanket. Others followed with Lila, Andrew, Evelyn, Adam, Ashley, Orin, Jackson, and William, nine prizes all in 180 a row. Their heads bobbed down or dropped to the side; their mouths were open in round O's of astonishment. They fell asleep, leaning on their neighbour or they struck out with spastic hands and hit his face without knowing.

The parents had their cameras ready. They began to shoot pictures, laughing all the while. The line of babies was the funniest thing people had 185 seen in ages. No one had imagined how funny it would be. The babies were startled. They looked not at each other but at the roomful of hysterical

adults. One toppled, and the one next to him fell over onto him. Then the whole line began to collapse. Strange creatures with faces like cabbages and changing goblin shapes, tightly rolled in blankets or drooping into
190 puddles of chin and stomach, they could have come from an alien star. The parents laughed, with relief at their babies' safe landing, and wonder at who they might be. The flashbulbs kept popping as the nine silly little bodies toppled and began to run together into a heap, until one of them, Evelyn, Ellen thinks it was, began to cry.

(2421 words)

Source: Govier, Katherine. "Sociology." *The Oxford Book of Canadian Short Stories in English*. Toronto: Oxford University Press, 1986. 398–403. Print.

READING FOR MEANING

→ Read the questions below.

→ Read the short story a second and a third time (or more), answering the questions as you do so.

1. The story takes place in four different settings in Cabbagetown, Toronto. Sequence these settings in the order they appear, writing 1 beside the first setting, 2 beside the second, 3 beside the third and 4 beside the fourth.

_____ In a boys' gymnasium in Cabbagetown

_____ In a Cabbagetown home

_____ In a hospital

_____ On the front porch of (and then inside) a Cabbagetown home

2. The story takes place in the 1970s or early 1980s. Over what period of time does it take place?

_____

_____

_____

3. How would you describe Ellen's reaction to the mugging (lines 1–38)?

_____

_____

_____

_____

4. What do the following two quotations reveal about Ellen's mental state?

a) "She [Ellen] was morbidly fascinated by the differences in circumstances between themselves and the next-door neighbour …" (lines 10–11).

b) "It had been her [Ellen's] fantasy during these last months that she would run into one of those maniacs who shot pregnant women in the belly or cut them open with a knife" (lines 32–34).

_____

_____

_____

5. Why is Ellen disappointed in the prenatal classes?

_____

_____

_____

_____

6. How is Robert's physical description (lines 68–69) seemingly in keeping with his character?

_____

_____

_____

7. What do the following quotations tell us about Ellen's viewpoint on pregnancy?

  a) "She'd thought their common predicament [being pregnant] would promote instant friendship ..." (lines 50–51).

  b) "But I don't feel bad. I feel—purified [after giving birth]" (line 99).

_____

_____

_____

8. Explain the significance of the following: "Ellen began to think of the others in the class and how it would be for them. 'I wonder what the odds are in ten births,' she said, holding her son" (lines 102–104). Hint: Consider what comes immediately before and immediately after this excerpt from the story.

_____

_____

_____

_____

9. The narrator informs us that Ellen calls the three couples who don't respond to her invitation because she wants to know how many paper plates to get for the potluck. Do you believe this is the real reason she calls the couples? If not, why do you think she calls them?

_____

_____

_____

_____

10. The word *sociology* is used twice in the short story, the first time as the title and the second in the following quotation: "Ellen got the sociology she wanted all along, and she was happy" (line 164). Define *sociology* and explain the significance of the quotation.

_____

_____

_____

_____

READING FOR RHETORIC

→ Answer the following questions.

1. The narrator begins the story with a **simile**, comparing Ellen to a pack horse (line 1). How is Ellen like a pack horse?

_____

_____

2. Explain how the first three quotations **foreshadow** the event alluded to in the fourth:

a) "By the end they would develop a limited closeness, like that of people stuck together in a train which is liable to go off the tracks" (lines 52–54).

b) "Her [June's] carriage was like that of a large and elegant bird, her head alert and still as if she were listening for an alarm" (lines 65–66).

c) "… the women made ready to go alone into the perilous future" (lines 87–88).

d) "It was as if a train had crashed and the person in the next seat had been crushed" (lines 173–174).

_____

_____

_____

3. Ellen is drawn to June, a woman Ellen compares to an oracle (line 71). Why would Ellen be drawn to an oracle?

_____

_____

_____

EXAMINING AN ELEMENT: Setting

Working with a partner, examine setting in "Sociology." Turn to pages 3–4 and 10–11 in the *Literary Handbook* for an explanation of setting and a worksheet on it. Complete a copy of the worksheet, applying it to the short story. Be prepared to discuss your completed worksheet with the rest of the class.

DISCUSSION

→ Discuss each of the questions below in small groups.

→ Be prepared to share your answers with the rest of the class and to explain them.

1. Why do you think Alec disapproves of his wife's curiosity about the others in her prenatal class (lines 58–59)? Do you, like Alec, disapprove of Ellen's curiosity?

2. After giving birth, Ellen compares childbirth to being mugged, an experience she and her husband, Alec, have at the beginning of the story (lines 1–38). Ellen then claims that childbirth (and, by association, mugging) made her feel purified, to which her husband Alec states, "Anyone who feels purified after a mugging has a bad case." Why would Ellen feel purified after being mugged? Do you share Alec's opinion that she has a bad case (i.e., that she is odd) because of this feeling?

3. At the gathering, the parents of babies who sleep through the night gloat. In general, why do people gloat (line 161)?

4. Consider the following French proverb: "There is something in the misfortune of our best friends that does not displease us." In light of the short story "Sociology," why should this be so?

5. What is the topic of "Sociology"? What is the theme?

A Question of PERSPECTIVE If you were one of the parents with a healthy baby, would you have wanted June and Robert to come to the party?

READING 3.2

Memoir: The Ring

Bernice Eisenstein (1949–) is a Toronto artist and author. Her memoir *I Was a Child of Holocaust Survivors* was a *Toronto Star* Best Book of the Year. "The Ring" is an excerpt from this memoir.

READING FOR INFORMATION

→ Read the memoir a first time, looking for the words matching the definitions in the chart on page 60.

→ When you find a word, underline it in the text, write it in the chart and indicate its part of speech.

PARAGRAPH (LINES)	DEFINITION	VOCABULARY
1 (1)	**1.** craving for the unattainable	
2 (2–15)	**2.** article of clothing	
2 (2–15)	**3.** tearing apart	
3 (16–22)	**4.** person who grieves someone's death	
3 (16–22)	**5.** inability to express	
5 (28–36)	**6.** possessions	
5 (28–36)	**7.** attach	
6 (37–46)	**8.** ugly object	
6 (37–46)	**9.** ungrateful person	
14 (83–86)	**10.** painful and pleasant	

The Ring

by Bernice Eisenstein

Death leaves a hole that grows covered with longing.

After my father was buried, I put aside the garment the rabbi had cut, symbolic of the rending of loss, a black slip that stays folded away in my dresser. When it was time to go through my father's clothing, in a closet
5 stuffed full from years of buying suits and ties and belts and hats, there were many items to be divided. Most of the clothing went to charity. I took home several polka-dot ties, wide ones and thin ones, depending on which era they came from, and bow ties that needed tying up, not the kind that simply clipped onto a collar. There was a suede vest my father always wore
10 when he drove his truck and made deliveries to people's homes of barbe-cued chickens and eggs. I took the vest with me and wore it at times, when sitting at my desk, delivering ink to paper. And an undershirt, the European kind, sleeveless, low at the neck and back, hanging below my waist, which I used to wear on overheated summer nights when I went to sleep. No
15 strange dark images disturbed those nights.

The thirty days following the burial of the dead is called *shloshim*. It is a time of transition for the mourner as he moves away from the inarticulateness of loss and returns to the familiar rhythm of everyday life. It is a time when memory can fill the hours of night and day. I dreamt often of my father
20 during that first month after his death. He accompanied my sleep. It had been difficult for me to be rid of the final image of his struggle but in my dreams he was always youthful and in good health.

LITERARY NOTE

Memoir and autobiography are related literary genres: memoir focuses on a particular aspect of a person's life (career, marriage, etc.) while autobiography encompasses the person's entire life.

On the eve of the thirtieth day, my father entered a cavelike dwelling and motioned me to him. We held on to each other and then he left. He did not
25 return to my nights for quite some time. Words do not come to fashion themselves around the appearance of my father in that dream, but it is the dream that accompanies me when I draw his face.

Years after my father's death, my mother sold her house and moved into a condominium. It was a practical decision and she carried it out with
30 impressive independence. During a visit to her new home, not long after she had moved, I found her in a closet, going through her jewellery, and she asked me if there were some things that I might want. I have always attached sentiment to possessions, unlike my mother, believing that a person's belongings hold power, can capture the essence of their owner.
35 Perhaps because all the things of value had been taken away from her during the war, my mother is unable to bind herself to any object.

From a little drawstring pouch, she pulled out a ring her father had always worn—small diamonds set in onyx—would I like to have it? I hesitated, not wanting to hurt her feelings. His ring should go to someone who had easy
40 thoughts of warmth whenever he was remembered. No thank you, let someone else have it. Would I like to have something that my grandmother had worn? She presented a ring with a gigantic stone that brought one word to my mind: *chalashes*, what an eyesore. Once again, but for a different reason, I thought this should go to someone other than myself. After we went
45 through the back-and-forth dance of the giver and the ingrate a few more times, she held out another ring—would I like to have this one?

Rarely has my mother surprised me, but it was hard to believe that she could so casually offer this to me. A plain gold band, not a perfect circle, slightly bent, made oval. My father's wedding ring.

50 "Now I will tell you its story," she said, and then we sat at her kitchen table with the ring placed between us.

My mother arrived in Canada long before the country became her new home. When she was in Birkenau, she would be marched daily with other

female prisoners to a section
55 of the camp named after a country for the abundance it held. For a short while, my mother worked there, in "Canada," in one of the many
60 storehouses. It was a place where the confiscated possessions of Jews were sorted— watches, shoes, clothing, books, kettles, bedding, eye-
65 glasses—separated into piles that constantly grew. Inmates became archaeologists, cataloguing the remnants of their dying culture. ············➤

70 One day, my mother was so cold she found the nerve to ask the guard if she could take a coat from the heap of so many, wear it just for the duration of her work duty. The guard nodded and gestured towards the pile of clothing.

My mother put the coat on and slid her hands into the pockets so as to have the luxury of momentary warmth. Inside, she felt something sewn into
75 the lining, and without attracting any attention to herself, she managed to slip out of its hiding place a ring—this golden ring she was giving to me now.

She hid the ring in her shoe and was able to keep it until the end of the war. It was the ring she gave to my father when they married, not long after Liberation. It was all that she had to give him and he wore it forever. It belongs
80 to my image of him as he lay dying.

The ring has an inscription—L.G. 25/II I4. A man had been married in February 1914, and had died in Auschwitz.

I once read that the Chinese treasure jade because it is believed that the spirit of the wearer enters the stone and can be passed on to the next
85 person. So, from a stranger to my mother, to my father as her gift to him, then to me, I wear the ring as a bittersweet inheritance.

My mother has always been able to give and receive the simpleness of touch, and I hold her in my arms and say thank you. I don't know if she truly comprehends what this gift has meant to me. For reasons that I'm not
90 sure I understand fully myself, I have never been able to form the words between us to explain it.

My father has come back to me, and I carry the spirits of the dead within a circle of gold. The ring holds all that I have come from.

(1096 words)

Source: Eisenstein, Bernice. "The Ring." *I Was a Child of Holocaust Survivors*. Toronto: McClelland & Stewart, 2006. 11–16. Print.

READING FOR MEANING

→ Read the questions below.

→ Read the memoir a second and a third time (or more), answering the questions as you do so.

1. What is *shloshim*?

_____

2. Explain the significance of the author's dream on the thirtieth day of *shloshim*.

_____

_____

_____

3. Why does the author's mother not form an emotional attachment to her possessions?

_____

_____

4. What expression in paragraph 10 (lines 70–73) means "found the courage (to do something)"?

_____

5. Why does the author describe the ring as a "bittersweet inheritance"?

_____

_____

READING FOR RHETORIC

→ Answer the following questions.

1. What **image** does the author associate with her father's grave?

_____

2. In paragraph 2 (lines 2–15), which object **symbolizes** "the rending of loss"?

_____

3. Copy out the two sentences in which the author **juxtaposes** her father's job with her own.

_____

_____

_____

_____

4. What does the ring **symbolize**?

_____

DISCUSSION

→ Discuss each of the questions below in small groups.

→ Be prepared to share your answers with the rest of the class and to explain them.

1. Is thirty days sufficient time to return to everyday life following the death of a loved one?

2. Why is loss so difficult to articulate?

3. Does the mother's taking of the ring constitute theft?

4. Do personal possessions hold power? Do they capture the essence of the owner?

5. What is the topic of "The Ring"? What is the theme?

**ost**

In this section, one short (100- to 150-word) and two long (550- to 600-word) writing activities are proposed. The first activity focuses on the memoir; the second, on essay writing using a close-reading approach; the third, on essay writing using a reader-response approach.

❶ Paragraph Writing: Memoir of a Moment

In this unit, you read "The Ring," an excerpt from Bernice Eisenstein's memoir *I Was a Child of Holocaust Survivors* (pages 60–62). In this activity, you are asked to relate a significant moment in your life, a moment that taught you something important—something that will help you thrive in life and not merely survive!

→ Write a 100- to 150-word paragraph in the first-person singular about your significant moment.

→ Choose a title for the paragraph that reflects the lesson learned, for example, "How I Learned It's Better to Give Than to Receive."

❷ Essay Using a Close-Reading Approach: Setting

LITERARY NOTE

In a close-reading approach, you examine a literary work by focusing on relevant literary elements and techniques, tracing their occurrence throughout the text to determine meaning.

→ Using a close-reading approach, write a formal analytical essay of approximately 550 words on the following subject:

Most of the action in the short story "Sociology" occurs inside buildings. Discuss the significance of setting the story in enclosed places.

→ In the Ponder section of this unit, you answered questions on the short story and applied Worksheet 3: Examining Setting to it (see pages 56–58). Before determining your thesis (your opinion), review your answers and completed worksheet.

→ Double space your work and revise it before submitting it. You can find information about researching, referencing and revising in Appendix C (page 198).

LITERARY NOTE

In a reader-response approach, you are asked to respond emotionally or intellectually to a literary work, making connections between the work and experiences you have had and agreeing or disagreeing with important ideas presented in the work.

❸ Essay Using a Reader-Response Approach

→ Using a reader-response approach, write a formal analytical essay of approximately 550 words in answer to one of the following questions:

1. What does it take to survive?

2. What does it take to thrive?

3. Some events in life are inevitable. Death and going over Niagara Falls (when you are an inch from the edge) are two examples examined in this unit. Why does the inevitable inspire peace in some and dread in others?

4. How do you survive the loss of a loved one?

5. Why do some survive while others die?

→ Justify your answer by referring directly to one or more of the following works: "Roger Woodward and Niagara Falls" (page 47); "Sociology" (page 51); "The Ring" (page 60).

→ Before determining your thesis (your opinion), review your answers to the questions about the literary work(s) in the Ponder section of this unit (pages 50–63).

→ Follow your teacher's instructions as to whether or not you may use the first-person singular when writing an essay using a reader-response approach.

→ Double space your work and revise it before submitting it. You can find information about researching, referencing and revising in Appendix C (page 198).

ⓟresent

In this section, a short (two-minute) and a long (seven- to ten-minute) speaking activity are proposed. The first activity focuses on setting; the second, on survival, the topic of this unit.

❶ *Where* and *When* Matter

Setting dictates human interaction (plot). The type of interaction that can occur in a boxing ring will differ from the type of interaction that can occur in a box at the theatre (or so one would hope).

In this activity, you and two or three classmates are asked to form a group and act as ethnographers—people who study individual human societies. The activity has two parts.

A Outside the Classroom

→ Pick a place (school cafeteria, gym, library, local store, bus, restaurant, etc.) in which human interactions occur.

→ Observe these interactions for as long as it takes to find a story: a moment of tension (conflict, problem, etc.) between two or more characters.

→ Determine who the characters are, the part each plays and the reason for the tension.

→ Analyze how the setting affects the interactions: the physical, the temporal and the psychological dimensions.

→ Make notes of your findings.

B Inside the Classroom

→ Prepare a group oral presentation to be given to other students in the class.

→ Choose how you will relate your findings: a group **narrative**, a computer presentation, a dramatic recreation of the events, etc. (Make sure that each person talks for approximately two minutes.)

→ End your presentation with a statement as to how setting influenced the characters' actions (plot).

Source: Smith, Michael W. & Jeffrey D. Wilhelm. *Fresh Takes on Teaching Literary Elements*. Toronto: Scholastic, 2010. 100–102. Print.

2 A Formal Analytical Speech about Survival

In this unit, you have read about survival: a little boy's miraculous trip over Niagara Falls, babies who survive childbirth (and a baby who doesn't) and the survival of a family and a people.

→ Reflect on these works and then develop a thesis statement on the topic of survival.

→ Photocopy "Outline of a Formal Analytical Speech" on page 196.

→ Complete the outline as you prepare a seven- to ten-minute formal analytical presentation in which you both state and support your opinion by referring to at least two of the following three works: "Roger Woodward and Niagara Falls" (page 47); "Sociology" (page 51); "The Ring" (page 60).

→ Submit your completed outline to your teacher, making another copy for yourself.

→ When called upon, give your speech.

Important tips

→ Do not read or recite your speech.

→ Refer to your outline appropriately, making sure you maintain eye contact with audience members.

→ Speak to the person farthest from you (so you are certain to be heard by all).

→ Respect your time limit.

Participate

In this section, you will work individually, with a partner and in a small group on understanding themes related to survival, the topic of this unit.

Storytelling

Storytelling is the oral expression of (often embellished) stories to entertain listeners and, more often than not, to instill moral values or transmit a message (theme). Essential to good storytelling are a well-defined setting, interesting characters and characters' actions (plot) and a universal theme.

In the Ponder section of this unit, you listened to "Roger Woodward and Niagara Falls," a survival story told by master storyteller Stuart McLean.

In this activity, you and a partner are asked to research and then tell a survival story to your classmates.

Procedure

A Research and Writing

1. Search for survival stories on the Internet and select a story of interest.

2. In point form, write down
   – a list of characters;
   – a plot summary;
   – a description of the setting;
   – a theme.

3. Optional: Indicate any embellishments you think would add to the story.

4. Submit what you have written to your teacher for evaluation.

B Telling

1. Tell (don't read) your survival story to your classmates as if you were telling a good story to a friend:
   – Set up the story (indicating where and when the story takes place).
   – Introduce the characters and relate the characters' actions (plot) in an interesting way.
   – Create tension by introducing complications (secondary conflicts), building toward a climax and ultimately a resolution.

2. Play with tone, pace and loudness: change your tone for effect, quicken or slow down the pace and raise or lower your voice.

3. Use gestures when appropriate. (Don't overdo it!)

4. At the end of your story, challenge your listeners to spot any embellishments you might have made and determine the theme (or moral) of your story.

**ursue**

The following related works may be of interest for continued study. Modern editions are available of all books listed.

TYPE OF LITERARY WORK	ANNOTATED TITLES
Film	*127 Hours*. Dir. Danny Boyle. Fox Searchlight Pictures, 2010. • Recounts the story of Aron Ralston, a mountain climber who became trapped by a boulder and had to amputate his arm to survive—not for the faint of heart! *28 Days Later*. Dir. Danny Boyle. Fox Searchlight Pictures, 2002. • Following the accidental release of a highly contagious virus, four survivors must come to terms with a new reality
Memoir	Paulsen, Gary. *Hatchet*. New York: Atheneum, 1987. Print. • Novel for teens and young adults about a thirteen-year-old stranded in the Canadian wilderness Wiesel, Elie. *Night*. Trans. Marion Wiesel. New York: Hill and Wang, 2006. Print. • A remarkable story of survival set in World War II (translated from French)
Novel	Boyne, John. *The Boy in the Striped Pajamas*. New York: David Fickling Books, 2006. Print. • A **metaphoric** tale of a friendship between a Nazi commandant's son and a young boy imprisoned in "Outwith" (Auschwitz) during World War II Govier, Katherine. *Angel Walk*. Toronto: Little Brown Canada, 1996. Print. • An internationally celebrated female photographer recounts her life as she sorts photographs with a son she had abandoned Martel, Yann. *Life of Pi*. Toronto: Knopf Canada, 2001. Print. • Fantasy adventure story about survival after a shipwreck McCarthy, Cormac. *The Road*. New York: Alfred A. Knopf, 2006. Print. • Post-apocalyptic tale of survival: haunting!
Short Story	Rule, Jane. "Slogans." *The Oxford Book of Canadian Short Stories*. Toronto: Oxford University Press, 1986. 218–225. Print. • Story about a woman with cancer • Written by the same author as "A Law Unto Himself" (pages 177–178) Vanderhaeghe, Guy. "Dancing Bear." *The Oxford Book of Canadian Short Stories*. Toronto: Oxford University Press, 1986. 404–417. Print. • Recounts an old man's final struggle—with his caregiver

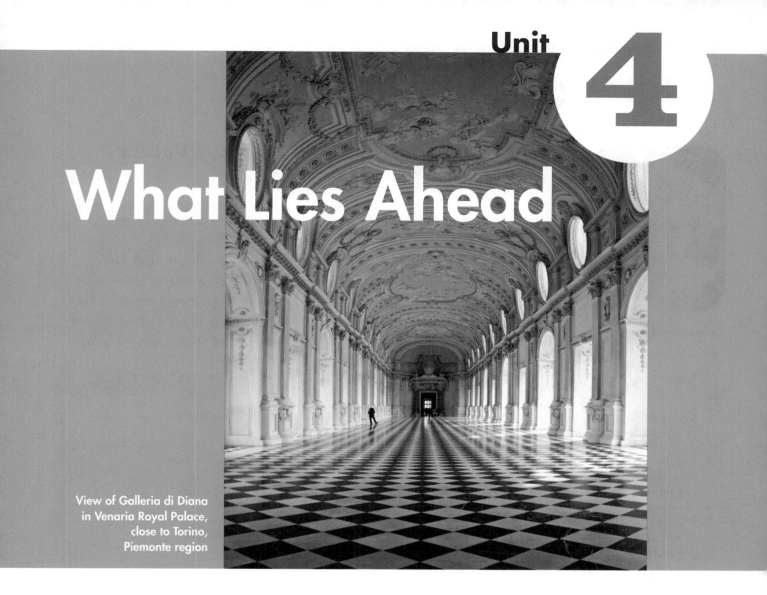

What Lies Ahead

View of Galleria di Diana
in Venaria Royal Palace,
close to Torino,
Piemonte region

review

No one knows what lies ahead.

We live our lives accumulating a past of present moments, headed toward a future that may not be there and about which we know naught.

For some, the future inspires fear; for others, hope.

In this unit, you will consider the future. You will read a poem about getting ready for it, a short story about wanting to know it and a memoir about creating it.

To discover what lies ahead, keep turning the pages.

𝒫repare

Margaret Atwood

Famous Writers' Thoughts about the Future

A Matching

→ Working with a partner, match the names of the famous writers below with the brief descriptions of their lives. Each description includes a famous quotation about the future attributed to the writer described.

a) Maya Angelou
b) Margaret Atwood
c) James Baldwin
d) Ray Bradbury
e) Pearl S. Buck

f) George Eliot
g) James Joyce
h) C. S. Lewis
i) W. Somerset Maugham
j) George Orwell

k) Edgar Allan Poe
l) William Shakespeare
m) George Bernard Shaw
n) Percy Bysshe Shelley
o) Tennessee Williams

DESCRIPTION	WRITER
1. Major English Romantic poet, married to the author of the Gothic novel *Frankenstein*. Quote: "Fear not for the future, weep not for the past."	
2. English author and journalist perhaps best known for his novels *Nineteen Eighty-Four* and *Animal Farm*. Quote: "He who controls the present, controls the past. He who controls the past, controls the future."	
3. Irish novelist and poet best known for *Ulysses*. Quote: "I am tomorrow, or some future day, what I establish today. I am today what I established yesterday or some previous day."	
4. Born Mary Anne Evans but better known by her male pen name. Author of *Middlemarch*. Quote: "I desire no future that will break the ties with the past."	
5. American author and poet known for his tales of mystery and the macabre. Quote: "It is by no means an irrational fancy that, in a future existence, we shall look upon what we think our present existence, as a dream."	
6. American writer who lived in China and wrote the Pulitzer Prize–winning novel *The Good Earth*. Quote: "One faces the future with one's past."	
7. Black American writer famous for the autobiographical *I Know Why the Caged Bird Sings*. Quote: "Prejudice is a burden that confuses the past, threatens the future and renders the present inaccessible."	
8. American playwright whose play *A Streetcar Named Desire* won the 1948 Pulitzer Prize for Drama. Quote: "The future is called 'perhaps,' which is the only possible thing to call the future. And the important thing is not to allow that to scare you."	
9. American writer and civil-rights activist whose novel *Giovanni's Room* stirred up controversy when it was first published in 1956. Quote: "The future is like heaven, everyone exalts it, but no one wants to go there now."	

DESCRIPTION	WRITER
10. Irish-born British novelist and academic famous for *The Chronicles of Narnia* and *The Screwtape Letters*. Quote: "The future is something which everyone reaches at the rate of sixty minutes an hour, whatever he does, whoever he is."	
11. English playwright, novelist and short-story writer whose notable works include *Of Human Bondage* and *The Razor's Edge*. Quote: "The future will one day be the present and will seem as unimportant as the present does now."	
12. Irish playwright and the only person to win both a Nobel Prize for Literature (1925) and an Oscar (1938). His work *Pygmalion* was adapted into the 1964 film *My Fair Lady*. Quote: "We are made wise not by the recollection of our past, but by the responsibility for our future."	
13. Widely regarded as the greatest writer in the English language. Quote: "We know what we are, but know not what we may be."	
14. Canadian poet, novelist, literary critic and essayist who wrote *Cat's Eye*, from which the following quotation was taken: "Potential has a shelf life."	
15. American fantasy, horror, science fiction and mystery writer best known for *The Martian Chronicles*, *The Illustrated Man* and *Fahrenheit 451*. Quote: "Without libraries what have we? We have no past and no future."	

B Questions about the Quotations

→ Respond to the questions.

→ Be prepared to discuss your answers.

1. Explain the following quotation from description 14, above: "Potential has a shelf life."

   _____

   _____

2. How does prejudice "threaten the future"?

   _____

   _____

3. Paraphrase C. S. Lewis's quotation about the future.

   _____

   _____

4. Which writer claims that our future selves are created today?

   _____

5. Which writer says that our future selves will view the present as a dream?

   _____

6. Which writers counsel us not to fear the future?

   _____

onder

Lorna Crozier (1948–) is a Canadian poet born and raised in Swift Current, Saskatchewan. She is the Chair of Writing in the Department of Writing at the University of Victoria. While Crozier's work deals with everyday life, "… it increasingly gestures towards a world of myth and magic that lies both within and beyond that everyday world" (Toye 133).

Packing for the Future: Instructions

by Lorna Crozier

Take the thickest socks.
Wherever you're going
you'll have to walk.

There may be water.
5 There may be stones.
There may be high places
you cannot go without
the hope socks bring you,
the way they hold you
10 to the earth.

At least one pair must be new,
must be blue as a wish
hand-knit by your mother
in her sleep.

15 Take a leather satchel,
a velvet bag and an old tin box—
a salamander painted on the lid.

This is to carry that small thing
you cannot leave. Perhaps the key
20 you've kept though it doesn't fit
any lock you know,
the photograph that keeps you sane,
a ball of string to lead you out
though you can't walk back
25 into that light.

In your bag leave room for sadness,
leave room for another language.

There may be doors nailed shut.
There may be painted windows.
30 There may be signs that warn you
to be gone. Take the dream
you've been having since
you were a child, the one
with open fields and the wind
35 sounding.

❁

Mistrust no one who offers you
water from a well, a songbird's feather,
something that's been mended twice.
40 Always travel lighter
than the heart.

(201 words)

Source: Crozier, Lorna. "Packing for the Future: Instructions." *Poetry: A Pocket Anthology*.
Ed. R. S. Gwynn and Wanda Campbell. Toronto: Pearson Education Canada, 2008. 318–320. Print.

VOCABULARY AND COMPREHENSION

→ You may wish to work with a partner as you answer the questions below.

1. Consider the title, "Packing for the Future: Instructions." To what is the future being compared?

_____

2. Complete the chart below. The first one has been done for you as an example.

ITEMS TO PACK	REASON FOR PACKING
a) Thickest socks	To help you walk when the walking gets difficult due to water, stones or high places (steep inclines)
b) Leather satchel[1]/ velvet bag	
c) Old tin box	
d) Childhood dream	

_____

1. small bag

3. Explain the meaning of the following **simile**: "At least one pair [of socks] … must be *blue as a wish hand-knit by your mother in her sleep*" (lines 11–14). (Hint: Consider the **symbolic** meaning of the colour blue in Western culture and literature.)

_____

_____

_____

_____

_____

4. Consider the following: "… you can't walk back into that light" (lines 24–25). What does "that light" refer to?

_____

_____

_____

5. With respect to lines 36–38, how would you describe someone who offers you:
   a) water from a well?

   _____

   b) a songbird's feather?

   _____

   c) something that's been mended twice?

   _____

6. Using your answers from the previous question, who should you not mistrust (lines 36–38)?

   _____

7. "A light heart lives long" is a well-known proverb. What is "a light heart"?

   _____

8. Interpret the meaning of the last two lines, considering your answer to the previous question.

   _____

   _____

DISCUSSION

→ Discuss each of the questions below in small groups.

→ Be prepared to share your answers with the rest of the class and to explain them.

1. The narrator advises you to take practical items (such as socks) and whimsical items (such as a key with no lock and a photograph). Why take items that are whimsical?

2. A dream can be a succession of images, thoughts or emotions passing through your mind while you are asleep. Remembering a pleasant dream can be comforting during difficult times. As a rule, do you remember your dreams? Is it important to try to remember them?

3. A dream can also be an aspiration. What is your most cherished dream?

4. Modern poetry is often ambiguous; that is, a modern poem is often open to several meanings or interpretations. Do you consider "Packing for the Future: Instructions" ambiguous? If so, does this ambiguity enhance or diminish the poem?

5. What is the topic of "Packing for the Future: Instructions"? What is the theme?

READING 4.1

Short Story: My Husband's Jump

Jessica Grant (1972–) is a Canadian writer living in St. John's, Newfoundland and Labrador. Her award-winning short story "My Husband's Jump" was republished in Grant's 2005 collection *Making Light of Tragedy*. Grant's novel *Come, Thou Tortoise* won the 2009 Books in Canada First Novel Award.

READING FOR INFORMATION

→ Read the short story a first time, underlining the words listed in the chart below and highlighting information essential to understanding the plot. (The vocabulary is listed in order of appearance in the text.)

→ Fill in the chart, defining the words according to their contexts. (You may need to refer to a dictionary.)

→ In sixty words or fewer, summarize the plot in the space provided.

VOCABULARY	DEFINITION	VOCABULARY	DEFINITION
1. begrudge (v.)		6. fumble (v.)	
2. forsaken (adj.)		7. feat (n.)	
3. doomsayer (n.)		8. quip (n.)	
4. insidious (adj.)		9. zealots (n.)	
5. gusto (n.)		10. deity (n.)	

My Husband's Jump

by Jessica Grant

My husband was an Olympic ski jumper. (*Is* an Olympic ski jumper?) But in the last Olympics, he never landed.

It began like any other jump. His speed was exactly what it should be. His height was impressive, as always. Up, up he went, into a perfect sky
5 that held its breath for him. He soared. Past the ninety- and hundred-metre marks, past every mark, past the marks that weren't really marks at all, just marks for decoration, impossible reference points, marks nobody ever expected to hit. Up. Over the crowd, slicing the sky. Every cheer in every language stopped; every flag in every colour dropped.

10 It was a wondrous sight.

Then he was gone, and they came after me. Desperate to make sense of it. And what could I tell them? He'd always warned me ski jumping was his life. I'd assumed he meant metaphorically. I didn't know he meant to spend (*sus*pend) his life mid-jump.

15 How did I feel? Honestly, and I swear this is true, at first I felt only wonder. It was pure, even as I watched him disappear. I wasn't worried about him, not then. I didn't begrudge him, not then. I didn't feel jealous, suspicious, forsaken.

I was pure as that sky.

20 But through a crack in the blue, in slithered Iago and Cassius and every troublemaker, doubt-planter, and doomsayer there ever was. In slithered the faithless.

Family, friends, teammates, the bloody IOC [2]—they had "thoughts" they wanted to share with me.

---

2. International Olympic Committee

₂₅ The first, from the IOC, was drugs. What did I think about drugs? Of course he must have been taking something, they said. Something their tests had overlooked? They were charming, disarming.

It was not a proud moment for me, shaking my head in public, saying no, no, no in my heart, and secretly checking every pocket, shoe, ski boot, cabi-₃₀ net, canister, and drawer in the house. I found nothing. Neither did the IOC. They tested and retested his blood, his urine, his hair. (They still had these *pieces* of him? Could I have them, I wondered, when they were done?)

The drug theory fizzled, for lack of evidence. Besides, the experts said (and why had they not spoken earlier?) such a drug did not, *could not*, exist. ₃₅ Yet. Though no doubt somebody somewhere was working on it.

A Swiss ski jumper, exhausted and slippery-looking, a rival of my husband's, took me to dinner.

He told me the story of a French man whose hang glider had caught a bizarre air current. An insidious Alpine wind, he said, one wind in a billion ₄₀ (what were the chances?) had scooped up his wings and lifted him to a cold, airless altitude that could not support life.

Ah. So my husband's skis had caught a similarly rare and determined air current? He had been carried off, against his will, into the stratosphere?

The Swiss ski jumper nodded enthusiastically.

₄₅ You believe, then, that my husband is dead?

He nodded again, but with less gusto. He was not heartless—just nervous and desperate to persuade me of something he didn't quite believe himself. I watched him fumble helplessly with his fork.

Have you slept recently? I asked. You seem jumpy—excuse the pun.

₅₀ He frowned. You don't believe it was the wind?

I shook my head. I'd been doing that a lot lately.

His fist hit the table. Then how? He looked around, as if he expected my husband to step out from behind the coat rack. *Ta da*!

I invited him to check under the table.

₅₅ Was it jealousy? Had my husband achieved what every ski jumper ulti-mately longs for, but dares not articulate? A dream that lies dormant, the sleeping back of a ski hill, beneath every jump. A silent, monstrous wish.

Yes, it was jealousy—and I pitied the Swiss ski jumper. I pitied them all. For any jump to follow my husband's, any jump *with a landing*, was now ₆₀ pointless. A hundred metres, a hundred and ten, twenty, thirty metres. Who cared? I had heard the IOC was planning to scrap ski jumping from the next Olympics. How could they hold a new event when the last one had never officially ended?

They needed closure, they said. Until they had it, they couldn't move on.

₆₅ Neither, apparently, could my Swiss friend. He continued to take me to dinner, to lecture me about winds and aerodynamics. He produced weather

maps. He insisted, he impressed upon me ... couldn't I see the veracity, the validity of ... look here ... put your finger here on this line and follow it to its logical end. Don't you see how it might have happened?

70 I shook my head—no. But I did. After the fifth dinner, how could I help but see, even if I couldn't believe?

I caught sleeplessness like an air current. It coiled and uncoiled beneath my blankets, a tiny tornado of worry, fraying the edges of sleep. I would wake, gasping—the *enormity* of what had happened: My husband had never
75 landed. Where was he, *now*, at this instant? Was he dead? Pinned to the side of some unskiable mountain? Had he been carried out to sea and dropped like Icarus, with no witnesses, no one to congratulate him, no one to grieve?

I had an undersea image of him: A slow-
80 motion landing through a fish-suspended world—his skis still in perfect V formation.

Meanwhile the media were attributing my husband's incredible jump to an extramarital affair. They failed to elaborate, or offer proof,
85 or to draw any logical connection between the affair and the feat itself. But this, I understand, is what the media do: They attribute the inexplicable to extramarital affairs. So I tried not to take it personally.

90 I did, however, tell one reporter that while adultery may break the law of *marriage*, it has never been known to break the law of *gravity*. I was quite pleased with my quip, but they never published it.

95 My husband's family adopted a more distressing theory. While they didn't believe he was having an affair, they believed he was trying to escape *me*. To jump ship, so to speak. Evidently the marriage was bad. Look at the
100 lengths he'd gone to. Literally, the *lengths*.

In my heart of hearts I knew it wasn't true. I had only to remember the way he proposed, spontaneously, on a chair lift in New Mexico. Or the way he littered our bed with Hershey's Kisses every Valentine's Day. Or the way he taught me to snowplough with my beginner's skis, making an upside-
105 down V in the snow, the reverse of his in the air.

But their suspicions hurt nonetheless and, I confess, sometimes they were my suspicions too. Sometimes my life was a country-and-western song: Had he really loved me? How could he just fly away? Not a word, no goodbye. Couldn't he have shared his sky ... with me?

110 But these were surface doubts. They came, they went. Like I said, where it counted, in my heart of hearts, I never faltered.

Herbert James Draper,
The Lament for Icarus, 1898

CULTURAL NOTE

In Greek mythology, Icarus attempts to escape from Crete by flying on wings made of feathers and wax. Icarus ignores instructions not to fly too close to the (heat of the) sun and falls to his death when the wax melts. The myth is an example of **hubris**.

The world was not interested in *my* theory, however. When I mentioned God, eyes glazed or were quickly averted, the subject politely changed. I tried to explain that my husband's jump had made a believer out of me. Out of *me*. That in itself was a miracle.

So where were the religious zealots, now that I'd joined their ranks? I'd spent my life feeling outnumbered by them—how dare they all defect? Now they screamed *Stunt*, or *Affair*, or *Air current*, or *Fraud*. Only I screamed *God*. Mine was the lone voice, howling *God* at the moon, night after night, half expecting to see my husband's silhouette pass before it like Santa Claus.

God was mine. He belonged to me now. I felt the weight of responsibility. Lost a husband, gained a deity. What did it mean? It was like inheriting a pet, unexpectedly. A very large Saint Bernard. What would I feed him? Where would he sleep? Could he cure me of loneliness, bring me a hot beverage when I was sick?

I went to see Sister Perpetua, my old high school principal. She coughed frequently—and her coughs were bigger than she was. Vast, hungry coughs.

Her room was spare: a bed, a table, a chair. Through a gabled window I could see the overpass linking the convent to the school. Tall black triangles drifted to and fro behind the glass.

You've found your faith, Sister Perpetua said.

I couldn't help it.

And then she said what I most dreaded to hear: that she had lost hers.

I left the window and went to her. The bed groaned beneath my weight. Beside me, Sister Perpetua scarcely dented the blanket.

She had lost her faith the night she saw my husband jump. She and the other sisters had been gathered around the television in the common room. When he failed to land, she said, they felt something yanked from them, something sucked from the room, from the world entire—something irrevocably lost.

God?

She shrugged. What we had *thought* was God.

His failure to land, she continued, but I didn't hear the rest. His failure to land. *His failure to land.*

Why not miracle of flight? Why not leap of faith?

I told her I was sure of God's existence now, as sure as if he were tied up in my backyard. I could smell him on my hands. That's how close he was. How real, how tangible, how furry.

She lifted her hands to her face, inhaled deeply, and coughed. For a good three minutes she coughed, and I crouched beneath the swirling air in the room, afraid.

It was a warm night in July. A plaintive wind sang under my sleep. I woke, went to the window, lifted the screen. In the yard below, the dog was softly whining. It was not the wind after all. When he saw me, he was quiet. He had
155 such great sad eyes—they broke the heart, they really did.

I sank to my knees beside the window.

I was content, I told him, when everyone else believed and I did not.

Why is that?

He shook his great floppy head. Spittle flew like stars around him.

160 And now all I'm left with is a dog—forgive me, but you are a very silent partner.

I knelt there for a long time, watching him, watching the sky. I thought about the word *jump*. My husband's word.

I considered it first as a noun, the lesser of its forms. As a noun, it was
165 already over. A completed thing. *A* jump. A half-circle you could trace with your finger, follow on the screen, measure against lines on the ground. Here is where you took off, here is where you landed.

But my husband's *jump* was a verb, not a noun. Forever unfinished. What must it be like, I wondered, to hang your life on a single word? To *jump*.
170 A verb ridden into the sunset. One verb to end all others.

To *jump*. Not to doubt, to pity, to worry, to prove or disprove. Not to remember, to howl, to ask, to answer. Not to love. Not even to *be*.

And not to *land*. Never, ever to land.

(1888 words)

Source: Grant, Jessica. "My Husband's Jump." *The Penguin Book of Contemporary Women's Short Stories.* Ed. Lisa Moore. Toronto: Penguin Canada, 2009. 147–152. Print.

READING FOR MEANING

→ Read the questions below.

→ Read the short story a second and a third time (or more), answering the questions as you do so.

1. In line 1, why does the author use both the past tense (*was*) and the present tense (*is*) to refer to her husband?

_____

2. After her husband disappears, various characters try to explain his disappearance. In the space provided, indicate the explanation offered by each. The first one has been done for you as an example.

CHARACTER	EXPLANATION
a) IOC	Drugs
b) Swiss ski jumper	
c) Media	
d) Husband's family	

3. How do you know the Swiss ski jumper is probably untrustworthy?

_____

_____

_____

4. In your own words, why does the narrator pity all ski jumpers?

_____

_____

5. The narrator was an atheist prior to her husband's disappearance.

☐ True   ☐ False

6. What are the "tall black triangles" referred to in lines 129–130?

_____

7. When do the nuns lose their faith in God?

_____

8. What causes the air to swirl in Sister Perpetua's room? Why do you think the narrator is afraid, crouched beneath the swirling air (line 150)?

_____

_____

_____

_____

_____

9. In lines 152–154, the narrator is awakened by her dog's whining and she talks to him, asking him why she was happy when everyone else believed in God and she did not. In response to this question, the dog "… shook his great floppy head. Spittle flew like stars around him. And now all I'm [the narrator is] left with is a dog …" (lines 159–160). How is this last sentence significant?

_____

_____

_____

10. Which form of the word *jump* is forever unfinished: a noun or a verb? Why is this significant?

_____

_____

_____

READING FOR RHETORIC

→ Answer the following questions.

1. Copy out an example of **personification** from lines 4–5. How is this example significant?

_____

_____

2. In paragraph 2, there is repetition of the words *up* and *past* and a repetition of structure in the last sentence: "Every cheer in every language stopped; every flag in every colour dropped." Why does the author use **repetition**?

_____

3. In line 20, the author makes an **allusion** to two literary figures: Iago and Cassius. How does this allusion enhance meaning? (Note: You may have to do some research to answer this question.)

_____

_____

_____

_____

_____

4. Consider the following: "… in slithered Iago and Cassius" (line 20). To what are Iago and Cassius being **metaphorically** compared? How does this comparison enhance meaning?

_____

_____

5. Consider the following: "It [sleeplessness] coiled and uncoiled beneath my blankets …" (lines 72–73). To what is sleeplessness being compared? How does this comparison enhance meaning?

_____

_____

_____

_____

6. Explain the possible **irony** of the following: "I had an undersea image of him: A slow-motion landing through a fish-suspended world—his skis still in perfect V formation" (lines 79–81).

_____

_____

7. Consider the following: "It was like inheriting a pet, unexpectedly" (lines 122–123). To what does the pronoun "it" refer? How does this **simile** add meaning to the text?

_____

_____

_____

8. Explain the **irony** of Sister Perpetua's name.

_____

_____

_____

9. In what way can "My Husband's Jump" be considered a Christian **allegory**?

_____

_____

_____

EXAMINING AN ELEMENT: Narrative Point of View

Working with a partner, examine narrative point of view in "My Husband's Jump." Turn to pages 4–5 and 12–13 in the *Literary Handbook* for an explanation of narrative point of view and a worksheet on it. Complete a copy of the worksheet, applying it to the short story. Be prepared to discuss your completed worksheet with the rest of the class.

DISCUSSION

→ Discuss each of the questions below in small groups.

→ Be prepared to share your answers with the rest of the class and to explain them.

1. Would knowing what happened to the husband weaken the story?

2. Did you find the story amusing? Odd?

3. Do you find the unknown frightening?

4. Are you optimistic or pessimistic about the future? About your future?

5. What is the topic of "My Husband's Jump"? What is the theme?

READING 4.2

Memoir: Waterworks

Timothy Findley (1930–2002) was an actor and writer who lived with William Whitehead, his partner of forty years, at Stone Orchard, their farm in Cannington, Ontario, and then in Stratford, Ontario. He is the author of critically acclaimed novels, collections of short stories and memoirs. Findley became an Officer of the Order of Canada in 1985 (Toye 184–186).

READING FOR INFORMATION

→ Read the memoir a first time, looking for the words that match the definitions in the chart below.

→ When you find a word, underline it in the text, write it in the chart and indicate its part of speech.

COMPANION
web+

PARAGRAPH (LINES)	DEFINITION	VOCABULARY
2 (2–9)	**1.** small amount	
2 (2–9)	**2.** periods of dry weather	
4 (14–18)	**3.** refuge	
7 (34)	**4.** doubtful	
10 (37–40)	**5.** deep hole	
11 (41–46)	**6.** incursions / advances	
11 (41–46)	**7.** swamp / soft, wet area of land	
15 (66–71)	**8.** successfully resist	
16 (72–78)	**9.** early evening / twilight	
19 (88–97)	**10.** sluggish inactivity	

Waterworks

by Timothy Findley

"We're going to have a real pond," Bill said. "Now."

We were out beyond the fence south of the garden. Our old pond lay behind us in a circle of willow trees and rushes. It was about the size of an average swimming pool—a shallow replica of the prairie dugouts of Bill's
5 Saskatchewan childhood. Every spring it filled to overflowing and through each summer its waters would slowly evaporate until, by autumn, there would only be a pittance left. What's more, recent years had produced a series of droughts, some of which had left the dugout nothing but a pit lined with dried, sun-cracked mud.

Prairie dugout

10 We had promised ourselves that the last major project at Stone Orchard would be a large, self-sustaining pond. This promise, first made in 1964, had been renewed so often that it had taken on the character of a New Year's resolution: *a promise made to be broken.*

For more than twenty-five years I had dreamed about this pond, this
15 water. Waking on summer mornings, I imagined it out beyond the spruce and willow trees, its shimmering surface already a part of the landscape— its wetness a haven to all kinds of creatures. But all I could see, in reality, was the muddy hollow we had, for years, tried to make into "our pond."

As if it were a desert mirage, the dream pond refused to let go of our
20 imaginations. Water is intrinsically part of human life—of who and what we are. The sight of it—the taste of it—the feel of it—even the thought of it is life sustaining. The fact is, the earth's great oceans are the amniotic fluid of the entire human race and all else that lives. Sinking into it—seemingly weightless—gives an almost immediate sense of peace and well-being. It is
25 not for nothing that for centuries, baths have been used to tranquillize the sick and pacify the mad.

Now, in spite of the continuing drought, Bill, the scientist, was making this bold declaration: the time had finally come to have our own body of

lasting water. And although I've always had faith in Bill's fund of scientific
30 knowledge, I was more than a little alarmed when he said we would go for
a depth of six metres and a width of almost forty. By the old count, in which
I still dream, this would be twenty feet deep and more than a hundred
feet wide!

"How will we fill it?" I asked, trying not to sound too sceptical.

35 "You'll see," he said.

Oh, sure. *If you dig it, the water will come …*

An excavator, two trucks and a backhoe rolled into the field one October
morning and the digging began. The pond was to be shaped like the letter
Q—with a small island in the middle and the old dugout forming a shallow
40 "tail." Two weeks later, we had a crater in our field. Huge—and empty.

All winter long, the dogs and I made forays into its depths. At six metres,
the excavators had expected to strike water. But the drought had lowered
the water table beyond their reach. And ours. Instead, the autumn rains
and snow had made a quagmire at the bottom and the island, with its willow
45 and cedar trees, stuck up out of the hole like some landscape gardener's
mistake—an aberration.

Eventually, the spring run-off began—at first, barely a trickle. I said
nothing—even though, at this rate, it would take at least three years to fill
the pond. Bill just said: *be patient* and gave his maddeningly self-confident
50 smile. Then, one night, the temperature rose and it began to rain. I was
awakened by a sound that up until that moment I had heard only in dreams.
It was the sound of rushing, pounding water—all the taps of heaven
seemingly opened by some mad angel thinking the time had come for the
Second Flood.

55 We went out with flashlights into the rain to see what was happening.
Niagara.

A virtual torrent of water was gushing from the culvert that drained the
fields to the east and was cascading down into the crater. Its great hollow
was already almost half-filled. Within another day—as the spring melt
60 continued—the pond was overflowing where Bill had created a buried run-
off culvert and the excavators had made a dip in the banks. The culvert
spilled its water along a streaming crease in the land, heading westward
towards the Beaver River—pausing it so happened, at the Khokar farm next
door to fill their pond. It seemed a miracle. Two ponds, not one, and ours a
65 dream that had finally come true.

What's more, the miracle has persisted. The run-off stream dries up
before the end of May, but now the pond itself, thanks to its six-metre depth,
holds enough water to withstand evaporation and maintain good levels
even through the hottest summer months. Moreover, having witnessed its
70 minimal loss of water, we believe there is seepage from the old springs, now
the water table has been revived.

Early April, the pond is pregnant with ten thousand lives—with frogs and
toads and snails; with crayfish, water striders, water boatmen and mayfly

larvae; with algae, plants and grasses and other botanical organisms
75 I cannot name. It is a magnet to everything living. The deer come up from
the woods at dusk and dawn; the foxes arrive after dark. Raccoons and
rabbits leave their tracks. Geese, ducks, herons return each year and king-
fishers, swallows and killdeer skim its surface.

All the pond lacked was fish. We decided on the most elegant and
80 colourful fish we knew—koi, the Japanese carp. Twenty-four fingerlings
from a nearby aquatic nursery were introduced. Black and gold and silver,
white and yellow and red. Added to these were sixteen goldfish, donated
by a friend whose own small backyard pond was overcrowded.

Last time we saw them, these fish had achieved new numbers hovering
85 around the three hundred mark. The largest koi now measure almost forty
centimetres, the goldfish, twenty-five. Obviously, their watery home is of a
size and has the resources to suit them all.

Most ponds have an ample supply of natural fish food—aquatic plants,
insect larvae and tadpoles. Still, we wanted to have some kind of active
90 relationship with the new arrivals, and decided on a daily feeding. Not
excessive—just enough to identify ourselves. We had been told at the fish
farm that lettuce and bread-crumbs—wholewheat, cracked wheat or rye—
were good for koi in the springtime, after a winter spent in relative lethargy
at the bottom of the pond. Otherwise, a special fish food that included
95 carotene, a colour enhancer, would suffice for both koi and goldfish.
As for "calling" the fish to feed, almost any signal would do, so long as it
was consistent.

There are wooden steps leading down to the water in front of the gazebo.
So it is here, every evening, that we bang three times with a stone—and the
100 fish appear. This is not unlike magic—and children are entranced by it.
Once, though, the feeding had a rather shocking pay-off, just when I was
about to show the fish to visitors.

I went to the steps with the food container, banged the required three
times with the stone, and there was the expected surge of movement
105 beneath the surface. A dozen fish—and then a dozen more—rose up and
began the usual feeding frenzy.

Well—it might have been the usual feeding frenzy, but it was not the
usual fish. Along with the koi and the goldfish, there were others. Small and
dark and obviously very young. Who the hell were they? Where had they
110 come from? The pond is land-locked, with the only flow of water coming
from the fields in spring, when the thaw is in full flood.

Bill suggested two possible answers. Fish eggs may have arrived from
the nearby Beaver River—either on the feet of one of our visiting herons,
or clinging to the water lilies we had transplanted to the pond. Or—during
115 the spring flood, it is just possible that small fish from the river may have
fought their way upstream. They would have to be extremely small to get
through the screening that keeps our fish from escaping through the
overflow. But ... who knows?

By June of its second season, we had asked Len Collins to design and
build a Victorian gazebo to be placed among the pond's bordering willows.
He made a wonder. It has an oriental cast, as so many Victorian and Edwar-
dian garden structures did, and has become the site of our summer evening
ritual. Alone or with friends, and always with wine glass in hand, we sit
there in silence, looking out over the water as the sun goes down. As the
birds retreat from the sky and the frogs and crickets begin to sing, the moon
and stars begin to rise. It is all one could ask for: peace.

Give the gift of water. Give the gift of life. Our pond *is* a gift. To us—and
from us. I look at it now and I wonder how I ever doubted its existence.
Everyone who sees it says: *it looks as if it has always been there.*

And yes—it does.

And yes—it has been. *If you dig it, it will come.* But only if you dream it first.

(1587 words)

Source: Findley, Timothy. *From Stone Orchard: A Collection of Memories*. Toronto: HarperPerennialCanada,
1998. 126–130. Print.

READING FOR MEANING

→ Read the questions below.

→ Read the memoir a second and a third time (or more), answering the
questions as you do so.

1. What had the author (and his partner) dreamed about for twenty-five years?

_____

2. Very briefly, how did the author and his partner make their dream come true?

_____

_____

READING FOR RHETORIC

→ Answer the following questions.

1. What is the "dream pond" compared to in line 19? Is the comparison a
simile or a **metaphor**? How does this comparison enhance meaning?

_____

_____

_____

_____

2. What are the world's oceans compared to in line 22? Is the comparison a **simile** or a **metaphor**? How does this comparison enhance meaning?

_____

_____

_____

_____

3. In line 36 and again in line 131, the author makes a cultural **allusion**. What is he alluding to? (Note: You may have to do some research.)

_____

_____

4. What **metaphor** is used in paragraph 12 (lines 47–54) to describe the "rushing, pounding water"? How does this metaphor enhance the work?

_____

_____

_____

5. In line 72, what is the pond compared to? Is this comparison a **simile** or a **metaphor**? How is this comparison similar to one used earlier?

_____

_____

6. Copy out the structural **repetition** in paragraph 25 (lines 127–129). How does this repetition enhance the text?

_____

_____

_____

DISCUSSION

→ Discuss each of the questions below in small groups.

→ Be prepared to share your answers with the rest of the class and to explain them.

1. What is a dream? How is it different from a goal? A fantasy? An illusion?

2. What dream(s) have you realized?

3. Have you let go of any dreams? Should you ever let go of a dream?

4. Are you ever too old to dream?

5. What is the topic of "Waterworks"? What is the theme?

ost

In this section, one short (100- to 150-word) and two long (550- to 600-word) writing activities are proposed. The first activity focuses on narrative point of view; the second, on essay writing using a close-reading approach; the third, on essay writing using a reader-response approach.

1A Analyzing One-Paragraph Narratives

→ Read both one-paragraph **narratives** and answer the questions that follow.

→ Be prepared to share your answers with the rest of the class and to explain them.

Narrative 1

My neighbour "old Mrs. Baxter" is such a nutcase. Every morning, I get up, get dressed, eat breakfast and walk my dogs. And every morning, she is at her window, glaring at me as I walk by. For the longest time, I couldn't figure out what her problem was—other than just being old and crotchety. Then a couple of weeks ago, she was outside talking with another neighbour, loudly complaining (for my benefit, I presume) how she was sick and tired of dogs "doing their business" on her front lawn. In the two years I have lived in the neighbourhood, my dogs have chosen her lawn as "the target" only a few dozen times. If she doesn't want dogs "doing what they do" on her lawn, she should move out of the city and go live in the country instead. I'm sure she'd be happier there.

(147 words)

---

1. What is the narrator's name?

   _____

2. What type of narration is used: first, second or third person?

   _____

3. Is the narrator omniscient or limited?

   _____

   _____

4. Is the narrator intrusive or unintrusive?

   _____

5. Is the narrator reliable or unreliable?

   _____

   _____

   _____

6. Is the narrator a participant in the story?

_____

> ### Narrative 2
>
> Those who saw her were struck by a physical beauty so intense that their senses could not fully comprehend the vision before them. Her beauty stirred warring emotions—a lethal combination of admiration and jealousy that attracted friends who wanted what she had but who quickly became vindictive, knowing they would never be so blessed. But that was many years ago now, and time had taken the raven hair, the porcelain skin and the exquisite body. And there she stands before the mirror, her reflection a reminder of what had once been and no longer was—her blue eyes alone salvaged from the storms of time, looking beseechingly at me and the pills in the palm of my hand.
>
> (118 words)

1. What is the narrator's name?

_____

2. What type of narration is used: first, second or third person?

_____

_____

3. Is the narrator omniscient or limited?

_____

_____

4. Is the narrator intrusive or unintrusive?

_____

_____

_____

5. Is the narrator reliable or unreliable?

_____

_____

_____

_____

6. Is the narrator a participant in the story?

_____

Source: Adapted from Smith, Michael W. & Jeffrey D. Wilhelm. *Fresh Takes on Teaching Literary Elements.* Toronto: Scholastic, 2010. 126–134. Print.

1B Writing a One-Paragraph Narrative

Using the **narratives** in part A as examples, write a one-paragraph 100- to150-word narrative. Your paragraph must be narrated in the first or third person. If using the first person, remember that a first-person narrator is intrusive; decide whether the narrator has total or limited omniscience and whether the narrator is reliable or unreliable. If using the third person, decide whether the narrator has total or limited omniscience, whether the narrator is intrusive or unintrusive and whether the narrator is reliable or unreliable.

LITERARY NOTE

In a close-reading approach, you examine a literary work by focusing on relevant literary elements and techniques, tracing their occurrence throughout the text to determine meaning.

2 Essay Using a Close-Reading Approach: Narrative Point of View

→ Using a close-reading approach, write a formal analytical essay of approximately 550 words in response to the following question:

> As the title implies, "My Husband's Jump" is narrated in the first person. Would the story be weakened or strengthened if it had instead been narrated in the third person and titled, "Her Husband's Jump"?

→ In the Ponder section of this unit, you answered questions on the short story and applied Worksheet 4: Examining Narrative Point of View to it (see pages 80–84). Before determining your thesis (your opinion), review your answers and completed worksheet.

→ Double space your work and revise it before submitting it. You can find information about researching, referencing and revising in Appendix C (page 198).

LITERARY NOTE

In a reader-response approach, you are asked to respond emotionally or intellectually to a literary work, making connections between the work and experiences you have had and agreeing or disagreeing with important ideas presented in the work.

3 Essay Using a Reader-Response Approach

→ Using a reader-response approach, write a formal analytical essay of approximately 550 words in response to one of the following questions:

1. Can you shape your destiny?

2. Would knowing the future enrich or impoverish your life?

3. Faith is a belief not based on proof. Does faith help or hinder the individual?

4. A leap of faith is sometimes necessary. Discuss.

5. With which of the following statements do you agree?
   a) When you stop dreaming, you stop living.
   b) When you stop dreaming, you start living.

→ Justify your answer by referring directly to one or more of the following works: "Packing for the Future: Instructions" (page 72); "My Husband's Jump" (page 76); "Waterworks" (page 85).

→ Before determining your thesis (your opinion), review your answers to the questions about the literary work(s) in the Ponder section of this unit (pages 73–89).

→ Follow your teacher's instructions as to whether or not you may use the first-person singular when writing an essay using a reader-response approach.

→ Double space your work and revise it before submitting it. You can find information about researching, referencing and revising in Appendix C (page 198).

Present

In this section, a short (two-minute) and a long (seven- to ten-minute) speaking activity are proposed. The first activity focuses on narrative point of view; the second, on the future, the topic of this unit.

❶ Telling the Tale from a Different Point of View

"Jack and Jill" is a classic English nursery rhyme, the lyrics to which are as follows:

> Jack and Jill went up the hill
> To fetch a pail of water.
> Jack fell down and broke his crown
> And Jill came tumbling after.
>
> Up Jack got and home did trot
> As fast as he could caper.
> He went to bed and bound his head
> With vinegar and brown paper.

→ Working with a partner or in a small group, retell the tale first from Jack's point of view and then from Jill's point of view. How does the change in narrative point of view affect the story?

→ Be prepared to share your retellings with the rest of the class and comment on how the retelling affected the story.

Source: Adapted from Smith, Michael W. & Jeffrey D. Wilhelm. *Fresh Takes on Teaching Literary Elements*. Toronto: Scholastic, 2010. 120–121. Print.

❷ A Formal Analytical Speech about the Future

In this unit, you have read about the future: getting ready for the future, the uncertainty of the future and dreaming about the future.

→ Reflect on these works and then develop a thesis statement based on the topic "the future."

→ Photocopy "Outline of a Formal Analytical Speech" on page 196.

→ Complete the outline as you prepare a seven- to ten-minute formal analytical presentation in which you both state and support your opinion by referring to at least two of the following three works: "Packing for the Future: Instructions" (page 72); "My Husband's Jump" (page 76); "Waterworks" (page 85).

→ Submit your completed outline to your teacher, making another copy for yourself.

→ When called upon, give your speech.

Important tips

→ Do not read or recite your speech.

→ Refer to your outline appropriately, making sure you maintain eye contact with audience members.

→ Speak to the person farthest from you (so you are certain to be heard by all).

→ Respect your time limit.

Famous Writers: Their Works and Influences on Their Works

In the Prepare section of this unit (page 70), you participated in an exercise in which you matched famous writers with their descriptions. In this activity, you will work with a partner to learn more about one of these writers.

Procedure

1. Select one of the fifteen writers listed and research his or her life and work, focusing on factors (gender, wealth, health, etc.) and experiences (both positive and negative) that may have influenced his or her writing.

2. Write a biographical sketch of the writer in which you include the following information:

   a) The writer's name

   b) Date and place of birth

   c) Date of death (if applicable)

   d) Nationality

   e) The type of work for which the writer is known (poetry, short stories, novels, essays, etc.)

   f) Most important works

   g) Factors and/or experiences that you believe influenced the writer's perspective (e.g., being a woman is an influencing factor for a feminist writer)

3. Revise and submit your biographical sketch, with a works-cited section, to your teacher for evaluation. (For information on researching, revising and referencing, see Appendix C.)

Note: Your teacher may schedule an appointment with you and your partner to discuss the writer chosen, your research and your choice of influencing factors and experiences.

Pursue

The following related works may be of interest for continued study. Modern editions are available of all books listed.

TYPE OF LITERARY WORK	ANNOTATED TITLES
Film	*Blade Runner*. Dir. Ridley Scott. Warner Brothers, 1982. • Science fiction based on the novel *Do Androids Dream of Electric Sheep?*, listed below *Field of Dreams*. Dir. Phil Alden Robinson. Universal Studios, 1989. • After seeing a vision, a farmer ploughs under a corn field to build a baseball diamond
Novel	Atwood, Margaret. *The Handmaid's Tale*. Toronto: McClelland & Stewart, 1985. Print. • Set in the near future, in a totalitarian theocracy that has overthrown the US government Bradbury, Ray. *Fahrenheit 451*. New York: Ballantine Books, 1953. Print. • Short novel about a futuristic society in which reading is outlawed Dick, Phillip K. *Do Androids Dream of Electric Sheep?* New York: Doubleday, 1968. Print. • The tale of an android bounty hunter set in a post-apocalyptic near future Findley, Timothy. *Not Wanted on the Voyage*. Toronto: Viking Canada, 1984. Print. • A retelling of the story of Noah Grant, Jessica. *Come, Thou Tortoise*. Toronto: Knopf Canada, 2009. Print. • An opinionated tortoise and an IQ-challenged narrator are caught up in a mystery
Short Story	Atwood, Margaret. "Simmering." *Murder in the Dark*. Toronto: Coach House Books, 1983. Print. • An unspecified time in the future when men's and women's roles are inverted Bradbury, Ray. "All Summer in a Day." *The Magazine of Fantasy and Science Fiction*. New York: Mercury Publications, 1954. Print. • Available online through *Wikipedia* • Set on the planet Venus, where the sun is visible for only two hours every seven years Eagleman, David. *Sum: Forty Tales from the Afterlives*. New York: Pantheon Books, 2009. Print. • An examination of forty unexpected afterlives

5

What Lies Beneath

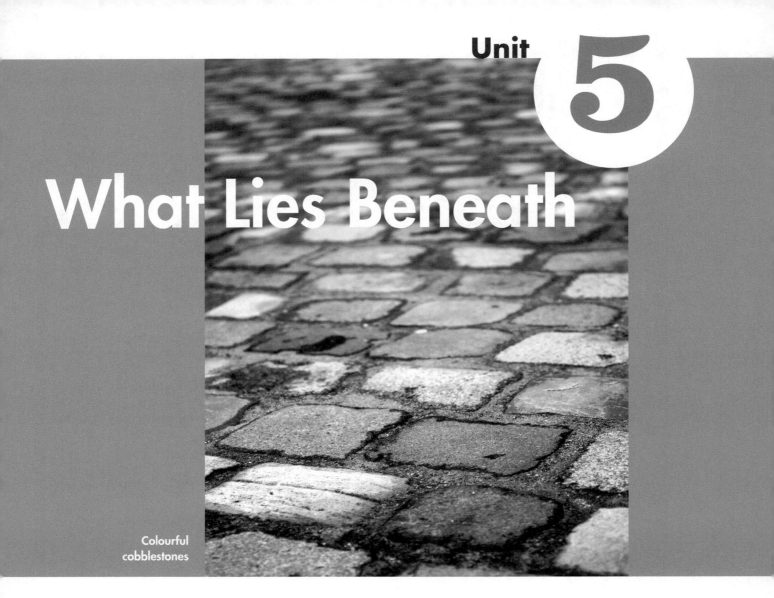

Colourful
cobblestones

𝒫review

In this unit, we're going to look at what lies beneath, and you're best forewarned: it isn't always a pretty sight!

You will see hatred, cruelty, distrust, insanity and evil.

You will also see love, kindness, trust, soundness and goodness—if you look hard enough!

Over the Toshogu shrine in Nikko, Japan are the "three wise monkeys," a pictorial representation of the proverb "See no evil, hear no evil, speak no evil."

Various meanings are given to the proverb, but it is often interpreted as a call to be of good mind, speech and action.

In this unit, you will see that not everyone heeds that call!

Behaving Badly

Many of the characters you will read about in this unit behave badly. Some behave so badly that the reader is left wondering whether the characters are crazy—or evil!

→ For each of the behaviours listed below, indicate with a check mark whether you would qualify the behaviour as bad, crazy or evil.

→ If none of these qualifiers applies, check *other* and indicate the qualifier that best describes the behaviour.

→ Be prepared to share your answers with the rest of the class and to explain them.

BEHAVIOUR	BAD	CRAZY	EVIL	OTHER
1. Abandoning your dog because you can't afford to keep him or her				
2. Taking pleasure from belittling your partner				
3. Cheating on your spouse and lying to cover up the affair				
4. Revealing extremely embarrassing information about a former boyfriend or girlfriend "to get even"				
5. Shoplifting inexpensive items for the thrill of it				
6. Scratching your neighbour's brand-new convertible with your car key to "take him down a notch"				
7. Lying to your parents (or friends) because they wouldn't approve of the truth				
8. Torturing insects				
9. Plagiarizing because you don't have time to complete an assignment on your own				
10. Intentionally transmitting a contagious, life-threatening disease				

Margaret Atwood (1939–) is an award-winning and internationally renowned writer whose career has spanned more than fifty years. Atwood is the author of collections of poetry and short fiction, novels and works of criticism (Toye 28).

Horror Comics

by Margaret Atwood

When I was twelve my friend C. and I used to pinch horror comics from the racks in drugstores. They were only ten cents then. We would read them on the way home from school, dramatizing the different parts, in radio voices with sound effects, to show we were above it. The blood was
5 too copious and lurid, the faces were green and purple, the screams overdone. We leaned against the low stone wall outside the funeral home, laughing so much that C., whose mother said she should never use the school toilets for fear of catching some unspecified disease, had to cross her legs and beg me to stop.

10 "I'm really a vampire, you know," I'd say in a conversational tone as we walked along, licking our lime popsicles. Those we paid for.

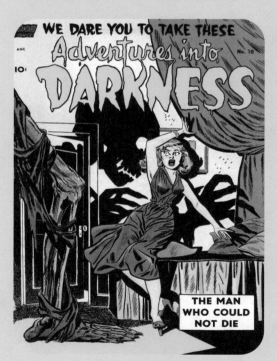

"No you aren't," C. said, her voice uncertain.

"You know I am," I said
15 quietly. "You don't have to be afraid of me though. You're my friend." I dropped my voice an octave. "I'm really dead, you know."

20 "Stop it," said C.

"Stop what?" I said innocently. "I'm only telling you the truth."

This occupied the four
25 blocks between the funeral parlour and the gas station. After that we would switch to boys.

In winter, when it was dark after school, we threw snowballs at grownups,
30 from behind, being careful to miss, doubling up with laughter because they
didn't even know they were being aimed at. Once we even hit someone, a
middle-aged woman in a muskrat coat. She turned around and looked at us,
white-faced and glaring. We ran away, shrieking with guilty laughter, and
threw ourselves backwards into a snow-bank around the corner, holding
35 our stomachs.

"The look on her face!" we screamed.

But we were terrified. It was the look on her face, pure hatred, real after
all. The undead walked among us.

(282 words)

Source: Atwood, Margaret. "Horror Comics." *Murder in the Dark*. Toronto: McClelland & Stewart, 1997. 16–17. Print.

VOCABULARY AND COMPREHENSION

→ You may wish to work with a partner as you answer the questions below.

1. Which words from the short story have the following meanings?

    a) steal: _____

    b) abundant: _____

    c) gruesome: _____

    d) staring angrily: _____

    e) screaming: _____

2. What does the following reveal about C: "'No you aren't [a vampire],' C. said, her voice uncertain" (lines 12–13)?

    _____

3. The characters throw snowballs intended to miss. What does this action reveal about them?

    _____

DISCUSSION

→ Discuss each of the questions below in small groups.

→ Be prepared to share your answers with the rest of the class and to explain them.

1. Are you a horror fan, or a horror phobic?

2. Do you enjoy scaring others?

3. Are humans essentially good or essentially bad?

4. What does "pure hatred" look like?

5. What is the topic of "Horror Comics"? What is the theme?

Short Story: The Woman Who Talked to Horses

Leon Rooke (1934–) is an American-born author living in Ontario. He is a prolific short-story writer, novelist and poet. Rooke was made a member of the Order of Canada in 2007 (Toye 536–537).

READING FOR INFORMATION

→ Read the short story a first time, underlining the words listed in the chart below and highlighting information essential to understanding the plot. (The vocabulary is listed in order of appearance in the text.)

→ Fill in the chart, defining the words according to their contexts. (You may need to refer to a dictionary.)

→ In sixty words or fewer, summarize the plot in the space provided.

COMPANION web+

VOCABULARY	DEFINITION	VOCABULARY	DEFINITION
1. emaciated (adj.)		6. haughty (adj.)	
2. standoffish (adj.)		7. bristled (v.)	
3. strutted (v.)		8. glean (v.)	
4. meek (adj.)		9. placid (adj.)	
5. tangible (adj.)		10. benign (adj.)	

PLOT SUMMARY

The Woman Who Talked to Horses

by Leon Rooke

"That's right," she said, "I talk to them. They will talk to me when they will talk to no one else."

"But they *can* talk," I said.

"Oh, sure."

5 "To each other?"

"All the time."

I looked over at the horses. They were in their stalls, eating hay, their rumps and hind legs about all I could see of them. They looked the same as they always had. I didn't believe they talked. I certainly didn't believe they
10 would talk to her.

"What's your fee?" I asked.

She looked off at the horses, too, then glanced at me, then worked one toe into the ground and looked at that. She was wearing blue cloth shoes with thick white shoelaces—all very clean. Too clean. She looked clean all
15 over. I didn't think she knew snot about horseflesh or about anything else. I figured she was a straight-out phoney.

"Your fee," I said.

She had a little itch behind one ear. She scratched there.

"Before we go into my fee structure," she said, "we need to have a quiet
20 discussion."

Fee structures? Holy Christ.

I had a good mind to turn and walk away.

"You won't tell me your fee?"

She pawed the ground again and the hand again went up to get at that
25 itch. I stared at that hand. She had long, slender fingers and white immacu-late skin with hardly any fuzz on it, and wrists no thicker than my thumb. All very feminine. She wasn't wearing a ring; I noticed that. I had her figured by this time. She was another one of those frail, inhibited, emaciated females who knew nothing about the real world but like to think they could tell you
30 about horses. One of those grim, pitiful creatures who was forever saying to themselves and to each other, *I can relate to horses.*

I'd had my share of that lot back when I had been boarding.

"I can't tell you my fee," she said, "until I know what you want of me and why you want it."

35 I nearly laughed in her face. The whole business was stupid. I didn't know why I'd let myself get talked into calling her. I wished now that she'd just get in her car and go away, so I could go into the house and tell Sarah, "Well, Sarah, you got any more of your dumb ideas? Let's hear them, Sarah." Something like that. And watch her shrivel up. Watch her mew and sob and
40 burn and hide away.

Christ, the time I was wasting. *All* the time I had wasted, listening to Sarah. Trying to take her seriously. Giving in when I knew it would prove a waste of time, all to keep a little peace in the house. To keep poor Sarah upright and not shrivelling.

45 I stared up at the house. Wondering if Sarah was watching. If she wasn't up there gritting her teeth, gnawing the woodwork, the broom in one hand, shoving hair out of her eyes with another, as she pressed her scared little face against a secret window. That was Sarah. Ever spying. The one way she had—so she'd tell it—of keeping her guard up.

50 "Mr. Gaddis?" the woman said.

"Yes, what is it?"

"All I need to know is what trouble it is you are having. With your horses. Then we can talk price."

"How about we talk *method*," I said. "*Then* price. You going to go up 55 and whisper sweet nothings in these horses' ears? Is that what I'm paying you for?"

The woman eyed me peculiarly. Her head tilted, her mouth a shade open. It wasn't dislike so much—though I knew she did. Nor was she making judgments. I didn't know what it was. A quiet distance. A watching.

60 Disapproval, too: that was there.

"I don't know what the trouble is," I said. "That's why I called you. I want to know what's going on. All I know is they've been acting funny lately."

"Funny how?"

"It's hard to say. Standoffish, maybe."

65 "Horses are like that. Can't horses have moods, Mr. Gaddis?"

"Not on my time," I said. "They're not producing. You'd think the bastards had gone on vacation. Zombies, the lot of them."

"I see," the woman said.

Bull. She saw nothing.

70 I stared at her open throat. She had on this soft cottony blouse, tinted like old rose, with a wide, folded collar, and at her throat a gold necklace no thicker than a fish line.

She had on these black britches.

Up at the house Sarah had all the 75 doors and windows shut up tight and outside not a hint of wind was stirring. Even the grass wasn't growing. It seemed to me all the life had gone out of that house. It looked dumb and 80 impenetrable and cold.

"Sure they can have moods," I said. "And they do. All the time. But this time it's different. This time it's affecting me."

She closed the blouse and held the hand at her throat.

85 "How do you mean?"

"I'm losing. I haven't had a horse in the running all year."

"That could be bad luck. It could be that the other horses are better."

"Could be but it isn't," I said. "These are good horses."

She glanced up at the house. Then she went on to the roofline and from
90 there up to the hills behind it. She wanted me to know she'd heard that
story a thousand times before. Every owner thought he had good horses.

I thought to tell her I had a fortune tied up in these horses. That they
were top dollar. Then I thought I had better not. You didn't talk fortune and
top dollar when some nut was trying to get it from you. Especially a nut
95 who imagined she could talk to horses.

"About fees," she said. "Naturally, if your horses that now are losing
begin winning after I've had my chat with them, then my fee will be higher."

"A chat!" I said. "You're going to have a chat with them?"

"A serious discussion. Do you like that better?"

100 "I don't like any of it," I said. "You wouldn't be here if—" I stopped. I didn't
see any point in raking up the family history.

"I didn't invite myself, Mr. Gaddis. You invited me."

She didn't say that with any anger. She was playing it very cool.

We both heard a door slam, and turned. Over at the back door of the
105 house my wife stood, splashing out water from a white enamel pot. Then
she swayed a little, standing there with her head bowed. Something must
have told her we were looking. She glared our way, then flung her pot into
the yard, and strutted back inside.

The woman beside me laughed.

110 I was pretty surprised myself. Sarah is prone to the odd explosion now
and then—for reasons totally incomprehensible—but she'd never done
anything like this before, not when someone else was around. Meek and
long-suffering: that was the word for Sarah.

"I gather your wife dislikes that pot," the woman said. She laughed again, a
115 velvety, softly arching laugh. I wanted to tell her it was none of her business.

"Forget Sarah," I said. "A minute ago you were saying something about
your fee structure and my hypothetical winnings."

"Was I?"

For no reason at all this woman suddenly squatted down on her legs and
120 began rooting through the thin grass with her long fingers. I couldn't make
it out. I couldn't tell whether she was searching for rock or flower or clover,
or for nothing at all. Maybe she had dropped a nickel. I had no idea what
the hell she was doing. I moved a little closer. I was tempted to step on her
hand. Her blouse ballooned out and I could see down her neckline to her
125 breasts. She wasn't wearing any brassiere.

Maybe that's why she was kneeling there.

She began speaking without lifting her head. "Yes," she said, "I think that's fair. Obviously much more is involved, more work for me, if I am to talk to your horses, root out their troubles, and get them winning. On the other hand, if you simply want me to walk over to the stalls and ask how they're doing today—"How you making it, kid," that sort of thing—and then come back here and simply repeat to you what they said, well in that case my fee would be minimum. Thirty dollars, let's say. Is that what you want?"

My wife was standing at the back door again. She had this fixed, zombielike expression which altered even as I watched. The skin reddened, her lips twitched, and in a moment she was twitching all over.

Then she pitched a pillow out into the yard. One of our big bed-pillows with the green slipcover still on it. Then she retreated.

The horse lady, down on the grass, hadn't noticed.

I had got around so that my back was to the door. "I was looking for something more solid," I told her. "Something tangible that I could act on. *Useful*, you know. Useful information. I *have heard* that you get good results."

She stood up. She turned and silently regarded the pillow in the yard.

"But you want my services for free, is that it, Mr. Gaddis?"

This made me mad. It was clear to me that this woman carried some sort of chip around on her shoulder. That she had no use for men. One of *those*, I thought.

"Now listen," I said. "George Gaddis pays for goods and services properly rendered, and he always has. He pays top dollar. But it's crazy for me to fork over hundreds of dollars just to watch you go over there for an hour or two and whisper into the ears of my horses."

She stopped studying the pillow and looked across at the door. No one was at the door. Sarah had closed the screen door, then she'd closed the cedar door behind it. It was quiet as a tomb in there.

"I don't often whisper, Mr. Gaddis," she said. "I speak distinctly and usually with some force, and if you'll allow me, most horses do the same."

Haughty and reproving. She seemed to think I deserved this.

"Their powers of articulation are quite well-developed, Mr. Gaddis. Perhaps more so than our own."

"They do talk?"

She bristled. "*Yes, they talk!*"

She struck off, moving down towards the fence at a determined pace.

She truly disliked me. There, she stood leaning up against the fence with her hands in her pockets. She had narrow shoulders and narrow bony hips that would fit in a cigar box. She was a woman all right, but she was too mean and skimpy for me.

"That filly I got from Quebec," I said, "she'd be speaking French, I suppose? *J'ai la mort dans mon â, J'ai la mort dans mon â, mon cœur se tend comme un lourd fardeau.*"

170　She spun and stared directly at me, her face burning. Mercy, one of the horses, plodded up to the fence and nuzzled her neck and shoulders. I wasn't impressed. Mercy was a dreamer. She liked people.

The woman strolled back, calm once more.

"We are getting nowhere," she said, "and my time is valuable. I did not
175 drive out here to give you a free estimate, or to illustrate my capabilities, or to listen to your troubles. No, Mr. Gaddis, the horses do not *talk* as such, not as we are talking, but they do think and develop their thoughts logically, except in dire cases. I am able, in a word, to read their minds."

"ESP, you mean?"

180　"Something like that." She fluttered a vague hand.

"You can guarantee this?"

"I do not give guarantees. I can swear to you that I shall talk to your horses, but the effectiveness with which you utilize the information I glean is clearly out of my hands."

185　"All right," I said. "Suppose I employ you and make good use of your information, and my horses begin winning. What's your standard contract? How much do you get?"

"Normally, ten percent."

"Good God! As much as that?"

190　"Yes. But in this instance I shall demand twenty-five."

She shot that out. She wasn't negotiating any more.

"You're out of your mind," I told her. "You got a screw loose."

"You are a difficult person to talk to," she said. "You are a distrusting person, a bullying one, and I should imagine your horses have picked up these
195 traits or are responding to them. It will make my job that much more difficult."

"Twenty-five *percent*!" I laughed. I still couldn't believe it. "Hell, lady, you'd be costing me more than my trainer does!"

"Then let your trainer talk to your horses."

It was my turn to walk down to the fence. Mercy saw me coming, and
200 plodded away.

"I'll have to think about this," I said. "I don't know if any of it makes any sense."

"You have my literature, sir," she said. "You have my testimonials. Call or not call, as you wish."

205　She started over to her car, a low convertible, red and shining and new, which stood in my driveway with the top down. Very expensive. Just as she was.

"I'd much prefer you *didn't* call," she said, stopping. "I don't believe I like you. Your situation does not attract my interest."

210　I waited until she got in the car.

"I don't suppose you like my horses *either*," I said. "I suppose you find them dull, too. I suppose you're one of those sanctified, scrubbed-out bitches who puts the dollar sign first. I don't suppose you care one crap about my horses' well-being."

215   Go for the throat, I thought. Get them in the old jugular.

She wasn't offended. Her expression was placid, composed, even a little amused. I knew that look. It was the look Sarah had when she found me in something foolish. The look would last about two minutes, then she'd begin slamming doors.

220   She started the engine.

I stayed by the fence, close to laughter, waiting to see if this was a woman who knew how to drive a car.

She cut the engine. She stared a long time over at my house, her hands still up on the wheel, that same benign, watchful, untroubled look in her 225 face. Then she turned in her seat and looked down at my fences and barn.

All four horses had come out. Mercy had her nose between the lowest boards, trying to get at grass, but the other three had 230 their necks out over the fence, looking at the woman in the car.

Something funny happened in the woman's eyes and in her whole face. She went soft. You 235 could see it soaking through her, warming her flesh.

"Go on," I said. "Get out of here."

She wasn't listening to me. 240 She seemed, for the moment, unaware of my presence. She was attuned to something else. Her jaw dropped open—not prettily ... she *was* a pretty woman—her brows went up, she grinned, and a second later her face broke out into a full-fledged smile.

245   Then a good solid laugh.

She had a nice laugh. It was the only time since her arrival that I had liked her.

"What is it?" I asked.

"Your stallion," she said. "Egorinski, is that his name? He was telling me a 250 joke. Not very flattering to you."

Her eyes sparkled. She was genuinely enjoying herself. I looked over at Egor. The damned beast had his rear end turned to me. His head, too. He seemed to be laughing.

She got her car started again and slapped it up into first gear. "I shall 255 send you a bill for my time," she said. "Goodbye, Mr. Gaddis."

As she drove out, down the narrow, circling lane, throwing up dust behind her and over the white fence, I could still hear her laughing. I imagined I heard her—sportive now, cackling, giving full rein to her pleasure—even as she turned her spiffy car out onto the highway.

260   Sarah was at the yard pump. She'd picked up the enamel pot and was filling it with water. She was wearing her print work-dress, but for some reason she'd put back on the high heels she'd been wearing last night. She'd put on her lipstick. The little scratch on her forehead was still there. It had swollen some.

265   She'd brought out a blanket and dumped that out in the yard beside the pillow.

As I approached, she glanced up, severe and meaning business. "Stay away," she said. "Don't touch me. Go on with whatever you were doing."

I could see now wasn't the time. That the time hadn't come. That maybe
270 it would be a long time before it did.

I went on down to the barn, scooted up the ladder, and sat on a bale of hay at the loft door. I looked out over the stables, over the fields, over the workout track and the further pasture and out over all of the long valley. I looked at the grey ring of hills. I wondered what had gone wrong with my
275 life. How I had become this bad person.

(2894 words)

Source: Rooke, Leon. "The Woman Who Talked to Horses." *The Oxford Book of Canadian Short Stories*. Ed. Margaret Atwood and Robert Weaver. Toronto: Oxford University Press, 1986. 263–269. Print.

READING FOR MEANING

→ Read the questions below.

→ Read the short story a second and a third time (or more), answering the questions as you do so.

1. Which of the following statements is *false*? Circle the letter of the correct answer.

   a) The narrator, George Gaddis, is the main character.

   b) From the start of the story, the main character is contemptuous of the female consultant.

   c) From the start of the story, the female consultant is contemptuous of the main character.

2. Why is it significant that no character other than George himself uses his first name?

   _____

   _____

3. Why is it significant that we never learn the name of the female consultant?

_____

_____

_____

4. George calls his horses "zombies" (line 67) and refers to his wife as "zombielike" (line 134). Why are all the creatures in George's world lifeless like zombies?

_____

_____

5. Explain the significance of the following: "Up at the house Sarah had all the doors and windows shut up tight and outside not a hint of wind was stirring. Even the grass wasn't growing. It seemed to me all the life had gone out of that house" (lines 74–79).

_____

_____

6. George describes the house as looking "dumb and impenetrable and cold" (lines 79–80). Which characters in the story would George (erroneously) describe this way? How is this significant?

_____

_____

_____

_____

_____

7. Why does Sarah put on lipstick and the high heels she'd been wearing the night before (lines 262–263)?

_____

_____

_____

_____

READING FOR RHETORIC

→ Answer the following questions.

1. It was Sarah's idea to consult with "the woman who talked to horses." George agrees to a consultation, "to keep poor Sarah upright and not shrivelling" (lines 43–44). How is this statement **ironic**?

_____

_____

2. During George's discussion with the female consultant, we get glimpses of George's wife, Sarah: we hear a door slam and see Sarah fling a pot into the yard; later, we see Sarah twitch and throw a pillow into the yard. What do these events **foreshadow**?

_____

_____

3. Explain the significance of the following **simile**: "It [the house] was quiet as a tomb in there" (line 154).

_____

_____

4. What is George's **epiphany**? What causes it?

_____

_____

_____

EXAMINING AN ELEMENT: Character and Characterization

Working with a partner, examine character and characterization in "The Woman Who Talked to Horses." Turn to pages 3 and 8–9 in the *Literary Handbook* for an explanation of character and characterization and a worksheet on it. Complete a copy of the worksheet, applying it to George Gaddis. Be prepared to discuss your completed worksheet with the rest of the class.

DISCUSSION

→ Discuss each of the questions below in small groups.

→ Be prepared to share your answers with the rest of the class and to explain them.

1. Is a person born bad, or does he or she become bad?

2. Which is easier: being good or being bad?

3. Do you think George will change?

4. Given his character, the narrator is not reliable. Sometimes his observations are accurate; sometimes, they are not. List two accurate observations and three inaccurate observations made by the narrator.

5. What is the topic of "The Woman Who Talked to Horses"? What is the theme?

A Question of PERSPECTIVE
If you were Sarah, would you leave George?

Short Story: The Nature of Pure Evil

Zsuzsi Gartner (1960–) is an award-winning Canadian author and journalist living in Vancouver. Her first collection of short stories, *All the Anxious Girls on Earth*, was published in 1999. Her short story "The Nature of Pure Evil" was included in this collection.

READING FOR INFORMATION

→ Read the short story a first time, underlining the words listed in the chart below and highlighting information essential to understanding the plot. (The vocabulary is listed in order of appearance in the text.)

→ Fill in the chart, defining the words according to their contexts. (You may need to refer to a dictionary.)

→ In sixty words or fewer, summarize the plot in the space provided.

VOCABULARY	DEFINITION	VOCABULARY	DEFINITION
1. mirth (n.)		**6.** gait (n.)	
2. impetus (n.)		**7.** whim (n.)	
3. gridlock (n.)		**8.** giddy (adj.)	
4. waifs (n.)		**9.** catatonic (adj.)	
5. squandering (v.)		**10.** bliss (n.)	

PLOT SUMMARY

The Nature of Pure Evil

by Zsuzsi Gartner

Hedy reaches for the telephone to make another bomb threat. In minutes, from the corner windows of this office on the nineteenth floor of the TD Tower, she will see people empty like ants from the art gallery across the way. Last week it was her own building, the week before an entire city
5 block—including the Hotel Georgia, Albear Jewellers and the Nightcourt Pub—and before that the Four Seasons Hotel. She knows it's illegal, but has convinced herself that it's not wrong, nor even harmful. It's a disruption of commerce, nothing more. Even the city gallery, with its reproductions shop and elegant little café, is a place of commerce. Hedy is like Jesus in the
10 temple, screaming, "Get out!"

Casting out the money-changers by Giotto (14th century)

Only, Jesus most likely wasn't seized with mirth after ordering the people out of the temple. Although Hedy's major acquaintance with the Saviour is not by way of the Bible, but through
15 the rock opera *Jesus Christ Superstar*, she can well imagine that Jesus didn't shake with uncontrollable laughter after knocking over tables of dovecotes[1] and chasing the money-changers and their customers into the street. And what would
20 Jesus think of the temples of today anyway, some of them as violently rococo[2] as the court of the Sun King, shamelessly passing their gilded collection plates at every opportunity? Her next target would be Christ Church Cathedral, no
25 question about it.

Hedy has to admit that her original impetus for disrupting daily commerce had not been half so noble as Jesus's. His was the sanctity of prayer. Hers was Stanley.

30 Hedy ironed the pleats of Stanley's white tuxedo shirt as he stood in the kitchen alcove in his undershirt, shaking Nuts 'n' Bolts into his mouth from the box and trying not to get any onto his freshly creased tuxedo pants. Hedy lifted the iron and it hissed like a small dragon. She pressed it down one more time. Stanley came over and traced her spine lightly with his
35 hand. "That's perfect, honey. Bang-on job."

After Hedy helped adjust Stanley's bow tie, she asked him one more time, "So how come I don't get to come to this wedding with you?"

---

1. compartmental structures for housing domesticated pigeons
2. style of architecture and decoration originating in eighteenth-century France and characterized by elaborate ornamentation

CULTURAL NOTE

Louis XIV (1638–1715) was known as the Sun King (*le Roi-Soleil*) and reigned more than seventy-two years, having ascended the throne at the age of four.

"Aw, Hedy, come on. Don't start with that again."

"I'm not starting with anything. It just seems funny."

40 Stanley shrugged. "I told you, I'm the only one invited."

"In that case, we'll see who has a better time. I'm going to curl up with a fat novel, my box of Quality Street[3] and some Bessie Smith.[4] I hate borscht, anyways."

"Atta girl," Stanley said and chucked her affectionately under the chin.

45 The next day, Hedy showed up at work with swollen eyes bulging like tennis balls. Tiny blood vessels had burst in her nose from a night of crying. "Allergies," Hedy said brightly in response to the receptionist's concerned look. Brigit, the salesperson at the next desk who had taken it upon herself to become Hedy's best friend, took one look at her and led her into the 50 Ladies. When Hedy told her Stanley had come home after the wedding, packed a suitcase and left because it had been his *own* wedding, Brigit put her hands over her mouth and looked like she'd stopped breathing.

"Oh, Hedy!"

"It's all right," Hedy sniffed.

55 "It's terrible. It's so weird. He must be insane."

Hedy shook her head. "He's quite normal."

"If he's not crazy, then he's pure evil."

Hedy looks to see if there's anyone within hearing distance and then starts to dial. At the time management company she works for, the employees 60 pride themselves on organizing their days effectively, conquering gridlock of the mind. They talk of things like Time Bandits and the Time Crunch Decade. By prioritizing their activities, they are seldom stuck working at their desks through the lunch hour. Instead, they are at liberty to go shop for the perfect wedding gift, pick up their dry cleaning, or stroll the mall, 65 a hot dog in hand, pretending to be free spirits while dodging skateboards piloted by heavily pierced and tattooed waifs. As a result, there is usually no one in the office at the tail end of the lunch hour, except for the substitute receptionist and employees organizing house parties who don't want to be caught squandering company time.

70 The first time Hedy called in a bomb threat, she did it without any fore-thought. She was on the telephone to a potential client, a paint wholesaler, on the verge of selling him a seminar package for his office staff, when through the big plate-glass windows of the nineteenth floor she saw Stanley walk into the Four Seasons, arm in arm with a woman.

75 She was sure it was Stanley. His red bomber jacket, his bouncy gait. This was one week after she had carefully ironed his white tuxedo shirt and sent him off to his own wedding. The iron had hissed with that reassuring sound she loved. She had even straightened his bow tie.

---

3. type of sweets
4. American blues singer (1894–1937)

She told the potential client that a colleague had just collapsed—heart
80 attack, cholesterol, angina, epilepsy, fish bone—it was hard to see from
where she was sitting, and she had better go. Her St. John Ambulance
training might be needed. Hedy surprised herself with her quick, bubbly lie.
She had always been the carefully honest one, the one who admitted to the
bus driver that her handful of change was a penny short of the fare, the one
85 who had always come home at least half an hour before curfew.

Her throat tightened at the thought of Stanley taking his bride to lunch
at Chartwell. They had gone to Chartwell, once, after they first moved in
together. The tomato-gin soup had tickled her nose and Stanley had made a
big show of choosing a martini "like Roger Moore would of drunk." In that
90 dark room, with fox-hunt wallpaper and sturdy chairs upholstered in tapestry,
Hedy had imagined they were now legitimately in love. What if Stanley and
his bride, his *wife*, now sat at the same table, toying with the same cutlery?
What if his wife put the very same silver fork into her mouth that Hedy had
used to pierce the crisp skin of her stuffed quail seven years ago?

95 Hedy opened the telephone book, looked up the Four Seasons, and dialled.

She had been surprised how easy it was. People pouring out onto
Georgia and Howe streets, dodging traffic and then standing, craning their
necks from across the road, waiting for the explosion. The police cars and
fire trucks whirring up from all directions, and Hedy standing alongside
100 her colleagues who anxiously lined the office windows wondering what in
the world was going on down there. She had pinched her forearms to keep
from laughing. All those people milling around on the sidewalks, scared,
excited, all because of her one little phone call. And there was Stanley,
standing by himself in the crowd, practically right below her window,
105 goosenecking for a better view, his new bride momentarily forgotten.

The newspapers wrote righteous and relieved editorials about the false
alarm. But Hedy realized that people had enjoyed the incident. They got to
go home and say, "You wouldn't believe what happened today!" People had
something to discuss while they waited at bus stops and SkyTrain stations.
110 They were *talking* to each other. By casting them out into the street, Hedy
had done them all a favour. Like Jesus.

As Hedy's best friend, Brigit felt compelled to launch a crusade to prove
Stanley was evil. Whenever Hedy insisted Stanley had never been the
slightest bit crazy, Brigit said, "Then he must be pure evil. There's no other
115 explanation for that kind of behaviour." Hedy found her friend's efforts on
her behalf embarrassing. Brigit would haul her up to a colleague's desk and
say, "Tell Tina/Shaffin/Morgan/Pascal, et cetera, exactly what Stanley did."
After Hedy finished the *Reader's Digest* version, with much prodding from
Brigit, Brigit would say, "Now, don't you find that insane?" The colleague
120 would agree, after glancing at Hedy, that yes, Stanley's actions sounded a
touch insane. "But if he's not crazy, then what?" Brigit would ask. "If he's
perfectly normal, wouldn't you say he was pure evil?"

Brigit showed Hedy magazine articles about people without consciences —people who, on a mere whim, crushed children's heads like melons, sold
125 fake and fatal remedies to the elderly, or were secretly polygamous. None of them showed any remorse. "It's not just the deed itself, it's the lack of remorse that makes them evil," Brigit said.

It was true Stanley had shown no remorse. "Gotta go, kiddo, Steph's waiting in the car," he had said as Hedy handed him his folded shirts, which
130 he carefully laid into the largest of their burgundy Samsonite bags, along with a handful of the fresh-smelling cedar eggs they kept in the underwear drawer. The luggage was a gift from her mother, who had felt sorry for them when they showed up at the airport one Christmas years ago with their clothes in an old Adidas hockey bag mended with silver duct tape. Hedy
135 considered the set of luggage theirs as opposed to just hers. That's what happens with things after you live together for seven years. She had wanted to ask what "their" song had been at the wedding. She needed to know it wasn't their song, Rod Stewart's "You're in My Heart, You're in My Soul." She sort of doubted it—Rod Stewart didn't seem to be held in high regard
140 these days. Still, some things remain sacred.

She wanted to ask whether Steph—or was it Stephanie?—knew about her, but she realized of course she must; he's up here packing his clothes and has asked her to wait downstairs. Hedy had felt giddy, almost hurrying him along, thinking, *His wife's waiting downstairs*, as if she was anxious not
145 to be labelled the other woman, some dame spread-eagled across the bed in filmy lingerie, cooing B-movie enticements.

Hedy had wanted to ask him why he was doing this. But she believed that if he knew, he probably would have told her.

"Hitler, Clifford Olson, David Koresh, those blond monsters in
150 St. Catharines, all anonymous albino hitmen everywhere," Brigit said, "and Stanley."

Hedy has it all down pat now. If she's not creepily specific, this may be the time they decide the caller is crying wolf. They might call her bluff. But then, perhaps they can't afford to take that chance. Not with all those children
155 in the art gallery, Hedy thinks, the ones there for the regular Wednesday children's tour.

Last time, she detailed the type of bomb and the group responsible, which resulted in an even quicker evacuation and a SWAT[5] team—*a SWAT team!* The entire TD Tower and adjoining mall had been emptied out. They
160 weren't allowed to take the elevators, for fear that might trigger the bomb, so everyone in the tower trooped down the stairs, some barely concealing their panic, others skeptical and cursing about sales they'd be losing to competitors. As Hedy was jostled down the stairs, she thought of the adulterers who might not be at work that day due to an illicit rendezvous
165 at Horseshoe Bay or the Reifel Bird Sanctuary. "Bob!" "Sue!" their innocent loves would say when they arrived home. "I was so worried about you

---

5. acronym for Special Weapons and Tactics

because of that bomb threat. I tried to phone but all the lines kept ringing busy." The adulterers, still in a postcoital haze, would let slip, "Bomb threat? What bomb threat?" And the cat, claws and all, would tumble out of the bag.

170 "Plastic explosives," Hedy says to the hysterical gallery attendant on the other end of the line. "Even trained dogs can't smell them." She knows enough to keep it short so the call can't be traced. Last week the employee who answered the phone at the TD branch downstairs had maintained the presence of mind to try to keep her on the line. "I have two little children,"
175 the woman had said. "Louise and Adrienne, two lovely girls. Do you happen to have any children, ma'am?" Hedy had hung up, admiring the woman's outward calm.

But this giddy gallery attendant has already dropped the receiver and is yelling something wildly in the background. Hedy hears the receiver bump
180 against the counter, once, twice, three times, and pictures it dangling on the end of its line, twisting a little like a freshly hooked fish. Someone picks up the receiver and Hedy hears the carefully varnished tones of a Kerrisdale[6] matron, "Who do you think you are?"

Didn't Jesus say, Let he who is without sin cast the first stone?

185 Everyone knows that from their elementary school catechism. And Hedy, well, she is without sin. She is the lamb.

"It's not like it was the love affair of the century," Hedy told Brigit. "We were just comfortable."

"That's still no excuse to treat you like that."

190 Hedy and Brigit entered the Frog & Peach, a lovely, rustic little French restaurant on the west side of the city.

"These women you're about to meet, they're very good people," Brigit said. "You'll like them. You spend way too much time alone. Women need female friends."

195 "Please promise you won't bring up Stanley."

Brigit made as if she was zipping up her mouth with her fingers and then tossing the key over her shoulder. She made such a show of it that Hedy could almost hear the key tinkle on the restaurant's terra-cotta tiles.

Hedy had finished her trout with persimmon chutney and sweet potato
200 gratin, and was toying with her fudge cake on raspberry coulis when Brigit brought up the subject of evil. To be fair, she didn't exactly bring it up, but grasped the opportunity when it arose. Mary Tam, who was a French immersion teacher, looked at the praline slice she'd ordered and said, "*Oh, c'est diabolique, c'est mauvais, je l'aime.*" Then she automatically translated,
205 out of habit: "It's devilish, it's evil, I love it."

"Would you say that people who do unspeakable things are plain crazy?" Brigit asked as if the thought just happened to descend on her from the pastoral fresco overhead. Her fork swayed dreamily above her lemon

---

6. a relatively affluent neighbourhood

mousse. "Or is there such a thing as pure evil?" Hedy picked up her knife
210 and made a quick sawing motion across her throat. Brigit ignored her.

"It depends on what you mean by evil," said Donna von something, who
was unbelievably thin despite her seven-month pregnancy. She had attended
university in the States and throughout dinner she fumed about an American
professor of hers named Bloom who had decried moral relativism. He had
215 even published a book on the topic, *The Closing of the American Mind*, or
something like that. When Hedy weakly joked that she thought the American
mind was already closed, Donna had looked at her with pity.

"What's evil in some cultures isn't considered evil in others." Donna's
tone implied she would mentally thrash all dissenters.

220 "By evil, I mean doing something that causes irreparable pain or harm to
innocent people," Brigit said. "I don't think it's relative at all."

"Female circumcision. That's brutal any way you look at it."

"Please, I'm still eating."

Mary put down her fork and took a big swallow of red wine. "Hurting
225 children is evil, rape is evil, eating people is evil."

"What if you eat someone to survive, like those rugby players that crashed
in the Andes? And look at how curious everyone was, wanting to know what
it tasted like." Hedy thought Donna's smile looked wickedly jejune,[7] as if she
had just scored a point at a high school debating tournament.

230 "When you've come into contact with pure evil, there's no mistaking it,"
Claudia, a practising family therapist, said slowly. She had been rather quiet
all through dinner and now the unexpected sound of her voice commanded
attention. "When I was living in Ottawa a few years ago, I went to an open
house one Sunday. It was a beautiful place in Sandy Hill, right near the
235 University of Ottawa. A three-storey sandstone, with enormous red maple
leaves brushing against the front windows because it was fall."

"Fall in Ottawa is fabulous," Brigit said. Everyone shushed her.

"It was full of people, and the real estate agent had put out a platter of
petits fours and was serving coffee in real china cups. It felt like some
240 exquisite afternoon salon as people wandered in and out of rooms, chatting,
sipping at coffee and nibbling little cakes. But there was this one room on
the third floor, sort of an attic bedroom, that people seemed to walk out
of really quickly. They came hurrying down the stairs, dribbling coffee
and crumbs."

245 Mary refilled the wineglasses. "I don't know if I can listen to this."

"I went up the stairs behind the real estate agent, who seemed almost
hesitant to show me that room. I walked right into it and immediately I felt
the hairs rise on the back of my neck and arms. The real estate agent stood
in the doorway, just outside the room, and tried to direct my view out the
250 window toward the Ottawa River. But something made me look up. The ceiling
was painted black, with thin red lines connected to form a pentagram."

---

7. childish

"Look, the hairs on my arms are standing up right now!" Mary held her thin arms out over the table. The black hairs glistened silver in the candlelight. The hairs on Hedy's arms were rising, too. She felt like she used to at sleepover parties when the girls tried to outdo each other with horror stories just before falling off to sleep. Maybe that's what evil was, just another party game.

Donna looked disdainful. "I find it really hard to believe they wouldn't have painted the ceiling over before attempting to sell such a prime piece of real estate."

"That's what I thought, too," Claudia said. "But I found out they had tried. They went through half a dozen professional painters and a couple of university students. Nobody could stay in that room more than five minutes. There was something evil in there, I could feel it. I've never come across a feeling like that before or since."

"I was talking about evil people," Brigit said, sounding irritated. "Not *spirits*."

Hedy looked up at the fresco and saw a bucolic scene of little satyrs chasing plump nymphs across faux-distressed plaster. The candlelight flicked shadows across it, creating the illusion that the creatures were moving, darting in and out of flames. She thought of Stanley and his bride, Stephanie, tousling on a king-size brass bed with jungle-motif sheets and decided that if Brigit brought up the subject of Stanley she would be forced to tip a burning candle into her lap.

"What about that person who's been calling in all those fake bomb threats?" Mary asked.

"Oh, that person," Brigit said. "That person's just nuts."

"I think we're talking about someone who desperately craves attention. Someone deprived of adequate affection in childhood."

"Original. I don't think you need a psych degree to figure that one out."

"I think it's pretty harmless."

"What if someone gets hurt, gets so scared they have a fatal heart attack right there on the street in front of their building?"

Hedy drifted in and out of the conversation. She thought about her childhood, a textbook case of love and understanding. Pork chops and applesauce, Snakes and Ladders, backyard swing sets, and a mother who hadn't been too embarrassed to hold a snowy white cotton pad in her hand and carefully explain what womanhood had to do with Hedy. She thought about Stanley, her affection for the springy rust-coloured hairs on his chest and his ability to bluster through most awkward social situations in an amiably anti-intellectual manner. But was that love?

"If hurting someone wasn't the intent, I would say it wasn't evil."

"Especially if they're sorry."

"What if they say they're sorry, but they're not."

"It's easy to say you're sorry."

"Only God really knows."

"What if you don't believe in God, or any gods?"

"Right."

God could really make people scurry, Hedy thought. God of Thunder, God of Lightning. Raining frogs down from the sky, now there was a feat.
300 Where had she heard that? How could a booming giant like God have had a gentle son like Jesus? But it was always the quiet ones who surprised everyone when they finally opened their mouths to roar, wasn't it? Or perhaps she was putting too much stock in the Jesus of Tim Rice and Andrew Lloyd Webber.[8]

305 "Evil has nothing to do with what's legal or illegal."

"I agree, I mean, there are so many unjust laws."

"Like which ones, for instance?"

"Always the devil's advocate."

"There's that word again."

310 "What word?"

"Devil."

"Ha ha."

Hedy stands at the window across the room from her desk, looking out toward the art gallery. A small person with green hair skateboards down
315 the granite steps. The Iranians are there, passing out their pamphlets, counting on the milk of human kindness. Others steal a moment from a busy day to sit on the steps and hold their faces to the sun. She feels happy, although she would never tell Brigit that. In Brigit's judgment, she has every right to feel paralysed with unhappiness, catatonic with indignation.
320 But Hedy has combed her heart and found no detritus,[9] no coiled reddish hairs, no rust flakes.

Brigit would find some fault with happiness, anyways. Yesterday, she showed Hedy a magazine article about a British psychiatrist who thinks happiness should be classified as a mental condition—because it's a highly
325 *abnormal* state of being. The psychiatrist wasn't referring to bliss, but a plain, old-fashioned level of contentment and calm. In which case perhaps Stanley is crazy after all, not evil, because he seemed so happy the last time Hedy saw him, unapologetically happy.

She wonders why people haven't started pouring out of the art gallery
330 yet. It's been almost ten minutes since her phone call, yet there are no signs of panic, no sirens piercing the air, no men in stiff black coveralls stealthily slipping through the side entrances of the gallery, their intricate bomb diffusion kits strapped to their belts. Hedy's mood loses a little of its fine buoyancy. She decides she must make the call again. She glances toward
335 her telephone, but sees that Brigit is back at the neighbouring desk.

"I was just listening to the CBC news in the car," Brigit says, as Hedy roots around in her top drawer for a quarter, "and did you know that

---

8. collaborators on *Jesus Christ Superstar*
9. debris

there's a trend away from accepting pleas of insanity in cases of aggravated assault? It's an acknowledgement of man's baser instincts. I mean men *and* 340 women, of course." Hedy nods as if she's paying attention, and then smiles as her fingers close around a quarter that's been nesting in a pile of paper clips. She tells Brigit that she's forgotten to pay an important bill and has to run down to the bank for a few minutes, just in case anyone asks. Brigit tut tuts, "Oh, those darn Time Bandits!" and waves her off with a 345 conspiratorial wink.

Hedy starts counting as she enters the elevator, needing to know how long it will take to get back upstairs. She wants to be there in time to watch all the people streaming out of the gallery, the panicked milling around with the merely curious, the emergency vehicles dramatically screeching 350 to a halt, the children noisily demanding to be told what's going on. As she walks through the shiny lobby toward the row of pay phones, Hedy feels positively grand. She is the one without sin striding quickly across the burning desert, thin sandals moulded to her calloused feet, the quarter hot and round and flat in the hollow of her hand.

(4038 words)

Source: Gartner, Zsuzsi. "The Nature of Pure Evil." *The Penguin Book of Contemporary Canadian Women's Short Stories*. Ed. Lisa Moore. Toronto: Penguin Canada, 2009. 127–138. Print.

READING FOR MEANING

→ Read the questions below.

→ Read the short story a second and a third time (or more), answering the questions as you do so.

1. In which Canadian city does the story take place? Hint: Research some of the place names referenced in the story.

   _____

2. Explain the significance of Hedy's next planned target: Christ Church Cathedral.

   _____

   _____

   _____

   _____

3. Who does Hedy blame for her behaviour (calling in bomb threats)? Why does she blame this person?

   _____

   _____

   _____

4. Hedy's first bomb threat was well-planned.

   ☐ True   ☐ False

5. Why did Hedy call in her first bomb threat?

_____

_____

_____

_____

_____

6. Consider the following: "Brigit showed Hedy magazine articles about people without consciences—people who, on a mere whim, crushed children's heads like melons, sold fake and fatal remedies to the elderly, or were secretly polygamous. None of them showed any remorse. 'It's not just the deed itself, it's the lack of remorse that makes them evil,' Brigit said" (lines 123–127). From Brigit's standpoint, would Hedy be considered evil?

_____

_____

_____

_____

7. Which of the following statements is _false_? Circle the correct answer.

a) After his marriage, Hedy helps Stanley pack, lets him leave with one of her suitcases and rushes him along so that his new wife, who is waiting in the car, doesn't suspect them of adultery.

b) Hedy thinks Stanley probably doesn't know why he behaved as he did.

c) Hedy equates Stanley with Hitler and other mass murderers.

8. Explain the significance of Hedy thinking about how adulterers would get caught by their mates as a result of her bomb threat (paragraph 32, lines 157–169).

_____

_____

_____

_____

9. Explain the significance of the following: "And Hedy, well, she is without sin. She is the lamb" (lines 185–186).

_____

_____

_____

10. From Brigit's standpoint, Hedy is a loner.

☐ True   ☐ False

11. Why is Brigit so keen on discussing the existence of pure evil?

_____

_____

_____

12. Brigit refocuses the discussion on the nature of evil from spirits (like the evil presence described in Claudia's story) to people.

☐ True ☐ False

13. Hedy blames her childhood for her behaviour (calling in bomb threats).

☐ True ☐ False

14. Explain the significance of the following: "But Hedy has combed her heart and found no detritus, no coiled reddish hairs, no rust flakes" (lines 320–321).

_____

_____

_____

_____

15. Explain the significance of the following: "'I [Brigit] was just listening to the CBC news in the car … and did you know that there's a trend away from accepting pleas of insanity in cases of aggravated assault? It's an acknow-ledgement of man's baser instincts. I mean men _and_ women, of course'" (lines 336–340).

_____

_____

_____

_____

READING FOR RHETORIC

→ Answer the following questions.

1. Explain a possible **irony** inherent in the title.

_____

_____

_____

2. The author uses several **similes**, which enhance the story by appealing to the reader's imagination. In the chart below, copy out five such similes, indicating the line number for each.

	SIMILE	LINE
a)		
b)		
c)		
d)		
e)		

3. In paragraph 31 (lines 152–156), an **allusion** is made to a well-known fable by Aesop. What is the fable?

_____

4. In paragraph 32 (lines 157–169), what **metaphor** (and idiom) is used to describe a secret infidelity revealed?

_____

5. Explain the **irony** of the following: "'Oh, that person [the person calling in fake bomb threats],' Brigit said. 'That person's just nuts'" (line 276).

_____

_____

_____

_____

EXAMINING AN ELEMENT: Character and Characterization

Working with a partner, examine character and characterization in "The Nature of Pure Evil." Turn to pages 3 and 8–9 in the *Literary Handbook* for an explanation of character and characterization and a worksheet on it. Complete a copy of the worksheet, applying it to Hedy. Be prepared to discuss your completed worksheet with the rest of the class.

DISCUSSION

→ Discuss each of the questions below in small groups.

→ Be prepared to share your answers with the rest of the class and to explain them.

1. Do people enjoy emergency situations?

2. Consider the following: "She [Hedy] thought about Stanley, her affection for the springy rust-coloured hairs on his chest and his ability to bluster through most awkward social situations in an amiably anti-intellectual manner. But was that love?" (lines 287–290). Well, was that love? Did Hedy love Stanley?

3. Is Stanley crazy or evil?

4. Is evil culturally relative?

5. What is the topic of "The Nature of Pure Evil"? What is the theme?

A Question of PERSPECTIVE If you were Hedy, would you tell Stanley's new wife about what he had done to you? *Could* you tell her?

In this section, one short (100- to 150-word) and two long (550- to 600-word) writing activities are proposed. The first activity focuses on character and characterization; the second, on essay writing using a close-reading approach; the third, on essay writing using a reader-response approach.

■ In-Role Writing

An in-role writing exercise requires that you "become" a literary character and write from that character's perspective.

→ Choose one of the in-role writing exercises below.

→ Write 100 to 150 words, writing as if you were the character, not yourself.

Short Story 1: "The Woman Who Talked to Horses"

1. Pretend you are George Gaddis. You are now in the barn, seated on a bale of hay. You have had a hard day: a woman who claimed she could talk to your horses and make them win drove off, laughing at you. Worse, she refuses to help you. Your wife threw your pillow into the yard and told you to "stay away" and not touch her. Now take a notebook and pen out of your shirt pocket and write about why you think nobody wants to be around you—and what you intend to do about it.

2. Pretend you are a female consultant. You spent a frustrating afternoon at Mr. Gaddis's place, talking to him about his horses. He is a really unpleasant man, and you decided not to help him. You're at home now. Take out your diary and write about your afternoon.

3. Pretend you are Sarah Gaddis. You asked George to consult with "the woman who talks to horses." She's outside right now, talking to George. Describe what you see, what you're thinking and how you're feeling.

Short Story 2: "The Nature of Pure Evil"

1. Pretend you're Brigit. Your colleague Hedy told you the most horrendous story at work today: her partner Stanley married another woman. And that's not the worst of it. He had Hedy unknowingly iron his wedding clothes. You're shocked. You have Stanley's e-mail address. Write Stanley an e-mail, telling him exactly what you think of what he did.

2. You're Stanley. You just received an e-mail from Brigit, your ex's colleague: she's angry because you left your ex and married another woman. She made a big deal out of the fact that you had Hedy unknowingly iron your wedding clothes for you. Respond to the e-mail, justifying your actions.

3. You're Hedy. You called the local art gallery, making a fake bomb threat while you were at work today. You had to make up an excuse to leave the office to make the call from a phone booth. You're at home now. Write an entry in your diary in which you write about how you felt making up the excuse, making the call and watching people flee.

Source: Adapted from Smith, Michael W. & Jeffrey D. Wilhelm. *Fresh Takes on Teaching Literary Elements*. Toronto: Scholastic, 2010. 53–54. Print.

2 Essay Using a Close-Reading Approach: Character and Characterization

→ Using a close-reading approach, write a formal analytical essay of approximately 550 words in response to one of the following questions:

1. Can George Gaddis become a good man?

2. Why does Hedy, herself a victim, victimize others?

→ In the Ponder section of this unit, you answered questions on the short stories and applied Worksheet 2: Examining Character and Characterization to George Gaddis and Hedy respectively (see pages 107–123). Before determining your thesis (your opinion), review your answers and completed worksheet pertaining to the character you have selected.

→ Double space your work and revise it before submitting it. You can find information about researching, referencing and revising in Appendix C (page 198).

3 Essay Using a Reader-Response Approach

→ Using a reader-response approach, write a formal analytical essay of approximately 550 words in response to one of the following questions:

1. Why do people enjoy horror stories?

2. Do people choose to be bad?

3. What is evil?

4. Why do people terrorize (or bully) others?

5. How does one stop others from terrorizing (or bullying) others?

→ Justify your answer by referring directly to one or more of the following works: "Horror Comics" (page 98); "The Woman Who Talked to Horses" (page 101); "The Nature of Pure Evil" (page 111).

→ Before determining your thesis (your opinion), review your answers to the questions about the literary work(s) in the Ponder section of this unit (pages 99–123).

→ Follow your teacher's instructions as to whether or not you may use the first-person singular when writing an essay using a reader-response approach.

→ Double space your work and revise it before submitting it. You can find information about researching, referencing and revising in Appendix C (page 198).

In this section, a short (two-minute) and a long (seven- to ten-minute) speaking activity are proposed. The first activity focuses on character and characterization; the second, on evil, the topic of this unit.

1 In the Hot Seat

Being "in the hot seat" means being in a very uncomfortable or embarrassing situation.

→ Form a small group with classmates.

→ Have a volunteer sit in the hot seat.

→ Role-play one of the following situations.

1. You (the volunteer) are George Gaddis from "The Woman Who Talked to Horses." The police have arrested you. Your wife, Sarah, phoned in a complaint, claiming that you physically, mentally and emotionally abuse her. You are now being interrogated by a team of officers (your group-mates). Answer their questions as if you were George.

2. You (the volunteer) are Hedy from "The Nature of Pure Evil." The police have arrested you for making fake bomb threats. You are now being interrogated by a team of officers (your groupmates). Answer their questions as if you were Hedy.

→ Before the role-play, give everyone a few minutes to prepare.

→ After the role-play, discuss what you learned about the chosen character and whether the volunteer always responded in character. If the volunteer did not always respond in character, indicate when she or he went out of character and explain why, in your opinion, the response was out of character.

→ Repeat the exercise, using the other role-play and another volunteer.

Source: Adapted from Smith, Michael W. & Jeffrey D. Wilhelm. *Fresh Takes on Teaching Literary Elements*. Toronto: Scholastic, 2010. 54. Print.

2 A Formal Analytical Speech about Malice

In this unit, you have read about malice (intent to harm): seeing malice, becoming malicious and behaving maliciously.

→ Reflect on the works you have read and then develop a thesis statement based on the topic "malice."

→ Photocopy "Outline of a Formal Analytical Speech" on page 196.

→ Complete the outline as you prepare a seven- to ten-minute formal analytical presentation in which you both state and support your opinion by referring to at least two of the following three works: "Horror Comics" (page 98); "The Woman Who Talked to Horses" (page 101); "The Nature of Pure Evil" (page 111).

→ Submit your completed outline to your teacher, making another copy for yourself.

→ When called upon, give your speech.

Important tips

→ Do not read or recite your speech.

→ Refer to your outline appropriately, making sure you maintain eye contact with audience members.

→ Speak to the person farthest from you (so you are certain to be heard by all).

→ Respect your time limit.

Participate

In this section you will work with a partner, further exploring character and characterization, the literary element examined in this unit (and in Unit 2).

Character-Study Films

A character study is a work of fiction in which the portrayal of the main character's personality is more important than plot. Many films can be classified as character studies, and forty of these are listed below.

A Streetcar Named Desire (1951)	*Nell* (1994)
All about Eve (1950)	*Nuts* (1987)
Amadeus (1984)	*One Flew Over The Cuckoo's Nest* (1975)
American Beauty (1999)	*Out of Africa* (1985)
As Good As It Gets (1997)	*Psycho* (1960)
Bagdad Cafe (1987)	*Raging Bull* (1980)
Born on the Fourth of July (1989)	*Rain Man* (1988)
Capote (2005)	*Rocky* (1976)
Casablanca (1942)	*Schindler's List* (1993)
Citizen Kane (1941)	*Six Degrees of Separation* (1993)
Cobb (1994)	*Sophie's Choice* (1982)
Dark Victory (1939)	*Sunset Boulevard* (1950)
Driving Miss Daisy (1989)	*The Dresser* (1983)
Forrest Gump (1994)	*The Lost Weekend* (1945)
Frances (1982)	*The Misfits* (1961)
Grey Gardens (2009)	*The Prime of Miss Jean Brodie* (1969)
Hannah and Her Sisters (1986)	*The Shining* (1980)
Man on the Moon (1999)	*The Talented Mr. Ripley* (1999)
Marty (1955)	*The World According to Garp* (1982)
My Dinner with André (1981)	*Unforgiven* (1992)

Procedure

1. Working with your partner, select one of the forty character-study films listed above. (You may wish to research these films to help you determine the one that interests you the most.)

2. Watch the film.

3. Write an analysis of the main character in which you do the following:
   a) Identify the film title, the director's name and the name of the main character.
   b) Describe the character, referring to specific details in the film to support your description.
   c) Determine whether the character changes during the film, explaining in detail why the character does or does not change.

4. Revise your film-character analysis and submit it to your teacher for evaluation. If applicable, include a works-cited section. (For information on researching, revising and referencing, see Appendix C.)

Note: Your teacher may schedule an appointment with you and your partner to discuss your film choice and character analysis.

 **ursue**

The following related works may be of interest for continued study. Modern editions are available of all books listed.

TYPE OF LITERARY WORK	ANNOTATED TITLES
Essay	Morrow, Lance. "The Unconscious Hums, Destroy!" *Time Magazine U.S.* 25 March 1996. Web. 24 July 2011. • Reflections on the nature of evil following the Dunblane massacre in 1996 • Available online through *Time Magazine*
Film	"Nightmare at 20,000 Feet." *The Twilight Zone*. Dir. Richard Donner. CBS, 1963. • Famous episode from Season 5 of the popular American TV series • Based on a short story by Richard Matheson, first published in *Alone by Night* *What Lies Beneath*. Dir. Robert Zemeckis. DreamWorks / Twentieth Century Fox, 2000. • American supernatural horror-thriller
Novel	Bradbury, Ray. *Something Wicked This Way Comes*. New York: Simon and Schuster, 1962. Print. • A nightmarish carnival comes to town Matheson, Richard. *I Am Legend*. New York: Gold Medal, 1954. Print. • Classic horror fiction novel, influential in the development of the zombie genre • Multiple film adaptations, the most recent of which was in 2007
Short Story / Short Story Collections	Gartner, Zsuzsi. *Better Living Through Plastic Explosives*. Toronto: Hamish Hamilton Canada–Penguin Group, 2011. Print. • The latest collection of deep and darkly humorous short stories from the author of "The Nature of Pure Evil," the short story reprinted on pages 111–119 of this unit Jackson, Shirley. "The Lottery." *New Yorker*. June 26, 1948. • Horror story set in a small American town • Available online in print at Classic Short Stories and audio through *Wikipedia* King, Stephen. *Nightmares & Dreamscapes, Volume I*. New York: Viking, 1993. Print. • Short story collection from the American master of horror and suspense Poe, Edgar Allan. "The Black Cat." *Saturday Evening Post* (Philadelphia) Aug. 19, 1843. • An unreliable narrator kills in fits of rage • Available online in print and audio through *Wikipedia* Poe, Edgar Allan. "The Tell-Tale Heart." *The Pioneer* (Philadelphia) Jan. 1843. Print. • An unnamed narrator murders an old man • Available online in print and audio through *Wikipedia*

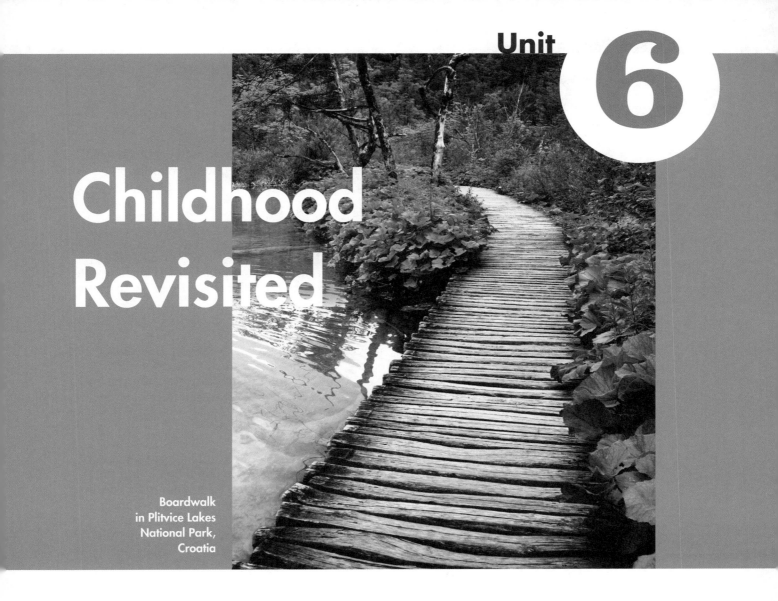

Childhood Revisited

Boardwalk
in Plitvice Lakes
National Park,
Croatia

review

The title of this unit takes its inspiration from the classic novel by English writer Evelyn Waugh, *Brideshead Revisited*, a story in which the narrator visits and revisits Brideshead, an aristocratic family's palatial home. Each time the narrator visits, the home and its occupants are never quite the same—for time changes things. Childhood memories are like this: they change each time we visit them in our minds.

In this unit, you will read a poem about one man's detachment from—and another man's attachment to—a childhood sport, a short story about one man's Christmas childhood memory and a memoir about one woman's attempt to create a childhood denied. All revisit their childhoods as adults and share interpretations of *what was*—portraits drawn by the hands of the people they have since become.

There's an old saying that states, "You can never go back." But that doesn't stop some from trying. Nor, dare I say, should it.

repare

→ Working with a partner, analyze the five scenarios below. In each scenario, you are asked to suggest a solution to a problem related to childhood, the topic of this unit.

→ Be prepared to share your suggestions and to explain them.

Scenario 1: Tell the Truth

Maggie is a sickly child who turned eight on December 15. At her birthday party, a couple of her little friends tell her that Santa Claus doesn't really exist. Upset, she runs to her dad and asks him to tell her the truth: Does Santa Claus exist? What should he say?

Scenario 2: Mama's Boy

Thirty-year-old Kevin is the youngest of six siblings, all of whom have left home, except for him. His parents envy their "empty-nester" peers and want Kevin to move out so that they can sell their too-big house in the suburbs and buy a chic little condo downtown. Kevin has no job, little education and no friends. Should they ask Kevin to leave?

Scenario 3: The Boomeranger

Stephen is a bright, charming young man in his twenties and a recent university graduate who had to move back into his parents' home when he couldn't find a job. After a week or so back home, his mom reverted to "mom mode," asking Stephen to clean his room, take out the trash and let her know his where-abouts at all times. Stephen doesn't pay room and board. Should Stephen confront his mother, telling her that he's a grown man and shouldn't be told what to do?

Scenario 4: Caught in the Middle

Raahi and his wife, Danna, immigrated to Canada from India fifteen years ago. They have twin daughters and a son: the girls are twelve and the boy, ten. They are very protective of their children, especially their daughters. Their next-door neighbour's twelve-year-old daughter Carla is having a sleepover, and she has invited the twins to spend the night. Raahi and Danna have refused. Carla and the twins are really disappointed, and they beg Carla's mother to call Raahi and Danna and ask them to reconsider. Should Carla's mother intervene?

Scenario 5: A Childhood Memory

Rita and Ryan have been dating for a few months, and things are starting to get serious. One day, Rita asks Ryan to tell her his first childhood memory. Ryan's first childhood memory is not a happy one: he was an abused child. Ryan never talks about his childhood, preferring to leave the past in the past. He tries to change the subject, but Rita won't let go of the question. What should he do?

onder

John B. Lee (1951–) is an award-winning author and poet from Ontario. He has numerous publications to his credit and in 2005 was named Poet Laureate of the City of Brantford.

My Father Quit Hockey One Night Late in His Youth

by John B. Lee

My father quit hockey
one night late in his youth.
Went home
and hung his skates in the shed
5 told his young bride
he was done with the game.

Done with the time he would race
a catalogue bent round each shin
and the wind in his face.
10 Done with the crack of the puck
and the rush-cut of the blade.
Done with the music of heart in the head.
Done with the sanguine age
when winter had a joy to rival the summer's sun.

15 He still tells the story
of one luckless player
who lived out his days a broken doll
heart quietly ticking
like a great clock lost in a corner.

20 But as for me
I feel a sadness that cannot grieve
and like a wicked son
I risk unmendable memory
and play the game beyond
25 the reach of wisdom in my ever collapsing years.

Source: Lee, John B. "My Father Quit Hockey One Night Late in His Youth." *Going Top Shelf: An Anthology of Canadian Hockey Poetry*. Ed. Michael P. J. Kennedy. Vancouver: Heritage House, 2005. 31. Print.

VOCABULARY AND COMPREHENSION

→ You may wish to work with a partner as you answer the questions below.

1. Which words from the poem have the following meanings?

   a) front part of leg, from knee to ankle _____

   b) confidently optimistic and cheerful _____

2. When does the narrator's father quit hockey?

   _____

3. Which word does the narrator **repeat** five times for artistic effect?

   _____

4. Why does the narrator's father quit hockey?

   _____

   _____

   _____

5. To what is the "luckless" player's life compared?

   _____

6. Explain the following **simile** (lines 18–19): "… [his] heart quietly ticking like a great clock lost in a corner."

   _____

   _____

   _____

7. Explain the last stanza (lines 20–25).

   _____

   _____

   _____

   _____

   _____

DISCUSSION

→ Discuss each of the questions below in small groups.

→ Be prepared to share your answers with the rest of the class and to explain them.

1. When you left your childhood, what did you leave behind? Is there anything you regret leaving behind?

2. Take a position for or against the following: It's important to act your age.

3. Differentiate *childlike* from *childish*.

4. Is the narrator childlike or childish?

5. What is the topic of "My Father Quit Hockey One Night Late in His Youth"? What is the theme?

Short Story: To Every Thing There Is a Season

Alistair MacLeod (1936–) was born in Saskatchewan and moved in 1946 to the family's ancestral farm in Cape Breton, a place that lies at the heart of his stories. MacLeod retired as professor of English at the University of Windsor and was appointed an Officer of the Order of Canada in 2007 (Toye 401–2).

READING FOR INFORMATION

→ Read the short story a first time, underlining the words listed in the chart below and highlighting information essential to understanding the plot. (The vocabulary is listed in order of appearance in the text.)

→ Fill in the chart, defining the words according to their contexts. (You may need to refer to a dictionary.)

→ In sixty words or fewer, summarize the plot in the space provided.

VOCABULARY	DEFINITION	VOCABULARY	DEFINITION
1. obliterated (v.)		**6.** frigid (adj.)	
2. unadulterated (adj.)		**7.** hearty (adj.)	
3. scant (adj.)		**8.** hoarding (v.)	
4. gnaws (v.)		**9.** doze (v.)	
5. boughs (n.)		**10.** pounce upon (v.)	

PLOT SUMMARY

To Every Thing There Is a Season

by Alistair MacLeod

I am speaking here of a time when I was eleven and lived with my family on our small farm on the west coast of Cape Breton. My family had been there for a long, long time and so it seemed had I. And much of that time seems like the proverbial yesterday. Yet when I speak on this Christmas 1977, I am not
5 *sure how much I speak with the voice of that time or how much in the voice of what I have since become. And I am not sure how many liberties I may be taking with the boy I think I was. For Christmas is a time of both past and present and often the two are imperfectly blended. As we step into its nowness we often look behind.*

10 We have been waiting now, it seems, forever. Actually, it has been most intense since Hallowe'en when the first snow fell upon us as we moved like muffled mummers[1] upon darkened
15 country roads. The large flakes were soft and new then and almost generous, and the earth to which they fell was still warm and as yet unfrozen. They fell in silence into the puddles and into
20 the sea where they disappeared at the moment of contact. They disappeared, too, upon touching the heated redness of our necks and hands or the faces of those who did not wear masks. We
25 carried our pillowcases from house to house, knocking on doors to become silhouettes in the light thrown out from kitchens (white pillowcases held out by whitened forms). The snow fell between us and the doors and was transformed in shimmering golden beams. When we turned to leave, it fell upon our footprints, and as the night
30 wore on obliterated them and all the records of our movements. In the morning everything was soft and still and November had come upon us.

My brother Kenneth, who is two and a half, is unsure of his last Christmas. It is Hallowe'en that looms largest in his memory as an exceptional time of being up late in magic darkness and falling snow. "Who are you going to
35 dress up as at Christmas?" he asks. "I think I'll be a snowman." All of us laugh at that and tell him Santa Claus will find him if he is good and that he need not dress up at all. We go about our appointed tasks waiting for it to happen.

I am troubled myself about the nature of Santa Claus and I am trying to
40 hang on to him in any way that I can. It is true that at my age I no longer

---

1. disguised merrymakers

really believe in him, yet I have hoped in all his possibilities as fiercely as I can; much in the same way, I think, that the drowning man waves desperately to the lights of the passing ship on the high sea's darkness. For without him, as without the man's ship, it seems our fragile lives would be so much
45 more desperate.

My mother has been fairly tolerant of my attempted perpetuation. Perhaps because she has encountered it before. Once I overheard her speaking about my sister Anne to one of her neighbours. "I thought Anne would *believe* forever," she said. "I practically had to tell her." I have somehow always
50 wished I had not heard her say that as I seek sanctuary and reinforcement even in an ignorance I know I dare not trust.

Kenneth, however, believes with an unadulterated fervour, and so do Bruce and Barry, who are six-year-old twins. Beyond me there is Anne who is thirteen and Mary who is fifteen, both of whom seem to be leaving
55 childhood at an alarming rate. My mother has told us that she was already married when she was seventeen, which is only two years older than Mary is now. That, too, seems strange to contemplate and perhaps childhood is shorter for some than it is for others. I think of this sometimes in the evenings when we have finished our chores and the supper dishes have
60 been cleared away and we are supposed to be doing our homework. I glance sideways at my mother, who is always knitting or mending, and at my father, who mostly sits by the stove coughing quietly with his handkerchief at his mouth. He has "not been well" for over two years and has difficulty breathing whenever he moves at more than the slowest pace.
65 He is most sympathetic of all concerning my extended hopes, and says we should hang on to the good things in our lives as long as we are able. As I look at him out of the corner of my eye, it does not seem that he has many of them left. He is old, we think, at forty-two.

Yet Christmas, in spite of all the doubts of our different ages, is a fine
70 and splendid time, and now as we pass the midpoint of December our expectations are heightened by the increasing coldness that has settled down upon us. The ocean is flat and calm and along the coast, in the scooped-out coves, has turned to an icy slush. The brook that flows past our house is almost totally frozen and there is only a small channel of
75 rushing water that flows openly at its very centre. When we let the cattle out to drink, we chop holes with the axe at the brook's edge so that they can drink without venturing onto the ice.

The sheep move in and out of their lean-to shelter, restlessly stamping their feet or huddling together in tightly packed groups. A conspiracy
80 of wool against the cold. The hens perch high on their roosts with their feathers fluffed out about them, hardly feeling it worthwhile to descend to the floor for their few scant kernels of grain. The pig, who has little time before his butchering, squeals his displeasure to the cold and with his snout tosses his wooden trough high in the icy air. The splendid young horse paws
85 the planking of his stall and gnaws the wooden cribwork of his manger.

We have put a protective barricade of spruce boughs about our kitchen door and banked our house with additional boughs and billows[2] of eel grass. Still, the pail of water we leave standing in the porch is solid in the morning and has to be broken with the hammer. The clothes my mother hangs on the line are frozen almost instantly and sway and creak from their suspending clothespins like sections of dismantled robots: the stiff-legged rasping trousers and the shirts and sweaters with unyielding arms outstretched. In the morning we race from our frigid upstairs bedrooms to finish dressing around the kitchen stove.

We would extend our coldness half a continent away to the Great Lakes of Ontario so that it might hasten the Christmas coming of my oldest brother, Neil. He is nineteen and employed on the "lake boats," the long flat carriers of grain and iron ore whose season ends any day after December 10, depending on the ice conditions. We wish it to be cold, cold on the Great Lakes of Ontario, so that he may come home to us as soon as possible. Already his cartons have arrived. They come from different places: Cobourg, Toronto, St. Catharines, Welland, Windsor, Sarnia, Sault Ste. Marie. Places that we, with the exception of my father, have never been. We locate them excitedly on the map, tracing their outlines with eager fingers. The cartons bear the lettering of Canada Steamship Lines, and are bound with rope knotted intricately in the fashion of sailors. My mother says they contain his "clothes" and we are not allowed to open them.

For us it is impossible to know the time or manner of his coming. If the lakes freeze early, he may come by train because it is cheaper. If the lakes stay open until December 20, he will have to fly because his time will be more precious than his money. He will hitchhike the last sixty or hundred miles from either station or airport. On our part, we can do nothing but listen with straining ears to radio reports of distant ice formations. His coming seems to depend on so many factors which are out there far beyond us and over which we lack control.

The days go by in fevered slowness until finally on the morning of December 23 the strange car rolls into our yard. My mother touches her hand to her lips and whispers "Thank God." My father gets up unsteadily from his chair to look through the window. Their longed-for son and our golden older brother is here at last. He is here with his reddish hair and beard and we can hear his hearty laugh. He will be happy and strong and confident for us all.

There are three other young men with him who look much the same as he. They, too, are from the boats and are trying to get home to Newfoundland. They must still drive a hundred miles to reach the ferry at North Sydney. The car seems very old. They purchased it in Thorold[3] for two hundred dollars because they were too late to make any reservations, and they have driven steadily since they began. In northern New Brunswick their windshield wipers failed, but instead of stopping they tied lengths of cord to the

---

2. bunches
3. city on the Niagara Escarpment in Ontario, about 2000 km from Cape Breton

130 wipers' arms and passed them through the front window vents. Since that time, in whatever precipitation, one of them has pulled the cords back and forth to make the wipers function. This information falls tiredly but excitedly from their lips and we greedily gather it in. My father pours them drinks of rum and my mother takes out her mincemeat and the fruitcakes
135 she has been carefully hoarding.

We lean on the furniture or look from the safety of sheltered doorways. We would like to hug our brother but are too shy with strangers present. In the kitchen's warmth, the young men begin to nod and doze, their heads dropping suddenly to their chests. They nudge each other with their feet
140 in an attempt to keep awake. They will not stay and rest because they have come so far and tomorrow is Christmas Eve and stretches of mountains and water still lie between them and those they love. After they leave we pounce upon our brother physically and verbally. He laughs and shouts and lifts us over his head and swings us in his muscular arms. Yet in spite of his
145 happiness he seems surprised at the appearance of his father, whom he has not seen since March. My father merely smiles at him, while my mother bites her lip.

Now that he is here there is a great flurry of activity. We have left everything we could until the time he might be with us. Eagerly I show him the
150 fir tree on the hill which I have been watching for months and marvel at how easily he fells it and carries it down the hill. We fall over one another in the excitement of decoration.

He promises that on Christmas Eve he will take us to church in the sleigh behind the splendid horse that until his coming we are all afraid to handle.
155 And on the afternoon of Christmas Eve he shoes the horse, lifting each hoof and rasping[4] it fine and hammering the cherry-red horseshoes into shape upon the anvil.[5] Later he drops them hissingly into the steaming tub of water. My father sits beside him on an overturned pail and tells him what to do. Sometimes we argue with our father, but our brother does everything he says.

160 That night, bundled in hay and voluminous coats, and with heated stones at our feet, we start upon our journey. Our parents and Kenneth remain at home, but all the rest of us go. Before we leave we feed the cattle and sheep and even the pig all that they can possibly eat, so that they will be contented on Christmas Eve. Our parents wave to us from the doorway.
165 We go four miles across the mountain road. It is a primitive logging trail and there will be no cars or other vehicles upon it. At first the horse is wild with excitement and lack of exercise and my brother has to stand at the front of the sleigh and lean backwards on the reins. Later he settles down to a trot[6] and still later to a walk as the mountain rises before him. We sing all the
170 Christmas songs we know and watch for the rabbits and foxes scudding[7] across the open patches of snow and listen to the drumming of partridge wings. We are never cold.

............➤

---

4. scraping
5. heavy iron block
6. gait between a walk and a run
7. moving quickly

When we descend to the country church we tie the horse in a grove of trees where he will be sheltered and not frightened by the many cars. We put a blanket over him and give him oats. At the church door the neighbours shake hands with my brother. "Hello, Neil," they say. "How is your father?"

"Oh," he says, just "Oh."

The church is very beautiful at night with its festooned branches[8] and glowing candles and the booming, joyous sounds that come from the choir loft. We go through the service as if we are mesmerized.

On the way home, although the stones have cooled, we remain happy and warm. We listen to the creak of the leather harness and the hiss of runners on the snow and begin to think of the potentiality of presents. When we are about a mile from home the horse senses his destination and breaks into a trot and then into a confident lope.[9] My brother lets him go and we move across the winter landscape like figures freed from a Christmas card. The snow from the horse's hooves falls about our heads like the whiteness of the stars.

After we have stabled the horse we talk with our parents and eat the meal our mother has prepared. And then I am sleepy and it is time for the younger children to be in bed. But tonight my father says to me, "We would like you to stay up with us a while," and so I stay quietly with the older members of my family.

When all is silent upstairs Neil brings in the cartons that contain his "clothes" and begins to open them. He unties the intricate knots quickly, their whorls[10] falling away before his agile fingers. The boxes are filled with gifts neatly wrapped and bearing tags. The ones for my younger brothers say "from Santa Claus" but mine are not among them any more, as I know with certainty they will never be again. Yet I am not so much surprised as touched by a pang of loss at being here on the adult side of the world. It is as if I have suddenly moved into another room and heard a door click lastingly behind me. I am jabbed by my own small wound.

But then I look at those before me. I look at my parents drawn together before the Christmas tree. My mother has her hand upon my father's shoulder and he is holding his ever-present handkerchief. I look at my sisters, who have crossed this threshold ahead of me and now each day journey farther from the lives they knew as girls. I look at my magic older brother who has come to us this Christmas from half a continent away, bringing everything he has and is. All of them are captured in the tableau of their care.

"Every man moves on," says my father quietly, and I think he speaks of Santa Claus, "but there is no need to grieve. He leaves good things behind."

(2705 words)

Source: MacLeod, Alistair. "To Every Thing There Is a Season." *Island: The Collected Stories.*
Toronto: McClelland & Stewart, 2000. 209–217. Print.

---

8. branches suspended in a curve between two points
9. leisurely canter (easy gallop)
10. curls

READING FOR MEANING

→ Read the questions below.

→ Read the short story a second and a third time (or more), answering the questions as you do so.

1. In the prologue (the *italicized* first paragraph), the author indicates that he is unsure as to how much of the story is told in the voice of the boy he once was and how much is told in the voice of the man he has since become.

   ☐ True   ☐ False

2. As indicated in the prologue, the story takes place in a small town on the west coast of Cape Breton. When does it take place?

   _____

   _____

   _____

3. In line 34, why is the darkness "magic" for MacLeod's younger brother Kenneth?

   _____

   _____

   _____

4. In paragraph 4 (lines 39–45), why does the narrator not want to let go of his belief in Santa Claus?

   _____

   _____

5. Why does the MacLeod family want the cold of Cape Breton to encompass the Great Lakes?

   _____

   _____

   _____

   _____

6. In line 107, why is the word *clothes* in quotation marks?

   _____

   _____

   _____

7. Explain the significance of the following: "He will be happy and strong and confident for us all" (lines 121–122).

   _____

   _____

   _____

8. Explain the significance of the following: "Sometimes we argue with our father, but our brother does everything he says" (line 159).

_____

_____

_____

_____

9. In line 177, why does Neil respond as he does when asked about his father?

_____

_____

_____

10. Why is the narrator invited by his father to stay up with the older members of the family?

_____

_____

_____

_____

11. Explain the significance of the closing lines (210–211): "'Every man moves on,' says my father quietly, and I think he speaks of Santa Claus, 'but there is no need to grieve. He leaves good things behind.'"

_____

_____

_____

_____

12. Paraphrase the following: "All of them are captured in the tableau of their care" (line 209).

_____

_____

READING FOR RHETORIC

→ Answer the following questions.

1. The author uses several **similes** that enhance the story by appealing to the reader's imagination. In the chart opposite, copy out three such similes, indicating the line number for each.

	SIMILE	LINE
a)		
b)		
c)		

2. Identify an example of **synecdoche** in paragraph 8 (lines 78–85).

_____

3. Identify the **onomatopoeic** words in paragraph 21 (lines 181–188).

_____

EXAMINING AN ELEMENT: Setting

Working with a partner, examine setting in "To Every Thing There Is a Season." Turn to pages 3–4 and 10–11 in the _Literary Handbook_ for an explanation of setting and a worksheet on it. Complete a copy of the worksheet, applying it to the short story. Be prepared to discuss your completed worksheet with the rest of the class.

DISCUSSION

→ Discuss each of the questions below in small groups.

→ Be prepared to share your answers with the rest of the class and to explain them.

1. If you once believed in Santa Claus or another childhood figment such as the Tooth Fairy, do you remember the moment when you stopped believing? Would you define this moment as the moment you left (at least part of) your childhood behind?

2. Is childhood shorter for some than it is for others?

3. Take a position for or against the following: You can never go back.

4. Can you ever completely leave your childhood behind?

5. What is the topic of "To Every Thing There Is a Season"? What is the theme?

A Question of PERSPECTIVE If you were the narrator as an adult (the author), would you want to relive your youth?

READING 6.2

Memoir: Girls Gone Mild

Rupinder Gill is a writer whose first book, a memoir titled *On the Outside Looking Indian*, was released in March 2011. In the memoir, Gill comically relates her experiences as she sets out to have the North American childhood she was denied while growing up in an Indian-Canadian household. The prologue to the memoir is reprinted opposite.

READING FOR INFORMATION

→ Read the memoir a first time, looking for the words that match the definitions in the chart below.

→ When you find a word, underline it in the text, write it in the chart and indicate its part of speech.

COMPANION
web+

PARAGRAPH (LINES)	DEFINITION	VOCABULARY
4 (21–25)	**1.** rough or boisterous activity	
4 (21–25)	**2.** silly behaviour	
9 (40–48)	**3.** childhood education / rearing	
9 (40–48)	**4.** anything that restricts freedom	
10 (49–55)	**5.** dull	
16 (96–102)	**6.** beat / was more important than	
17 (103–108)	**7.** arrogant	
21 (137–147)	**8.** extracted	
23 (155–162)	**9.** lying in an enjoyable way	
26 (180–196)	**10.** desperate or frenzied	

Girls Gone Mild

by Rupinder Gill

There is a phenomenon in Amish culture called *Rumspringa*, in which Amish adolescents are permitted to break free from their modest traditional lifestyles and indulge in normally taboo activities. They dress however they want, go out if and when they please, smoke, drink, and party like it's 1899.
5 At the end of their Springa Break they decide whether they will maintain their new lifestyles or return and join the Amish church.

Amish courting buggy

In Indian adolescence you never break free of the rules. You cook, clean, babysit, clean, get good grades, clean, be silent, clean, and
10 don't challenge your parents in any way— especially while cleaning. This was my life. I grew up in a town whiter than snow, about an hour outside of Toronto. Like most children of immigrants, I was raised by the rules of one
15 culture and looked longingly at those living a distinctly different way.

I didn't have time for a continent-wide census, but from what I know, this is how typical North American kids spend their summer va-
20 cations growing up:

July—summer camp, family trip, or cottage. Activities include swimming, canoeing, travelling, laughter, horseplay, tomfoolery, and general merriment. Mother makes glazed ham while father reads Russian
25 classics and smokes a pipe. Kids dance around maypoles.

August—return home and play with friends, have sleepovers, take weekend trips, and shop for fabulous new back-to-school clothes while dreading the inevitable return to academia.

Here is how I spent my summer vacations growing up:

30 *July*—TV room. Activities include hanging out with my sisters and watching anything and everything on television, including *Welcome Back, Kotter*, *Who's the Boss?*, *227*, and various other programs offering canned laughter and some much-needed escapism. Brief breaks for housecleaning and being nagged for not cleaning enough.

35 *August*—basement TV room (much cooler). Count down the return to school. Find blank VHS tapes on which to tape *Days of Our Lives* (dying to know if Patch and Kayla will get together!). Fight with parents about their annual two shirts, two pants back-to-school shopping policy. Pray that sideburns spontaneously fall off by Labour Day.

CULTURAL NOTE

A "maypole" is a tall wooden pole for spring and other festivals. Today, it is most often associated with May Day celebrations, which take place on May 1. The origins of the maypole are unclear, but its use in Europe dates back to the Middle Ages.

40 If an Indian version of *Rumspringa* existed—a *Ram-Singha* of sorts—I would bet my last rupee[11] that at the end of it, only one out of every hundred kids would return to their traditional Indian upbringing. The rest of us would be hanging out at the mall in acid-washed jeans, schooling the younger members of the group in how to undo their parental shackles and

45 integrate into Western society. Sessions would be set up for courses such as You Are Not Your Cousin Ravi: How to Function in a Culture That Doesn't Compare You Against Everybody Else's Kids and Less is More: A Workshop in Applying Men's Musk Oil Cologne.

Unfortunately no such program existed during my adolescence, so my

50 parents raised us by the standard rules of northern Punjab[12] nunneries. I don't wholly blame my parents for my lacklustre childhood. Having been to India, I am aware that the majority of kids there don't spend their summers singing around campfires or learning to play the flute. From a young age you are expected to make a contribution to the house, not simply to hang

55 up your favourite cartoon posters in it.

Whenever we complained, my parents liked to remind us that they hadn't grown up like Richie and Joanie Cunningham[13] either. "When I was a kid, we made toys out of mud," my dad once said. This was the Indian equivalent of the walking-two-miles-to-school tale that white parents used as their

60 trump card. According to my dad, they would fashion mud cars, mud guns, or mud animals and pray it didn't rain before they finished their game of cops and robbers.

Since their own childhoods were so limited, I understood why they didn't see value in the things we were missing out on. But what they seemed to

65 miss was that they weren't living in India anymore. They tried desperately to hold on to their culture. For years the only friends they had were fellow Indians. I took the opposite approach.

From the musical *Bollywood Love Story*, Barcelona, Spain, 2009

Growing up, I had friends, but I didn't have a single Indian friend. This was due

70 partly to the fact that there were only two other Indians in our primary school, but also because I was not interested in all things Indian. I grew bored of Bollywood films, didn't listen to Indian music, and ate

75 cereal for dinner so I didn't have to eat saag.[14] I viewed the fact that I was Indian as the reason I was living my life hanging out in my basement. It was the reason I couldn't go to dances, go to movies past five p.m., take

80 singing lessons, or be friends with boys, so I wasn't really interested in embracing any more of the culture than was required.

11. common unit of money in India and Pakistan
12. a region located in both India and Pakistan
13. characters from the American TV show *Happy Days* (1974–1984)
14. spinach- or mustard leaf-based dish eaten in India and Pakistan

In high school there were a few other Indian kids at my school. They all hung out together, but I never made it into the fellowship. I didn't know the first thing about the latest and greatest bhangra[15] tracks and couldn't roll out samosa[16] dough to save my life.

That left my white friends as my only source of comparison, and it seemed fairly clear that we had very different lives. For starters, they had two distinct eyebrows, while above my eyes I had one hibernating slug. Their parents knew the names of their kids' friends and welcomed them into their homes. But more important, they had freedom—my version of freedom at least. They had the luxury of indulging their interests. They went to "lessons" and "hung out" on weekends. They went on family trips and actually had stories to tell in September when the teacher asked us what we did on our summer vacations.

I wanted that, and didn't understand why I couldn't have it. Suffice it to say, my parents were strict. I was rarely allowed to go out. I wasn't allowed to take lessons or to talk on the phone with boys, or for extended periods with girls. I was discouraged from being too involved in extracurricular activities. I was expected to get good grades, although cleaning and taking care of the needs of houseguests trumped homework. I was not allowed to attend sleepovers, nor were my friends ever invited into our home.

I was, however, permitted to watch hours upon hours of television, because television kept us quiet and indoors. Unfortunately for my parents, it just exposed us further to the lives that other kids were leading. Those TV kids had even cooler clothes and adventures than the real kids I knew, pushing my sense of injustice into feelings of anger. I wanted to punch the TV every time those smug Cosby kids were on it.

One sunny August weekend not too long ago, my high school friends and I went up to our friend Jessie's cottage. We were celebrating her and our friend Johanna's upcoming weddings. As I sat on the dock and watched them swimming in the crystal-clear lake, I felt envious—not for their marriages, but for their ability to swim. I couldn't swim. I had spent my whole life sitting on the pool deck, standing in the shallow end, or simply avoiding the situation altogether. If we'd been at an ice-skating rink instead of a lake, I wouldn't have been able to participate there either. Ditto for skiing, tennis, gymnastics, camping, swapping stories about family vacations, and reminiscing about teenage love. I didn't have any camp friends or photos of me dressed as a bumblebee in a dance recital. Never having been on a team, I didn't have a shiny Little League trophy.

I had always joked about my boring and uneventful childhood. That day, the reality of it truly hit me. I had lost hundreds of hours of my childhood and missed countless experiences as I sat in front of that television. It may have been that I had just turned thirty, an age that makes you evaluate your

---

15. form of dance and music from the Punjab region
16. pastry stuffed with potatoes, onions, peas, coriander and lentils or ground beef or chicken

125 life whether you want to or not. It may also have been that I was surrounded by the very friends I had watched have the childhood experiences I wanted.

For years I believed that childhood experiences (or the lack thereof) were strictly once-in-a-lifetime. I always thought, *When I have my own kids, they will do all the things I never did.* But that day, as I contemplated risking

130 death for a few minutes of feeling the water lap around me, I didn't care about those hypothetical future kids. Those jerks weren't going to put me through eighteen hours of labour and be rewarded for it with clarinet lessons. From a childhood lived in a fun-proof cave had grown an adult who didn't take chances, who didn't boldly go anywhere, and who was, well,

135 quite bored with my routine-filled life. I needed to experience for myself what I had missed, or I would forever live a life of sitting on the sidelines.

When I got back to the city, I vowed I would finally learn to swim. As I researched lessons in my neighbourhood, I started to get excited at the thought of diving into a pool on a hot day, the way they do in diet soda

140 commercials. I also started thinking about all the other lost experiences of youth. There were so many other things I wished I had done as a kid, so whenever I thought of a new one, I would write it down. Soon I became overly ambitious. As summer gave way to the cool of fall and the fall gave way to the bitter cold of winter, my list grew. I culled some items because

145 I really didn't think it was that important to learn to tie-dye my own scrunchies[17] or backpack through Europe like Mike Seaver in *Growing Pains*, and soon I had created a workable list of goals.

It wasn't until January that I started to take action on the list. It was a new year and I was thirty—it felt like the perfect time for a new start. The

150 items on the list were some of the missing links between the life I had and the one I wanted. A few were life skills, some were just desires, but all of them were important enough that I felt they warranted pursuing. I could have added a million more items, but I started by setting five concrete goals to tackle. The list read as follows, in no particular order:

155 1. LEARN TO SWIM. Indians don't swim. They don't have cottages, they don't go on cruises, and they are rarely seen basking in the sun at the beach. Indian girls especially don't swim, because only a fool would think that learning a life-saving skill is more important than keeping your body hidden forever. No doubt the Indian

160 women's swimming team practises in full snowsuits with matching glittery bracelets. This was a life skill I had just assumed I would never have; it was time to change that thinking.

2. TAKE LESSONS. Oh, how I wanted to take lessons when I was a kid. How I wanted to hate my piano teacher and do dance routines

165 in the junior high talent show like all the other girls. What I would have given to say "I can't—I have karate" or "No, thanks, I have to get to gymnastics," instead of "I have to go. It is my night to clean the stove!"

---

17. fabric-covered elastic hair ties

3. VISIT DISNEY WORLD. Yes, I know not every kid visited Disney
World, but I always dreamed of it. Like many children with boring
home lives, my fantasy life was incredibly vivid, and it involved
many imaginary characters from the Disney catalogue, children's
stories, and various nonsensical cartoons. We would record
Disney specials from TV onto VHS tapes and watch them over and
over, fast-forwarding through the commercials for Hypercolor[18]
shirts and Mini Pop Kids albums. We never did family trips longer
than two days, and even those overnighters would be simply to
see family. I didn't want to see another uncle I had never met—
I wanted to see Goofy.

4. GO TO CAMP. I longed to sleep on a flea-infested mattress set
on wooden planks, swim amongst leeches, and sing "Kumbaya"
while up roasting s'mores to perfection. In my seventh grade the
junior school offered an end-of-the-year camp trip. Two weeks
before the deposit was due, I took the permission slip to my dad
and offered him a sales pitch straight out of *Glengarry Glen Ross*.[19]
"Forget it," he told me. I was always advised to forget whatever
I wanted. If only he could have forgotten to say no, just once.
As a desperate measure I went to my mom, who simply asked
what my father had said. Two days before the application was
due, I grew frantic. All my classmates had already committed,
and the only people outstanding were ethnic girls and suspected
bedwetters. Knowing that both my parents would have left for
their jobs by six thirty a.m., I woke up at six and went downstairs
for one last effort. At least they were considerate enough to yell
"No!" in less than a minute, allowing me to go back to bed and get
another hour of sleep before school.

5. OWN A PET. I have wanted a dog my whole life. All my sisters
have too. We would take out library books on dog breeds, buy
dog magazines, cut pictures of cute pups out of them, and dream
of the day that our parents' tundra hearts would melt. My mom
always had the same response: "I have enough animals in this
house already!" It was a killer joke in the Indian mothers' circle.
But I was out of her house now, and what could make my house
a home more than a furry foot-warmer to sit with me while
I watched *Seinfeld* reruns?

I typed out my list the same way I had typed out hundreds of lists before
it. And, as with every list I had ever made, I wondered how in hell I was
going to really achieve any of it.

"Set one new New Year's resolution for each year until you are done," my
friend Madeleine suggested.

"You know how that goes," I said.

---

18. clothing line consisting mostly of T-shirts and shorts that changed colour with heat
19. 1992 American film, based on the play by David Mamet, about four salesmen who will do almost
anything to make a sale

Madeleine and I met in college. We had created a deep friendship based on a mutual love of eating, complaining about our weight, and each year swapping lists of New Year's resolutions that we had abandoned like clock-
215 work by January 15.

I don't think I had ever achieved one of my New Year's resolutions. I never learned to do the worm[20] (1988), alphabetized my VHS movie tapes (1994), read every book on the *New York Times* fiction list (1998), or lost ten pounds (2001, 2002, 2003, 2004, 2005, 2006). If I tried to do only one item on the list
220 each year, I would have one foot in a ballet shoe and the other in the grave by the time I got around to them all. There was only one logical solution I could think of—I would have to do them all at once.

This was a bit of a goal-setting stretch for someone who had not achieved the vast majority of goals she set for herself, but if I pulled it off, perhaps
225 I could finally stop looking at the past and move gracefully into the future. Thirty seemed as good an age as any to finish off my youth. And if I had time left at the end, maybe I would learn to do the worm.

(2602 words)

Source: Gill, Rupinder. "Prologue: Girls Gone Mild." *On the Outside Looking Indian: How My Second Childhood Changed My Life*. Toronto: McClelland & Stewart, 2011. 1–10. Print.

READING FOR MEANING

→ Read the questions below.

→ Read the memoir a second and a third time (or more), answering the questions as you do so.

1. In your own words, what is *Rumspringa* (line 1)?

_____

_____

_____

_____

2. Which of the following statements is *false*? Circle the correct answer.

The narrator (the author)

a) had a restricted upbringing;

b) believes that, given the chance, most Indian children would opt for a Western upbringing over a traditional Indian upbringing;

c) blames her parents completely for her restricted childhood;

d) resisted Indian culture while growing up.

3. What (more formal) expression in paragraph 16 (lines 96–102) means "let's just say"?

_____

_____

---

20. dance move associated with breakdancing in which the subject lies face down and forms a rippling motion through his or her body

4. What made the author finally decide to seek out the experiences she had missed in childhood?

_____

_____

_____

_____

_____

5. The author wrote her "childhood experiences to do" list in a day.

☐ True   ☐ False

6. Why did the author set out to have all her missed childhood experiences at once and not treat them as New Year's resolutions to be fulfilled one at a time, one per year, year after year?

_____

_____

_____

_____

READING FOR RHETORIC

→ Answer the following questions.

1. What famous song is (comically) **alluded** to in the first paragraph?

_____

2. In paragraph 2 (lines 7–16), which word is **repeated** for comic effect?

_____

3. Identify and explain the **metonym** in paragraph 2 (lines 7–16).

_____

_____

_____

_____

4. When describing the childhoods of her non-Indian peers (lines 21–28), the author uses **hyperbole** for an added touch of humour. Provide one example.

_____

_____

5. Identify and explain the **metaphor** in line 89: "… above my eyes I had one hibernating slug."

_____

_____

_____

6. Sarcasm often involves **irony**. Identify and explain the sarcasm in paragraph 23 (lines 155–162).

_____

_____

_____

_____

_____

DISCUSSION

→ Discuss each of the questions below in small groups.

→ Be prepared to share your answers with the rest of the class and to explain them.

1. Rumspringa is a period during which Amish adolescents are left to "sow their wild oats." Why do you think the elders permit this? Does your culture have a Rumspringa? Should your culture have a Rumspringa?

2. Do you agree or disagree with the following statement? Parents raise their children the way they themselves were raised.

3. Why do people tend to take stock of their lives when they turn twenty, thirty, forty, and so on?

4. Can an adult experience Disney World or camp as a child would?

5. What is the topic of "Girls Gone Mild"? What is the theme?

 **Post**

In this section, one short (100- to 150-word) and two long (550- to 600-word) writing activities are proposed. The first activity focuses on setting; the second, on essay writing using a close-reading approach; the third, on essay writing using a reader-response approach.

▮ Setting the Stage

In the first paragraph (lines 1–9) of the short story "To Every Thing There Is a Season," the reader learns when the story takes place, where the story takes place and the psychosocial space (the atmosphere) that exists between the characters (page 134).

Examine the pictures opposite. Select one of the pictures and write the introductory paragraph to a short story written in the first person. By the end of your paragraph, the reader must know when the story takes place, where the story takes place and the psychosocial space (the atmosphere) that exists between you and at least one other character. Write approximately 150 words and use descriptive language.

Source: Adapted from Smith, Michael W. & Jeffrey D. Wilhelm. *Fresh Takes on Teaching Literary Elements.* Toronto: Scholastic, 2010. 80. Print.

LITERARY NOTE

In a close-reading approach, you examine a literary work by focusing on relevant literary elements and techniques, tracing their occurrence throughout the text to determine meaning.

❷ Essay Using a Close-Reading Approach: Setting

→ Using a close-reading approach, write a formal analytical essay of approximately 550 words in response to the following question:

The warmth that exists between the characters of "To Every Thing There Is a Season" is in sharp contrast to the coldness of the physical setting in which the story takes place. Discuss.

→ In the Ponder section of this unit, you answered questions on "To Every Thing There Is a Season" and applied Worksheet 3: Examining Setting to it (see pages 139–142). Before determining your thesis (your opinion), review your answers and completed worksheet.

→ Double space your work and revise it before submitting it. You can find information about researching, referencing and revising in Appendix C (page 198).

3 Essay Using a Reader-Response Approach

→ Using a reader-response approach, write a formal analytical essay of approximately 550 words in response to one of the following questions:

1. Is it possible to be childlike without being childish?

2. When is childhood over?

3. Is childhood beautiful?

4. Explain the following quotation: "To every thing there is a season …" (Ecclesiastes 3:1).

5. Take a position for or against the following: You can never go back.

→ Justify your answer by referring directly to one or more of the following works: "My Father Quit Hockey One Night Late in His Youth" (page 131); "To Every Thing There Is a Season" (page 134); "Girls Gone Mild" (page 143).

→ Before determining your thesis (your opinion), review your answers to the questions about the literary work(s) in the Ponder section of this unit (pages 132–150).

→ Follow your teacher's instructions as to whether or not you may use the first-person singular when writing an essay using a reader-response approach.

→ Double space your work and revise it before submitting it. You can find information about researching, referencing and revising in Appendix C (page 198).

Present

In this section, a short (two-minute) and a long (seven- to ten-minute) speaking activity are proposed. The first activity focuses on the influence of setting on characters' actions (plot); the second, on childhood, the topic of this unit.

1 Improvisation: "I Have Something to Tell You …"

An improvisation (or "improv") is a short dramatic sketch composed on the spur of the moment.

There are five basic rules to improv:

1. Go with the flow.

2. Don't ask open-ended questions.

3. Don't try to be funny.

4. Try to make your partner look good.

5. Tell a story.

Procedure

1. Form a small group of four or five.

2. Establish which two group members will volunteer to start the improv.

3. Decide who is the first volunteer and who is the second. The first volunteer plays him- or herself; the second volunteer chooses to play one of the following:

    a) A priest in church

    b) A loved one in a hospital examination room

    c) A teacher at his or her retirement party

    d) A police officer in an interrogation room

    e) A mugger in a back alley

4. The first volunteer begins with the line, "I have something to tell you," and the second volunteer responds with the line, "What is it?" The rest of the dialogue is improvised and can last no longer than two minutes.

5. Repeat the activity, this time using two new volunteers, with the second volunteer choosing a new character and setting.

6. As a group, discuss how the different settings influenced the dialogues.

Source: Adapted from Smith, Michael W. & Jeffrey D. Wilhelm. *Fresh Takes on Teaching Literary Elements*. Toronto: Scholastic, 2010. 87 and 89. Print.

❷ A Formal Analytical Speech about Childhood

In this unit, you have read about childhood: letting go of childhood, remembering childhood and reinventing childhood.

→ Reflect on the works you have read and then develop a thesis statement based on the topic "childhood."

→ Photocopy "Outline of a Formal Analytical Speech" on page 196.

→ Complete the outline as you prepare a seven- to ten-minute formal analytical speech in which you both state and support your opinion by referring to at least two of the following three works: "My Father Quit Hockey One Night Late in His Youth" (page 131); "To Every Thing There Is a Season" (page 134); "Girls Gone Mild" (page 143).

→ Submit your completed outline to your teacher, making another copy for yourself.

→ When called upon, give your speech.

Important tips

→ Do not read or recite your speech.

→ Refer to your outline appropriately, making sure you maintain eye contact with audience members.

→ Speak to the person farthest from you (so you are certain to be heard by all).

→ Respect your time limit.

When Was It?

When reading literary works, *when*, like *where*, matters: what a character can do in 1895 differs from what a character can do in 1995. Sometimes a reader is given the exact date when a story takes place: the story "1933" (page 26) is an obvious example. However, sometimes a reader is not given this information and must infer the date (or the time period) from details in the story. For instance, we know the story "To Every Thing There Is a Season" (page 134) is set in 1947 from information in the author's profile and the prologue to the story; however, even without this information, we could have placed the story in the 1940s or 1950s by paying attention to certain details.[21]

In this pair activity, you are asked to infer the *when* of some family photos by examining clues related to setting.

Procedure

1. Working alone, find five family photos from five different time periods. You may use pictures of your own family or go online and find pictures of other families. Go to *awkwardfamilyphotos.com* or type "historic family photos" into the search engine of a photo-sharing website. Make a note of the year each photograph was taken.

2. Working with a partner, show each other your pictures. Have your partner guess the year (or time period) of each photo by making inferences based on furnishing, clothing, hairstyles, vehicles, home decorations, and so on.

3. Write a report on the activity, including the following information:
   a) The types of details by which you were able to date the photos
   b) The accuracy of your inferences
   c) A list of the skills needed to date a picture
   d) An appraisal of the similarity between these skills and those needed to date a story

4. Revise your report and submit it to your teacher for evaluation. If applicable, include a works-cited section. (For information on researching, referencing and revising, see Appendix C.)

Note: Your teacher may schedule an appointment with you and your partner to discuss your report.

Source: Adapted from Smith, Michael W. & Jeffrey D. Wilhelm. *Fresh Takes on Teaching Literary Elements*. Toronto: Scholastic, 2010. 80–83. Print.

---

21. The "strange car" the young men purchase to make their 2000 km trek home places the story in the 1900s at the earliest, and the oldest brother shoeing the horse on Christmas Eve in preparation for a sleigh ride to church along a "primitive logging trail" suggests the story is probably not within the last fifty or sixty years.

Pursue

The following related works may be of interest for continued study. Modern editions are available of all books listed.

TYPE OF LITERARY WORK	ANNOTATED TITLES
Film	*The Sweater*. Dir. Sheldon Cohen. NFB, 1980. • Animated short based on *The Hockey Sweater* by Roch Carrier • Available online at NFB
Novel	Atwood, Margaret. *Cat's Eye*. Toronto: McClelland & Stewart, 1988. Print. • A woman's childhood memories Clarke, Arthur C. *Childhood's End*. New York: Ballantine Books, 1953. Print. • Story of a peaceful alien invasion • Considered one of the British novelist's best works MacLeod, Alistair. *No Great Mischief*. Toronto: McClelland & Stewart, 1999. Print. • Acclaimed novel by the author of "To Every Thing There Is a Season," a short story reprinted in this unit (page 134) Mitchell, W. O. *Who Has Seen the Wind*. Toronto: MacMillan, 1947. Print. • Classic coming-of-age novel set in the Canadian Prairies during the 1930s • Adapted for film in 1977 Waugh, Evelyn. *Brideshead Revisited*. UK: Chapman and Hall, 1945. Print. • A young man's encounters with eccentric British aristocrats over roughly twenty years from 1923
Memoir	McBride, James. *The Color of Water: A Black Man's Tribute to His White Mother*. New York: Riverhead Books, 1996. • Portrait of an interracial child growing up in a black neighbourhood
Short Story / Short Story Collections	MacLeod, Alistair. "The Boat." *Island: The Collected Stories*. Toronto: McClelland & Stewart, 2000. 1–25. Print. • Story about a young boy growing up in a Cape Breton fishing family in the 1940s • First published in the *Massachusetts Review*, 1968 Thien, Madeleine. "Simple Recipes." *Simple Recipes: Stories*. New York: McClelland & Stewart, 2001. • The daughter of Asian-Canadian immigrants recounts a turbulent moment from her childhood Welty, Eudora. "A Visit of Charity." *The Collected Stories of Eudora Welty*. Boston: Houghton Mifflin Harcourt, 1980. 113–118. Print. • A young girl visits a residence for elderly women and is changed by the experience • First published in *Decision* in 1941; available online through Google books

Leaving

Amphibious
vehicle
leaving a beach

𝒫review

Most days we leave someone, somewhere or something, and most days we return to the someone, somewhere or something we left behind.

Sometimes, however, the leaving is permanent: on that most uncommon of days, there is no returning.

This is the case when a romance is ended, a loved one dies or a death is hastened—three topics that will be examined in this, the last unit.

"Parting," as Shakespeare wrote, "is such sweet sorrow, that I shall say good night till it be morrow."

Prepare

The words in the crossword puzzle below were taken from songs about leaving and being left. Read the clues and fill in the corresponding blanks. You may wish to work with a partner.

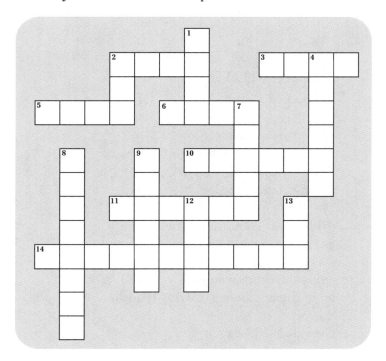

Across

2. Line from 1978 hit song "Life's Been Good" by Joe Walsh (of Eagles' fame): "It's hard to leave when you can't find the _____." A satire of the rock-star lifestyle.

3. Number one hit from 1961, made famous by Ray Charles: "Hit the Road _____."

5. Song included on the 1969 debut album by Led Zeppelin: "_____ I'm Gonna Leave You."

6. "I Will Remember You," Grammy award-winning song by Sarah McLachlan containing the repeated line, "_____ not for the memories."

10. One of Johnny Cash's signature songs: "Folsom _____ Blues."

11. Song originally sung by Elton John in honour of Marilyn Monroe and later remixed in tribute to Diana, Princess of Wales: "_____ in the Wind."

14. Line from "I Will Always Love You," a song written and recorded by Dolly Parton in the early 1970s and recorded by Whitney Houston in 1992: "_____ memories, that is all I'm taking with me."

Down

1. Song featured on Queen's 1984 album, *The Works*: "I Want to Break _____."

2. Final line from "Fast Car," written and recorded by Tracy Chapman: "Leave tonight or live and _____ this way."

4. Jazz standard "Send in the _____," performed by Judy Collins, Frank Sinatra, Barbra Streisand and many other famous artists.

7. Line from Orchestral Manoeuvres in the Dark's biggest US hit, "If You Leave" (1985): "I won't let go at any _____."

8. "_____ Train to Georgia," a 1973 number one hit for Gladys Knight and the Pips.

9. Ballad written by Eric Clapton and Will Jennings following the death of Clapton's four-year-old son: "Tears in _____."

12. Refrain from a 2006 pop song by Nelly Furtado, "All Good Things (Come to an End)": "Flames to _____ / Lovers to friends / Why do all good things come to an end?"

13. Song written by John Denver, made famous by folk rock group Peter, Paul and Mary: "Leaving on a _____ Plane."

℗onder

Fiona Tinwei Lam (1964–) is a Vancouver writer born in Scotland. She is the author of two books of poetry, and her prose and poetry have been published in more than a dozen anthologies (Crozier and Peacock 130).

Aquarium

by Fiona Tinwei Lam

Delicate, unworldly
seahorses behind the coral.
The grey one holds high
a noble, elaborate head.
5 The white one, belly full of young,
drifts near. Their tails entwine
as hands, even their unravelling
a slow caress. One hovers
while the other wanders
10 amid the anemones' waving tendrils.

Outside the glass,
my young son and I stand rapt
before this little paradise
as if it were a film
15 we must memorize
or perish.

His father has left us.
Probably for good.

(79 words)

Source: Lam, Fiona Tinwei. "Aquarium." *The Best Canadian Poetry in English 2010*. Ed. Lorna Crozier. Toronto: Tightrope Books, 2010. 37. Print.

VOCABULARY AND COMPREHENSION

→ You may wish to work with a partner as you answer the questions below.

1. Which words from the poem have the following meanings?

   a) twist around each other: _____

   b) untwisting: _____

   c) loving touch: _____

   d) lingers or remains: _____

   e) fascinated: _____

2. The poem has three stanzas. Where is the action set in the first stanza? In the second and third stanzas? Which physical setting is more pleasing to the narrator?

   _____

   _____

   _____

   _____

3. How do the second and third stanzas contrast with the first stanza?

   _____

   _____

   _____

   _____

DISCUSSION

→ Discuss each of the questions below in small groups.

→ Be prepared to share your answers with the rest of the class and to explain them.

1. The third stanza is the shortest. What impact does this have on the reader?

2. How did reading the poem make you feel?

3. What do you think of the poem?

4. The poem is very short. Would it be more or less effective if it were longer?

5. What is the topic of "Aquarium"? What is the theme?

Short Story: Last Rites

Moyez G. Vassanji (1950–) was born in Nairobi, Kenya, and grew up in Dar es Salaam, Tanzania. He obtained his PhD in physics from the University of Pennsylvania in 1978 and came to Canada that same year to work in Chalk River, Ontario. In 1980, he moved to Toronto, where he still resides. In 1989, he ceased lecturing in physics at the University of Toronto and became a full-time writer. In 2004, he was made a Member of the Order of Canada. Much of Vassanji's early writing is an attempt to reclaim and express the experiences of his community, which had emigrated from India to East Africa in the early 1900s (Toye 643).

READING FOR INFORMATION

→ Read the short story a first time, underlining the words listed in the chart below and highlighting information essential to understanding the plot. (The vocabulary is listed in order of appearance in the text.)

→ Fill in the chart, defining the words according to their contexts. (You may need to refer to a dictionary.)

→ In sixty words or fewer, summarize the plot in the space provided.

COMPANION
WEB+

VOCABULARY	DEFINITION	VOCABULARY	DEFINITION
1. glib (adj.)		6. indictment (n.)	
2. ordeal (n.)		7. inanities (n.)	
3. conundrum (n.)		8. turmoil (n.)	
4. eerily (adv.)		9. petered out (v.)	
5. quandary (n.)		10. hefty (adj.)	

PLOT SUMMARY

Last Rites

by M. G. Vassanji

"Shamshu *mukhi*," she said, "how are you?"

I had just stepped out of the front doorway of the Don Mills[1] mosque[2] and onto the stoop, where she had been standing, waiting.

"Hale and hearty, and how is the world treating you, Yasmin," I replied
5 jovially. The formal address *mukhi* always provokes an exaggerated, paternal sort of cheeriness in my manner that I can't quite curb and (as I've realized over the years) don't wish to either, because it is what people expect, draw comfort from. But no sooner had my glib response escaped my lips than I was reminded by her demeanour that lately the world had not been treating
10 Yasmin Bharwani very kindly.

I asked her, more seriously: "And how is Karim—I understand he's in hospital?"

A pinprick of guilt began to nag. It was more than a week now since I heard that her husband, who had been a classmate of mine, had been admitted
15 for something possibly serious. I had not seen Bharwani in years, our paths having diverged since we ended up in this city; still, I had meant to go and do my bit to cheer him up for old times' sake. Only, with this and that to attend to, at home and away, that good thought had simply sieved through the mind.

20 She nodded, paused a moment to look away, before turning back to reply, "He's at Sunnybrook. I've come to ask, can you give him *chhanta*? ... "

"Now, now, Yasmin, don't talk like that. It can't be serious—he's young yet, we all are." (That irrepressible bluster again—who was I kidding, since when has the Grim Reaper given a hoot about age?) "And what will your unbeliev-
25 ing husband Karim say to my giving him chhanta—he will scream murder."

---

1. neighbourhood in the North York district of Toronto
2. Muslim place of worship

Chhanta is the ceremony at which a person is granted forgiveness by his mukhi on behalf of the world and the Almighty. You join hands and supplicate once a month at new moon, and then finally at death's bed. I recall a sceptical Bharwani from our boyhood days arguing with hotheaded arro-
30 gance, "What have I done against the world that I should crave forgiveness all the time?" And some of us replying, "If nothing else, you might have stepped on an ant and killed it, *ulu*[3]—even an angel commits at least seven sins daily, and what do you think, that you are better than an angel?" We called him "Communist" in those teen years, which nickname he rather
35 relished, for it had intellectual connotations and set him apart from the rest of us, all destined for the heavenly embrace.

"Try, please," his wife now begged me. "He's dying … and there's another matter too …"

At this moment Farida joined me, and we invited Yasmin to come home
40 and have supper with us, when she could also unburden her mind. We had anticipated a quiet Sunday evening together, but such sacrifices of privacy have been our pleasure, having brought meaning to our lives as we approach what are called our more mellow years. It is a traditional responsibility that I hold, as presider of a mosque, father to its community; nothing could
45 seem safer for someone so conventional, indeed mediocre, as I, until Yasmin and Karim Bharwani put me through an ordeal from which I don't think I recovered.

Yasmin must be some five years younger than both my wife and I; she is petite and trim, fair complexioned, with short dark hair. She was dressed
50 smartly that night, though perhaps a bit sternly. She had her own car, so we met in the lobby of our building and went up together. At first we discussed anything but the gloomy subject at hand, her husband's illness. Finally, over a swiftly put-together supper, an assortment of leftover and fresh, I said to Yasmin, who was waiting for just such a prompt, "Now tell us what's
55 this other matter that you mentioned."

She looked anxiously at me and said all in a rush: "My husband wishes to be cremated when he dies."

I spluttered out a quite meaningless "But why?" to which nevertheless she answered, "I don't know why, I don't understand his reasons—he has
60 plenty of them and I don't understand them."

"But surely you've not given up hope yet," Farida said, "it's too soon to talk of …" Her voice trailed off. We watched Yasmin break down silently, large tears flowing down her cheeks. Farida went and sat beside her, poured her a glass of water. "Pray for him," she whispered. "We will, too."

65 "You must come and give him chhanta … now," the grieving woman answered, wiping away her tears.

The three of us drove to Sunnybrook Hospital, Farida going with Yasmin in the latter's car.

---

3. word used in South Asia, meaning "fool"

Trust Karim Bharwani to pose a conundrum such as this one. Always
the oddball, always the one with the dissenting opinion: why this way and
not the other? Because the world is so, eh *chodu*,[4] we would laugh him off.
There were times when we vilified him, mercilessly, and tried to ostracize
him, when he had wounded our pietistic[5] feelings with one of his poisoned
utterings. But he was too much one of us, you might as well cast out a part
of your body. Now here he was, saying cremate me, don't bury me. The
trouble is, we don't cremate our dead, we bury them, according to the Book,
the same way Cain first disposed of his brother Abel.

I wanted to say to him, as I saw him, Look, Bharwani, this is not the time
for your smart, sceptical arguments. This is real, this is how you leave the
world; at least this once, walk along with the rest of us.

He had been washed. His face was flushed, but creased, and he looked
exhausted and frail. He had always had rather prominent eyes behind big
black-framed glasses; now his eyeballs were sunken deep inside their
sockets, where two tiny black pools of fire burned with fervid life. There
was barely any flesh on the cheeks. He reminded me rather of a movie
version of an extraterrestrial. He said, in answer to his wife's concerns, that
he had been taken for a short walk; yes, he had eaten a bit of the awful food,
to keep his strength; and today the pain was less. He would die for a curry;
he attempted a laugh. He sounded hoarse and a little high-pitched. He had
let an arm drop to the side of the bed; I picked it up, cold, and squeezed it.
"Ey, Bharwani, how are you?"

"It's been a long time," he said, meaning presumably the time since we
last met. He smiled at Farida, who had gone and sat at the foot of the bed.
"Mukhi and Mukhiani," he said to the two of us, with an ever so slight mock
in his tone, "so have you come to give me chhanta?"

I threw a look at Yasmin, who turned to him with large, liquid eyes.
"Let them," she pleaded. "In case. It's our tradition."

He said nothing for a moment, apparently trying to control himself. Then,
in measured tones: "Doesn't it matter what I believe in or desire for myself?"

She had no argument, only the desperate words of a beloved: "For my
sake …"

He fell back exhausted, closed his eyes; opened them to stare at me.
I saw my chance then, in that helpless look, and drove home my simple
argument: "Karim, it can't hurt, whatever it is you believe in." With a laugh,
I added: "Surely you don't believe you have nothing to ask forgiveness for?"

He grinned, at me, at his wife, and said, "You have a point there."

I proceeded with the ceremony, having brought the holy water. When we
had finished, he joked, "I should go to heaven now."

"You *will* go to heaven," Yasmin said happily, "when the time comes.
But it was only a formality now." She smiled and her look seemed to drench
him in love. "And you'd not asked forgiveness from God in years."

---

4. somewhat vulgar Hindi slang meaning "idiotic"
5. adjective form of "piety," a reverence for God

"But I asked forgiveness from you, not from Him."

"Oh." But she was not bothered.

"But I am firm about the other thing, I tell you. I insist. These two people
115 here are witnesses to my wish. I would like to be cremated when I die, not
buried in that cold ground at Yonge and Sheppard called Immigrant's Corner."

"But why, Karim, why?" For the first time, her voice animated, passionate.

"Because I *want* it so."

"It's not right."

120 "What difference does it make? I'll be *dead*. Doesn't it matter to you how
I want to be treated in death, what I believe in?"

She wiped away tears, looked straight at him and said, "All right. But I'll
have the prayers said over you by Mukhisaheb. A proper service."

"All right, Shamshu can say his juju[6] over my body—if they let him."

125 He knew it would not be a simple matter fulfilling his last wish. And so for
him I was a godsend, a witness to that wish who had known him in the past
and was not unsympathetic, and who was also a mukhi, with connections.
He also used the presence of me and my wife to extract grudging
acquiescence from his own wife. There the matter stood when Farida and
130 I took leave of the couple in the dingy, eerily quiet hospital room, our
footsteps echoing hollowly down the long, white corridors. We both
believed there was time still, for Bharwani and Yasmin to wrangle further
on the issue, for his other close family members to be brought into the

discussion, for him to be pressured into
135 changing his mind. Cantankerous Bharwani,
however, died suddenly the following day,
bequeathing me such a predicament that it
would seem as if I was caught inside a maze
from which there was no exit.

140 Once a death reaches notice of the community
organs, as somehow it does almost immediately,
the funeral committee goes into high gear.
Cemetery management is requested to prepare
the next available site, the body is sent for
145 ritual washing and embalming, the funeral date
is set and announced; relatives in different
cities in the world learn about the death within hours and arrange for
services in their local mosques. This is the way it always is.

"What should I do," Yasmin said to me over the phone from the hospital.
150 "They have taken over, and I don't know what to say to them ..."

If I had said, Nothing, she would surely have been relieved. It is what I felt
strongly inclined to say—Do nothing, let them take over; he's dead anyhow,
it won't make any difference to him. But it does make a difference to us, the
living, how we dispose of the dead.

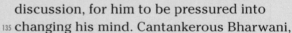

6. incantations

155 Does that sound right?

"What do you think you should do?" I probed her gently.

"My conscience tells me to follow his wishes, you know I promised I would. But I don't know what's right. I don't want him to go to hell or some such place because of his arrogance. Is there a hell, Mukhisaheb? What
160 exactly do we believe in?"

She had me there. I had learned as a child that hell was the name of the condition in which the human soul could not find final rest in the Universal Soul; in that case the body was simply useless and disposable baggage. I was also told of a Judgment Day, when the body would be raised, and of a
165 heaven where you had a lot of fun, presumably with many pretty young women, and in contrast a hell where you went to burn for your sins while giant scorpions gnawed at your guts. I was inclined toward the more sublime approach to the hereafter—though who has returned from the world of the dead to describe conditions there? It seemed a safe bet simply
170 to follow tradition, to go with the blessings and prayers of your people. But mere tradition was not enough for Karim Bharwani; he liked to make up his own mind. He had never played it safe. How were we going to send him off, and into what?

I didn't answer her question. "Your husband has put us into a real
175 quandary, Yasmin," I said instead. "Give me some time to think. Perhaps we can delay the funeral by a day, let me try and arrange that."

"His family has already started arriving, for the funeral ... it's a big family ... two brothers and two sisters and cousins and aunts and uncles, and his mother. What am I going to say to them?"

180 "Say nothing for now."

"I don't know what I would have done without you, you truly are a godsend."

Isn't that what I was supposed to be? But I found myself confounded, I didn't know what to do, where my duty lay.

185 I called up Jamal and Nanji, two other classmates from way back, to talk about "Communist" Bharwani's death, and we reminisced some. It was the first death to strike our group from school, not counting a tragedy in grade eleven, when a friend was hit by a truck. They told me that Alidina, Kassam, Samji, and perhaps a few others would also be arriving, from out of town,
190 for the funeral. Bharwani was lucky, so many of his former classmates would be present to pay him their respects. Would he appreciate that? We believed so.

He was always intense, always controversial. Broad shouldered and not very tall, he had a habit of tilting his head leftward as he walked. He parted
195 his thick black hair in the middle and, even more outrageous for the time (this was high school), wore suspenders to school. He spoke English with a twang that made people laugh, for its foreign imitation, until they heard what he was saying, which always seemed profound. He was our star

debater and actor. One day he brought in a four-page indictment of God,
200 obviously culled from books of literature, and presented the typescript to
our hapless religion teacher, one Mr. Dinani, who broke into tears and
called Bharwani "Lucifer," which thrilled him ever so much. Mr. Dinani lives
in Scarborough now, an insurance salesman recently awarded a plaque
by his company for record sales. I lost touch with Bharwani when he went
205 to England for university. When I saw him years later in Toronto, he seemed
distant and perhaps even a bit disdainful; I gathered that my vocation as
a real estate agent and my role as community worker did not meet his
standards of achievement.

That night there was the usual sympathy gathering of family and friends,
210 after services in my mosque, where I met my former classmates, six in all.
Yasmin sat in the midst of the large Bharwani clan, beside her mother-in-law,
a severe-looking though diminutive woman with hennaed hair furiously and
silently counting her beads. Mr. Dinani too was present, and in his familiar,
overwrought manner, was already in tears. But my former friends and
215 I gathered afterwards at Jamal's lavish house on Leslie Street and gave
ourselves a great reunion party, at which we remembered old "Communist."

Alidina, a heart surgeon in Kingston, recalled how Bharwani used to
read and edit his English compositions at school. Once a small guy, fondly
nicknamed "Smidgin," Alidina was now simply broad and short, a recently
220 divorced man turned out in an expensive suit. According to a rumour
I'd heard, he had been accused by his wife, at a reconciliation hearing,
of almost strangling her. His imitation of Bharwani's arrogant manner was
predictably hilarious. Nanji gave us a story the rest of us had never heard
before. Late one afternoon, after classes were long over, while he was
225 walking along a corridor he had chanced upon Bharwani and the new
chemistry teacher Mr. Sharma sitting together in a classroom at the
teacher's table; Mr. Sharma was in tears and Bharwani was patting him on
the hand to comfort him. What to make of that? Bharwani with a tender
heart was not an image we were familiar with.

230 The stories wove on, recalled after many years, inevitably embellished;
the evening wore on, a good portion of the people getting progressively
drunk, sentimental, louder. At these moments I always find myself adrift in
my soberness. I debated briefly with myself whether to let them in on
Bharwani's last wish, but decided the moment was not quite the right one
235 to request intelligent input from my friends. I left, taking my secret with me,
though I could not help warning Jamal in somewhat mysterious fashion that
I might need his legal advice on a serious matter. As I drove through Jamal's
gate, the question of the funeral seemed ever more urgent. Time was short.
Wouldn't it be better just to let things be, let the burial proceed? No one
240 would be the wiser, but for Yasmin, Farida, and me.

Messages were waiting for me when I arrived home. In one, I had been
confirmed to preside over the funeral ceremony, which according to
another message had been postponed from the next day to the one
following, as I had requested. There was a frantic appeal from Yasmin—
245 Please call, any time.

"I met with my in-laws today, to discuss procedures for the funeral ceremony," she told me when I called.

"Did you tell them of Karim's wish?"

"I didn't know what to say. I was waiting for your advice."

250 "What do your children think?"

"I've told all three of them. The older ones want to meet with you."

We agreed that I should go to meet her and the children early the next morning at her house.

The house is in an area of north Toronto called Glencedar Park, a locale
255 so devoid of coloured faces—except for the nannies pushing strollers—as to appear foreign to the likes of me. A cul-de-sac, with access to it limited by one-way streets, the neighbourhood might remind the cynical minded of a fortress. There are not many such neighbourhoods left. I have taken clients to inspect houses in Glencedar Park, who after a single drive
260 through it have instructed me simply to hasten out to somewhere else. Having parked my car and come out on the sidewalk, I met the curious though not unfriendly eyes of a couple of heads of households in long coats, each with a briefcase in hand and a folded paper under an arm, striding off to catch the subway on Yonge Street. I told myself this is where
265 Bharwani had come to seek refuge from his people.

"How do you like the area?" I asked Yasmin when she opened the door.

"Very much," she said. "We've had no problems. Some of the neighbours are rather nice. The others keep to themselves."

All three children were waiting for me in the living room. The oldest,
270 Emil, was a broad, strapping young man, conspicuously crowned with a crop of thick black hair slicked and parted in the middle, which reminded me of his father in his youth. He was at university. The second, Zuleikha, with the slim and toned looks of her age, resembled neither parent; she was finishing high school. The third child, Iqbal, was nine and rather delicate
275 looking. They stood up and I went and embraced each in turn. I reminded myself that this was their time of sorrow, they had lost a father, who to me was only Bharwani, from a shared past, calling upon which he had put me in a delicate spot.

I muttered some inanities in praise of their father, my arm around the
280 shoulders of little Iqbal, beside whom I had sat down, when Emil, after a nod from his sister, went straight to the point. "Mukhisaheb," he said, "our mother has told us about Dad's desire to be cremated. We would like to know what you think."

"Your father expressed that wish to me and your mother. I believe the
285 ultimate decision is the family's."

"I think cremation's the best way," Zuleikha spoke up, sounding frivolously like an ad, which wasn't her intent. She had evidently not had much sleep, and she had spent time crying. There was a mild look of defiance in the glare she then awarded me. I have come to believe, in the few years

290 I've held communal office, that to the young people I am a little like a cop, whom they would like to come to for help but whom they also resent.

"I differ," Emil said stiffly. "But of course Dad's wishes matter."

"I don't want Dad to be burnt," broke the quivering voice of young Iqbal beside me and I held him tight at the shoulders as he gave a sob. His 295 mother, saying to him, "Come," took him from me and out of the room.

This is a close family, I observed to myself. I thought of my own son, who had left home soon after graduating from school and was now in Calgary, never quite having looked back; and of my daughter, the same age as Zuleikha, who had grown distant from Farida and me.

300 "The problem is," I told Emil and Zuleikha, "that cremating is not in our tradition—you know that. It might even be forbidden on theological grounds. The community will not allow it. And there are other family members—your father's mother, and his brothers and sisters. They will have something to say, too."

305 "But he was *our* father, we have the right to decide," the girl said emphatically.

"What can the community do?" asked her brother.

"They can refuse the final rites to the body," I told him.

"Does that matter?" asked Zuleikha. "It wouldn't have mattered to Daddy. 310 He would have refused them anyway, if he could."

"Your mother wishes the final rites and prayers."

Their mother brought in fresh brewed coffee and a plate of cookies. "He'll be all right," she told me, with a smile, referring to Iqbal. "I'm trying to explain to him that his father lives on in spirit." She quickly averted her 315 eyes, so expressive of the turmoil and grief beneath her surface. In a cream cardigan over a dark green dress, she reminded me of how young women used to dress back in Dar[7] a long time ago, during the cooler hours of the day. She had been trained as a librarian, as I was aware, and now worked in government. Ever since her call to tell me that her husband had closed his 320 eyes for the last time while in the midst of chatting with her and Iqbal, she seemed to have kept her emotion in check.

Emil said: "Mum, what would *you* like to do, regarding Dad?"

"It sounds silly, I know, but I only want to do what is right."

"What is right is what *he* wanted," her daughter insisted, and tossed 325 another glare at me. I could imagine her as Daddy's favourite, always ready at his defence during conflicts.

"Let's all give it a few more hours," I told them. "The funeral is tomorrow.

Meanwhile … if you wish, you could inquire about cremation procedures and costs …"

330 By that evening the community leadership had caught wind of Bharwani's last wish, and I received a stream of phone calls, all intended to sound me

---

7. Dar es Salaam

out regarding rumours already in circulation. No, I was certain, I replied, that the family was not considering alternative funeral arrangements. The ceremony would take place tomorrow, as announced. And, yes, I had seen Karim in hospital, delivered chhanta to him, he had not been out of his mind, ranting ignorant things. Finally came the call from the very top, the chummy but very commanding voice of our Chairman. "What is there to these rumours, Shamshu—something about the deceased's wish to be cremated. Word is that he spoke to you before he died, and that you are close to his family." I explained to him what the situation was and told him that since I was a witness to that last wish of the dead man, I felt somewhat obligated by it. The last remark was wilfully ambiguous, and I waited for his response. "We understand your personal predicament, Shamshu," the Chairman answered impatiently, "but first and foremost you are a mukhi; not just a presider but a representative of God. You know what is right. Just because the deceased had deviated from the right path—that's what I hear, he had become a communist—does that mean it is not our duty to try and save him? And it seems to me that this is the perfect opportunity, when he has fallen back into our hands. You said he let you do chhanta; that means he had a semblance of faith still left in him. Then let's save him. Otherwise he dies without the prayers of his people to go with him."

His was the kind of pompous, authoritarian voice that prompts one to rebel. What did the man know of the right path except that it was the official path, I caught myself asking, echoing Bharwani perhaps.

"It's his wife's and children's desire to fulfill his wish," I said.

"Then obviously they are misled. You can convince them as to what is right, can't you? If not, I'll give them a call myself."

He didn't wait, though, for twenty minutes later, while I prevaricated and sounded out Farida on what to do, Yasmin called.

"Mukhisaheb, the Chairman himself called. There doesn't seem much choice now ..." Her voice petered out.

All she wanted was to be told what was right. The Chairman had done that, but she wanted to hear it from me. At that moment I made up my mind.

"Listen, Yasmin," I told her. "You and the children should decide for yourself. I can't advise you what to do. But the funeral ceremony will happen tomorrow. It's up to you and your children whether you choose to bury or cremate their father."

She took a long moment before saying, "All right."

Emil called that evening, and we talked for a while. Then Zuleikha called and said, "Thank you, Mukhisaheb. I know my father was right to depend on you." She added, just before hanging up: "You know what? Some of my uncles have found out about this, and may try to stop us. But we are ready. The law is on our side, isn't it?"

"I believe so," I answered, having checked with my legal expert Jamal in the meantime.

"If your conscience wills it that way," was Farida's response to my decision. Bharwani's desire to be cremated had appalled her, actually; she saw it as mischievous and divisive. But she, if anyone, knew that my resolution had not been an easy one to arrive at; and we both were too aware that the final
380 outcome tomorrow was far from certain, and repercussions in the days ahead would yet have to be faced.

Laid out before me and my associate performing the funeral rites, Bharwani looked a meagre, helpless rendition of his old self in the funeral casket. In small groups selected members of the congregation came and knelt
385 before him, on his other side, and went through the ritual in which the dead is forgiven of sins. Earlier on I had spotted Iqbal and gone to give him a comforting pat on the shoulder. I had developed a possessive, protective instinct for him. We stood together, and when I went to take my place for the ceremonies he came and sat down beside me on the carpet, watching
390 people come and kneel before his dead father.

Yasmin was wearing a white shalwar kameez,[8] a dupatta[9] covering her head—a mode of dressing that was never traditionally ours but, ironically, has been recently acquired in Canada. Beside her sat her mother-in-law pulling at her beads frantically, her head lowered, and the sisters-in-law.
395 Bharwani's two brothers and other male relations sat grimly in a large group directly in front of me, ready for battle; somewhat to the side and quite distinct from them sat Emil with a few young men. It took me a while to find Zuleikha, also sitting away from her family.

8. dress (tunic and loose pants) worn by men and women in South Asia and Central Asia and traditionally worn in Pakistan and Bangladesh
9. long, multi-purpose scarf worn by South Asian women; a symbol of modesty

The ceremony over, I stood up, motioning for the casket to be left as it was,
400 and made a short speech. I said that our brother Karim Bharwani had made
his wish known at his deathbed that he wanted to be cremated. Karim,
who was a classmate of mine, was a deep-thinking and not frivolous man.
I had been told that his wife and children wished to respect our dead
brother's last wish. Whatever our own beliefs were, we should open our
405 hearts and respect their decision.

I motioned to the funeral committee to pick up the coffin and begin the
chant, so that the male family members and congregation could carry it
away. The women of the family began to weep.

"We do not cremate our dead, it is a sin!" boomed a deep voice from the
410 back of the hall. It was the Chairman.

For moments nothing moved, there came only the moaning, sobbing
sounds of the women. I was the person officially in charge, and the weight
of all stares was upon me. I nodded to Emil, whereupon he and two hefty
friends stepped forward to lift the casket. They gathered at the front end,
415 somewhat nervously awaiting reinforcements, when promptly the dead
man's brothers and a third man came and took hold of the back. The coffin
was raised—and there ensued a tug-of-war.

At first, equal forces applied from the front and the back, the coffin hung
still. Then it lurched forward, where the greater strength of the younger
420 men lay. But these boys relaxed their hold and a sudden pull came from
behind, where two large women had now joined forces. A fair crowd had
gathered and was pulling aggressively at the back, having sensed victory
for that side, ready to hand it charge—but two or three of those at the very
back tripped and fell, bringing their end of the coffin with them. Poor
425 Bharwani, after being buffeted this way and that in his box, was brought to
rest at a forty-five-degree angle.

There was stunned silence, and then the eerily thin quivering sound of
a snicker that turned heads. It was Yasmin, caught in a hysterical fit.
Tears streamed down her face as she laughed, Zuleikha holding on to her
430 shoulders. The women around them had moved away in fear.

In disgust I turned to Bharwani's relations: "Is this what you wish for him,
this circus? To what holy end?"

Shamefaced, they retreated from the coffin, which was brought back to
rest on the floor. Then Jamal, Nanji, and the rest of the classmates at one
435 end, and Emil and two pals in front, unescorted by anyone else, the coffin
bearing Bharwani slowly made its way to the door, outside which two
hearses awaited to carry the dead to either of the two arrangements which
had been made for him.

Bharwani, you won, I muttered, as I closed the door of my car on Iqbal,
440 who was accompanying me to the crematorium. There were four cars in
the procession that left the mosque, far fewer than would normally have
accompanied the cortège, and our escorting policemen sped us through
the traffic in no time.

My new friend Iqbal was chatty in the car. "When a person dies, he leaves
445 the body, isn't that so? So the body is just flesh, and even begins to smell
and rot."

I nodded. "Yes. That's why we have to bury it or ... cremate it, as soon as
possible." Or leave it exposed for vultures to eat, I said to myself.

"My dad is alive somewhere, I know."

450 "I know that too."

(5453 words)

Source: Vassanji, M. G. "Last Rites." *The Penguin Book of Canadian Short Stories*. Sel. Jane Urquhart.
Toronto: Penguin, 2007. 78–88. Print.

READING FOR MEANING

→ Read the questions below.

→ Read the short story a second and a third time (or more), answering the
questions as you do so.

1. From the context in which it is used, what is a "mukhi"?

    _____

    _____

    _____

    _____

    _____

    _____

2. In paragraph 8 (lines 26–36), identify two adjectives the narrator uses to describe Karim Bharwani's character during his boyhood.

    _____

3. The narrator qualifies Karim Bharwani as a nonconformist.

    ☐ True   ☐ False

4. The narrator is a religious zealot, a strong adherent to the teachings of his
faith.

    ☐ True   ☐ False

5. Explain the significance of the following: "Isn't that [being a godsend] what
I was supposed to be? But I found myself confounded, I didn't know what to
do, where my duty lay" (lines 183–184).

    _____

    _____

    _____

6. In paragraph 51 (lines 193–208), identify four adjectives the narrator uses to describe Karim Bharwani's character in high school.

_____

7. In paragraph 51 (lines 193–208), how does the narrator describe Karim Bharwani when they meet up "years later" in Toronto?

_____

8. From paragraph 52 (lines 209–216), which formal term means "in the middle of"?

_____

9. Explain the significance of Karim Bharwani comforting Mr. Sharma (lines 227–229).

_____

_____

_____

_____

10. In paragraph 54 (lines 230–240), why does the narrator not tell his friends about Karim Bharwani's last wish?

_____

_____

_____

_____

11. Why did Karim Bharwani choose to live in the racially homogeneous neighbourhood of Glencedar Park?

_____

_____

12. The narrator lies to members of his community.

☐ True   ☐ False

13. The Chairman's voice is described as "chummy" and "commanding" (line 337), "pompous" and "authoritarian" (line 352) and "deep" (line 409). The Chairman's physical appearance is not described. Explain the significance of the Chairman being heard, but not seen.

_____

_____

14. Explain the significance of the clothing Yasmin wears to the funeral.

_____

_____

_____

_____

15. Each of the characters reacts in one of the following ways to Karim Bharwani's request to be cremated and not follow tradition: with complete support (CS), with reluctant support (RS) or with complete opposition (CO). Complete the chart below, indicating how each character reacts to Karim's request. Justify your responses.

CHARACTER	CS	RS	CO	REASON
a) Shamshu, the narrator				
b) Yasmin Bharwani, Karim Bharwani's wife				
c) Farida, the narrator's wife				
d) Karim Bharwani's extended family[10]				
e) Karim Bharwani's former classmates[11]				
f) Emil, Karim Bharwani's elder son				
g) Zuleikha, Karim Bharwani's daughter				

---

10. two brothers, two sisters, cousins, aunts, uncles, mother
11. Jamal (lawyer), Nanji (heart surgeon), Alidina, Kassam, Samji and one unnamed classmate

CHARACTER	CS	RS	CO	REASON
h) Iqbal, Karim Bharwani's younger son				
i) The Chairman, important figure at the mosque				

READING FOR RHETORIC

→ Respond to the following questions:

1. What is the **personification** of death **alluded** to in paragraph 7 (lines 22–25)?

_____

2. Copy out an example of **foreshadowing** from paragraph 10 (lines 39–47). Explain the significance.

_____

_____

_____

_____

3. How is it **ironic** that Karim Bharwani's eyes "burned with fervid life" (line 84)?

_____

_____

_____

4. In paragraph 37 (lines 125–139), what **simile** is used to help the reader visualize the seriousness of the predicament in which Shamshu finds himself?

_____

_____

5. Explain the **symbolism** of the tug-of-war incident at the funeral.

_____

_____

_____

DISCUSSION

→ Discuss each of the questions below in small groups.

→ Be prepared to share your answers with the rest of the class and to explain them.

1. Was it fair for Yasmin Bharwani to coerce her husband into receiving chhanta?

2. The narrator qualifies Karim Bharwani as cantankerous. Do you agree with this qualifier?

3. Do you feel sorry for the religion teacher, the "hapless" Mr. Dinani?

4. Do you agree that the decision to either cremate or bury Karim Bharwani belonged to his immediate family?

5. What is the topic of "Last Rites"? What is the theme?

A Question of PERSPECTIVE If you were Karim Bharwani, would you have enjoyed your funeral?

READING 7.2

Memoir: A Law Unto Himself

Jane Rule (1931–2007) was an American-born Canadian author of essays, novels and short stories on lesbian themes. One of her best-known novels, *Desert of the Heart* (1964, reprinted 1991) was made into the film *Desert Hearts* in 1985. In 2007, Rule was made a Member of the Order of Canada (Toye 545–6). "A Law Unto Himself" was one of her last written works.

READING FOR INFORMATION

→ Read the memoir a first time, looking for the words that match the definitions in the chart opposite.

→ When you find a word, underline it in the text, write it in the chart and indicate its part of speech.

PARAGRAPH (LINES)	DEFINITION	VOCABULARY
1 (1–11)	**1.** minor physical illnesses	
1 (1–11)	**2.** unintentionally/unwittingly	
1 (1–11)	**3.** distress	
2 (12–18)	**4.** confined to bed	
2 (12–18)	**5.** disdainfully/arrogantly	
3 (19–23)	**6.** noisy/boisterous	
5 (28–32)	**7.** confused	
7 (36–37)	**8.** wake	
8 (38–44)	**9.** encumber	
11 (58–62)	**10.** stole from / swindled	

A Law Unto Himself

by Jane Rule

{ March 2007 }

I did not like my grandmother's doctor, and I didn't understand why she did. He was a tall, arrogant, ugly man who assumed he was attractive to all females, not because he bothered to charm them but simply because he
5 offered them his random, condescending attention. Grandmother was charmed. She had half a dozen chronic ailments, any one of which might require hospitalization. He so overcharged her for his many house and hospital calls, she claimed to have built one wing of the local hospital. He told her she subsidized his work with the poor. She also inadvertently
10 overfed his large dog, who often stole steaks or a roast from the kitchen counter, to the dismay of the cook and the disappointment of dinner guests.

I did not have much to do with him until the summer I moved in with my grandparents after my grandfather had had a stroke and was bedridden. I was only fourteen, but it was during the war and no nurses were available.
15 The doctor came in once a week to check on both old people. He gave no instructions. He cast no more than an appraising sexual eye on me. Once I tried to confide in him that I was frightened I wouldn't know what to do in an emergency. He said dismissively, "Death isn't an emergency."

Years into her widowhood my grandmother said she didn't mind all her
20 physical handicaps, but she would really hate to lose her mind. In the last year of her life, she did, had lurid sexual fantasies about her aging nurses'

imagined lovers, became rowdy and unreasonable until the help quit, and my parents moved in with her to cope.

25 Her doctor had begun to raise money to build a retirement home for people like my grandmother, with plenty of money but without the ability any longer to run an establishment of her own. He tried to persuade her to invest in it, but she was beyond such considerations by then.

Restless, bewildered, longing to be allowed to go home, which was for her the home of her childhood, she went nights without sleep. My mother,
30 trying to comfort and quiet her, sat through one whole night singing with her, Grandmother still remembering the words of popular songs of the last seventy years.

The next morning, when she finally slept, the doctor came. "I've kept her alive to see her grandchildren grown, her first great-grandchild born,"
35 he said. "It's enough."

He gave her a shot and told my parents not to try to rouse her. Hours later she died in that sleep.

The doctor saw his elegant senior's residence built, the first of many that followed. In time my parents moved there to be sure they wouldn't burden
40 their children with the infirmities of their old age. Every time I visited them there, I had to pass a portrait of the doctor hanging in the front hall, dead now in his turn. I found myself wondering if one of his several doctor children had taken the responsibility of his death as he had probably taken the responsibility of many others.

45 Arrogant men like him are not as free now to play god with their patients. Such doctors can be charged and tried as criminals. I have heard some doctors complain that those who lobby for assisted suicide have cast too much light on the suffering of the dying and taken the right of mercy killing out of doctors' hands where it should belong, outside the law since so
50 many of the dying, like my grandmother, are beyond choice. The doctor's decision, in the face of great distress and suffering, may be, in order to do no more harm, to end a life.

My mother, after my father's stroke and heart attack, could ask to have life-support discontinued. "I promised him I wouldn't let him be a vegetable."
55 Though she would have liked to shorten her own dying, she could only starve herself against her cancer because there was no one with the knowledge or courage to help her die. My grandmother's doctor would have.

That ugly, arrogant man, a law unto himself, fleeced the rich, served the poor, built an elegant retirement home for the comfort and dignity of the
60 old, and kept alive and killed as he saw fit. I did not like the man. But I have never forgotten what he so long ago, and I thought callously, told me, "Death is not an emergency."

(753 words)

Source: Rule, Jane. "A Law Unto Himself." *Loving the Difficult.* Toronto: Hedgerow Press, 2008. 166–168. Print.

READING FOR MEANING

→ Read the questions below.

→ Read the memoir a second and a third time (or more), answering the questions as you do so.

1. How were the doctor and his dog similar?

_____

_____

_____

2. How did the author come to meet the doctor?

_____

_____

3. Why was the doctor unable to get the grandmother to invest in his retirement home?

_____

_____

4. The doctor gave the grandmother an overdose.

☐ True   ☐ False

5. Paraphrase the following: "… some doctors complain that those who lobby for assisted suicide have cast too much light on the suffering of the dying and taken the right of mercy killing out of doctors' hands where it should belong, outside the law since so many of the dying, like my grandmother, are beyond choice" (lines 46–50).

_____

_____

_____

_____

6. The author ends her **narrative** in support of doctor-assisted suicide.

☐ True   ☐ False

7. Explain the significance of the last sentence.

_____

_____

_____

READING FOR RHETORIC

→ Respond to the following:

Explain the **irony** of the grandmother losing her mind.

_____

_____

DISCUSSION

→ Discuss each of the questions below in small groups.

→ Be prepared to share your answers with the rest of the class and to explain them.

1. Is death ever an emergency?

2. Were the author's parents complicit in the grandmother's death?

3. Was the doctor callous or humane?

4. The author's father could legally have life-support removed, but the author's mother could not legally have medical personnel end her life. Is this fair?

5. What is the topic of "A Law Unto Himself"? What is the theme?

In this section, one short (100- to 150-word) and two long (550- to 600-word) writing activities are proposed. The first activity focuses on narrative point of view; the second, on essay writing using a close-reading approach; the third, on essay writing using a reader-response approach.

❶ Rewriting from a Different Perspective

→ In a paragraph of 100 to 150 words, respond to one of the following:

1. Revisit the hospital scene from M. G. Vassanji's "Last Rites" (pages 163–164). Rewrite the scene from Karim Bharwani's perspective.

2. Revisit the funeral scene from M. G. Vassanji's "Last Rites" (pages 170–171). Rewrite the scene from Karim Bharwani's perspective.

3. Pretend you are the doctor from Jane Rule's "A Law Unto Himself" (page 177). Your patients' fourteen-year-old granddaughter has just told you she is frightened of her grandfather's impending death and wouldn't know what to do in an emergency. Rewrite the scene from the doctor's perspective, ending with the line, "Death isn't an emergency."

❷ Essay Using a Close-Reading Approach: Narrative Point of View

→ Using a close-reading approach, write a formal analytical essay of approximately 550 words in response to the following question:

Shamshu, the narrator of "Last Rites," is a dramatized narrator: he is a character in the story being told. What are the advantages and disadvantages of using a dramatized narrator to tell this story?

→ In the Ponder section of this unit, you answered questions on "Last Rites" and applied Worksheet 4: Examining Narrative Point of View to it (see pages 172–176). Before determining your thesis (your opinion), review your answers and completed worksheet.

→ Double space your work and revise it before submitting it. You can find information about researching, referencing and revising in Appendix C (page 198).

❸ Essay Using A Reader-Response Approach

→ Using a reader-response approach, write a formal analytical essay of approximately 550 words in response to one of the following questions:

1. Is it easier to leave or be left?

2. What are the advantages and disadvantages of following one's traditions?

3. It is foolish to blindly follow tradition. Discuss.

4. Does a person's body belong to him or her?

5. Take a position for or against the following: Access to assisted suicide should be a human right.

→ Justify your answer by referring directly to one or more of the following works: "Aquarium" (page 158); "Last Rites" (page 161); "A Law Unto Himself" (page 177).

→ Before determining your thesis (your opinion), review your answers to the questions about the literary work(s) in the Ponder section of this unit (pages 159–180).

→ Follow your teacher's instructions as to whether or not you may use the first-person singular when writing an essay using a reader-response approach.

→ Double space your work and revise it before submitting it. You can find information about researching, referencing and revising in Appendix C (page 198).

℗resent

In this section, a short (two-minute) and a long (seven- to ten-minute) speaking activity are proposed. The first activity focuses on narrative point of view; the second, on leaving, the topic of this unit.

❶ Retell It *My* Way!

→ Form a group of four or five students.

→ Assign each member of the group one of the following roles from "Last Rites": Kamil, Yasmin, Farida, the Chairman or one of Kamil and Yasmin's children (Emil, Zuleikha or Iqbal).

→ Retell the story, each in turn, from the perspective of the assigned character.

→ After the retellings, reflect on and discuss the impact that a change of narrator has on the story.

→ Be prepared to share your reflections with other groups.

LITERARY NOTE

In a reader-response approach, you are asked to respond emotionally or intellectually to a literary work, making connections between the work and experiences you have had and agreeing or disagreeing with important ideas presented in the work.

2 A Formal Analytical Speech about Leaving

→ In this unit, you have read about leaving: firstly, being left; secondly, dying; thirdly, being "mercifully" killed.

→ Reflect on the works you have read and then develop a thesis statement based on the topic "leaving."

→ Photocopy "Outline of a Formal Analytical Speech" on page 196.

→ Complete the outline as you prepare a seven- to ten-minute formal analytical speech in which you both state and support your opinion by referring to at least two of the following three works: "Aquarium" (page 158); "Last Rites" (page 161); "A Law Unto Himself" (page 177).

→ Submit your completed outline to your teacher, making another copy for yourself.

→ When called upon, give your speech.

Important tips

→ Do not read or recite your speech.

→ Refer to your outline appropriately, making sure to maintain eye contact with audience members.

→ Speak to the person farthest from you (so you are certain to be heard by all).

→ Respect your time limit.

⑨articipate

The narrator of "Last Rites" is a dramatized narrator who shares certain similarities with the author of the short story, M. G. Vassanji: they have a similar cultural heritage and both spent time in Dar es Salaam, Tanzania. The two are not one and the same; however, Vassanji's fictional character is most certainly inspired by real-life events.

→ Write a short short story (no more than 600 words) on the topic of leaving, narrated by a dramatized narrator who is very similar to you. Include one other character and incorporate dialogue into the narrative.

→ When you are satisfied with your first draft, find a partner and edit each other's stories.

→ Refer to Appendix C: Researching, Referencing and Revising (page 198) and the Grammar and Style Guide (page 205) to assist you with the editing process.

→ Submit your short short stories to your teacher for evaluation.

**ursue**

The following related works may be of interest for continued study. Modern editions are available of all books listed.

TYPE OF LITERARY WORK	ANNOTATED TITLES
Film	*The Awful Fate of Melpomenus Jones*. Dir. Gerald Potterton. National Film Board of Canada, 1983. • Amusing animated short about a curate who cannot say goodbye • Based on the Stephen Leacock short story of the same name and available for purchase from the NFB
Memoir	Gilbert, Elizabeth. *Eat, Pray, Love*. New York: Penguin, 2007. Print. • A woman leaves everything behind to discover what she truly wants from life
Novel	Brookner, Anita. *Leaving Home*. London: Viking–Penguin, 2005. Print. • A woman gains new insight after leaving home Gaines, Ernest J. *A Lesson Before Dying*. New York: Knopf, 1993. Print. • Story about a black man on death row • Set in a small Cajun community in the 1940s Ishiguro, Kazuo. *Never Let Me Go*. Toronto: Knopf Canada, 2005. Print. • Two young women and a young man must leave their boarding school to learn its secret
Short Story / Short Story Collection	Gallant, Mavis. "The End of the World." *The Selected Stories of Mavis Gallant*. Toronto: McClelland & Stewart, 1997. 346–353. Print. • A man sits with a dying father who had deserted the family some years before McLean, Stuart. "Maynard Helmer." *The Vinyl Cafe Notebooks*. Toronto: Viking–Canada, 2010. 260–267. Print. • Heartwarming tale of a man mourned by many Richler, Mordecai. "Bambinger." *The Street*. Toronto: McClelland & Stewart, 2002. 70–76. Print. • A lodger's brief stay with a Montreal family leaves a lasting impression Vanderhaeghe, Guy. "Dancing Bear." *The Oxford Book of Canadian Short Stories in English*. Eds. Margaret Atwood and Robert Weaver. Toronto: Oxford University Press, 1986. Print. • Haunting tale of a man whose only way out is death Watson, Sheila. "Rough Answer." *A Father's Kingdom: The Complete Short Fiction*. Toronto: McClelland & Stewart, 2004. 1–8. Print. • The new school mistress leaves shortly after she arrives

The Formal Analytical Essay

In the Post section of each unit in *Perspectives Plus*, you were presented with one short and two long writing activities: writing a paragraph and writing a formal analytical essay on a literary work using either a close-reading or a reader-response approach. In Unit 1, you learned about writing a paragraph (pages 15–16); in this appendix, you will learn about writing a formal essay in which you analyze a literary work.

Definition, Categories and Approaches

Writing a formal analytical essay about a literary work gives you the opportunity to learn more about the human condition and the human experience. While challenging, writing a literary analysis is also highly satisfying: the writing process sharpens your critical-thinking and analytical skills and rewards you with insights into living a fuller and richer life (Mulvaney and Jolliffe 103).

A literary analysis is, obviously enough, the analysis of a literary work (or works) or parts thereof. It is not a retelling of the work beyond the necessary references to situate the reader of the essay: the writer may assume the reader has read the work prior to reading the analysis.

There are two basic categories of literary analysis:
1. The self-created analysis
2. The secondary-source analysis (Mulvaney and Jolliffe 103–104)

As the names imply, the self-created analysis refers only to the literary work itself, while the secondary-source analysis refers to the literary work and other sources, such as articles of literary criticism, journal articles, book reviews, lecture notes, author biographies, etc. When using secondary sources, remember to include a works-cited section at the end of your analysis and to reference sources correctly. (For more information, see Appendix C: Researching, Referencing and Revising, page 198.)

Two common approaches to literary analysis include the following:
1. The close-reading approach
2. The reader-response approach (Mulvaney and Jolliffe 103)

In the close-reading approach, the writer focuses on one or more literary elements and their relation to the overall meaning or theme of the literary work. When adopting this approach, do not use the first and second persons (*I*, *my*, *me*, *we*, *our*, *us*; *you*, *your*, etc.); maintain an impersonal stance throughout the analysis. In the reader-response approach, the writer focuses on the effect the literary work has had on him or her from an emotional or an intellectual standpoint. When adopting this approach, it is permissible to use the first person (while advisable to avoid the second person) and to relate personal experiences pertinent to the analysis.

LITERARY NOTE

Many educators frown on using the first-person singular or plural (in any of its forms) in a formal essay. It is possible to adopt a reader-response approach when writing an essay and still not use the first person, as shown in the following examples:

• Avoid the first-person singular: ~~I think that Mrs. Turner is admirable.~~ ➡ *Mrs. Turner is admirable.*

• Refer to yourself in the third person: ~~From my experience . . .~~ ➡ *From the writer's experience . . .*; ~~From our perspective . . .~~ ➡ *From a young person's perspective . . .*

• Use the indefinite pronoun: ~~You can never truly know yourself.~~ ➡ *One can never truly know oneself.*

LITERARY NOTE

It is important not to confuse the terms *topic* and *thesis*. A thesis is an essay writer's opinion about a topic in the same way that a theme is a **narrative** writer's opinion about a topic. (For more information on topic and theme, see page 2 in the *Literary Handbook*.)

Elements and Structure

Regardless of the category or approach used, a literary analysis must be constructed around a *thesis statement*, a declarative statement that expresses the writer's opinion about the topic of the essay.

For a thesis statement to be effective, it must be based on a topic that is *single*, *significant*, *specific* and *supportable* (Norton and Green 24, 29, 31, 113). In other words, the topic on which the thesis statement is based must pass the "4-S" test.

THE 4-S TEST

To pass the 4-S test, a topic must be:

1. Single

A formal analytical essay deals with one topic—and only one topic. As a consequence, the thesis statement—upon which the entire essay is constructed—must express the writer's opinion on one, and only one, topic.

2. Significant

A formal analytical essay is written to be read. In an educational setting, the reader is typically your teacher and perhaps one or more of your classmates. Your teacher and your classmates deserve to read essays on meaningful topics.

3. Specific

A formal analytical essay is brief. The more specific your thesis statement, the more justice you can do to the topic selected; for example, instead of writing about love, write about the love parents have for their newborn child.

4. Supportable

An academic essay requires that you prove your point (your thesis). If you can't support your thesis statement, change it!

Even when assigned a topic, you will likely have to refine it so that it passes this very important test.

The thesis statement is placed at the end of the introduction to the formal analytical essay, an essay that typically consists of four or five paragraphs: the introductory paragraph, the two- or three-paragraph development and the concluding paragraph. (See the diagram on the next page.)

Formal Analytical Essay

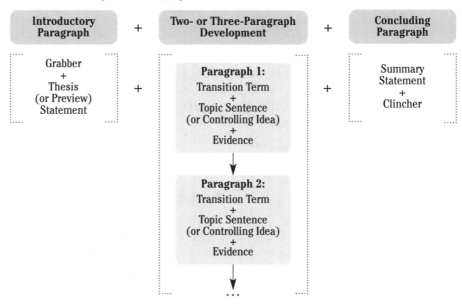

Introductory Paragraph

The first sentence of the introductory paragraph should grab the reader's attention. Not surprisingly, this first sentence is often referred to as a *grabber*. Effective grabber techniques include (but are not limited to) using quotations, definitions and facts.

The introductory paragraph must end with a thesis statement (the author's opinion on a single, significant, specific and supportable topic—see previous page), and this statement may be followed by a list of two or three main points to be used to support the thesis. When a thesis statement is followed by a list of main points, it is referred to as a *preview statement*.

Two- or Three-Paragraph Development

The first sentence of each paragraph in the development is the *topic sentence*, a statement that supports the thesis statement. The topic sentence is the controlling idea of the paragraph. Each topic sentence begins with a transition term, such as *first*, *second*, *third*, *to begin*, *to continue* and *finally*, and is backed up with evidence: statistics, an expert opinion or an example. Ideally, different types of evidence are used in the development.

Transition Terms

Transition terms lend coherence to a text, indicating relationships between ideas. The following list provides examples of commonly used transition terms and the functions of these terms:

FUNCTION	EXAMPLES
To add an idea	additionally, also, furthermore, in addition (to), in the same way, likewise, moreover, similarly
To conclude	all in all, briefly, by and large, in brief, in conclusion, in short, in summary, to conclude, to sum up

To emphasize an idea	indeed, in fact
To provide an example	for example, for instance, to illustrate
To sequence	after, earlier, finally, first, in the beginning, next, now, once, second, third, throughout, to begin with, to continue
To show a contrast	although, even though, however, in contrast, nevertheless, on the contrary, on the other hand, otherwise, yet
To show a result	as a result, because, consequently, hence, so, therefore, thus
To show priority	above all, for one reason, in the first place

Concluding Paragraph

The first sentence of the concluding paragraph is the *summary statement*, a paraphrase of the thesis statement and topic sentences. The summary statement begins with a transition term such as *to sum up*, *in summary*, *to conclude* or *in conclusion*.

The last sentence of the concluding paragraph is the *clincher*, used to encourage the reader to reflect on the essay. Effective clincher techniques include (but are not limited to) connecting with the introduction, asking a rhetorical question and offering a suggestion.

LITERARY NOTE

A literary analysis, such as the one presented below, is a formal piece of writing; for this reason, contractions (*he's, they're, we're, don't, doesn't,* etc.) are not used.

Model Literary Analysis and Exercises

The following text is an analysis of Margaret Atwood's short story "Happy Endings," a work the reader is assumed to have read prior to reading the analysis itself. ("Happy Endings" appears at the end of this appendix, on page 192.) Following the model analysis, you will find a series of questions that will help you evaluate how well you have learned the material covered in this appendix.

"Happy Endings": A Didactic Work on Plot

by Brent Davis Reid

The first rule for plot is this: "something happens" (Rabinowitz, qtd. in Smith and Wilhelm). In "Happy Endings," Canadian author Margaret Atwood underscores this truism by creating six plots, each of them variations on a theme. Plot A is the "happy ending," and while Plots B, C, D, E and F deviate
5 from this plot for a time, each returns—indeed, *must* return—to Plot A, which ends with the deaths of the main characters. Atwood's work is a didactic work that instructs the reader of literary works to focus less on the "what" of a narrative and more on the "how" and "why."

To begin with, the "what" of the six plots is of greater or lesser interest.
10 Significantly, Plot A—the happiest of the "happy endings" plots—is by far

the most mundane: John and Mary fall in love, get married, have children and die. Their names reflect the banality of their lives, which, in spite of being happy, are excruciatingly boring to read about on the printed page. The plot is mercifully short, and Atwood makes an interesting point: happy lives are not necessarily interesting lives. However, interest levels do rise in the remaining plots, which describe a one-sided relationship in which the female partner commits suicide (Plot B); a love triangle that ends in a murder-suicide (Plot C); a human-against-the-elements story of survival (Plot D); a struggle-to-survive story in which one romantic partner dies, leaving the other to carry on (Plot E); and a story of intrigue set in Canada (Plot F). Nevertheless, the only authentic ending to any story is the death of the characters involved, and as such, story endings (as well as story beginnings and the "stretch in between") can rapidly be dismissed by the reader: "The only authentic ending is the one provided here: *John and Mary die. John and Mary die. John and Mary die*. So much for endings."

To continue, a rereading of the plots, focusing on "how" and "why," transforms the tediousness of the initial "what" (or surface) reading experience into a richer and more rewarding one. Why are some satisfied with living "the American dream" (Plot A)? Why do some women allow men to treat them shabbily? And why do they think they can change such men (Plot B)? Why do some middle-aged men cheat on their wives (Plot C)? Why do some survive while others perish (Plot D)? How does one carry on after a loved one has passed away (Plot E)? Why do some challenge the system while others embrace it (Plot F)? The answers to such questions cannot be found in plot; they can be found only in other literary elements such as character and characterization, setting, narrative point of view and theme—elements left undeveloped by Atwood to make the point that knowing the "what" *informs* while knowing the "how" and "why" *transforms*.

To conclude, Atwood counsels the reader of literary works not only to read the lines but to read between them. Reading literary works must be more than "story-driven" (Chatman, qtd. in Smith and Wilhelm); it must be "point-driven" (Vipond and Hunt, qtd. in Smith and Wilhelm). It must focus not only on the story level but on the discourse level as well. Discourse implies a discussion, a conversation between a reader and an author who relates something that happened—something that demands pondering, merits understanding and offers personal enrichment to the reader who both ponders *and* understands.

(576 – 25 = 551 words)

Work Cited

Smith, Michael W. & Jeffrey D. Wilhelm. *Fresh Takes on Teaching Literary Elements*. Toronto: Scholastic, 2010. Print.

LITERARY ANALYSIS EXERCISES

Each of the following exercises has two parts: questions in part A pertain to information about the formal analytical essay, presented on page 184, while questions in part B are specific to the model literary analysis on page 187, "'Happy Endings': A Didactic Work on Plot."

EXERCISE 1

Part A

→ Indicate with a check mark whether each statement is true or false.

1. A literary analysis is a summary of the literary work.

   ☐ True   ☐ False

2. A self-created analysis requires a works-cited section at the end of the analysis.

   ☐ True   ☐ False

3. You may use the first-person singular when adopting a close-reading approach.

   ☐ True   ☐ False

Part B

→ Answer each of the following questions.

1. Is the essay "'Happy Endings': A Didactic Work on Plot" an example of a self-created analysis or a secondary-source analysis? Explain.

   _____

   _____

   _____

2. Which approach is used in the example analysis: a close-reading approach or a reader-response approach? Justify your response.

   _____

   _____

EXERCISE 2

Part A

→ Indicate with check marks whether each of the following topics meets the criteria of the 4-S test. (If you cannot put a check mark beside "single," "significant," "specific" *and* "supportable," the topic fails the test!)

1. Literature and sport

   ☐ Single   ☐ Significant   ☐ Specific   ☐ Supportable

2. My first academic composition

   ☐ Single   ☐ Significant   ☐ Specific   ☐ Supportable

3. Setting

☐ Single   ☐ Significant   ☐ Specific   ☐ Supportable

4. The impact of setting on plot in the short story "Mrs. Turner Cutting the Grass"

☐ Single   ☐ Significant   ☐ Specific   ☐ Supportable

5. The future of Canadian literature

☐ Single   ☐ Significant   ☐ Specific   ☐ Supportable

Part B

1. What is the topic of the literary analysis "'Happy Endings': A Didactic Work on Plot"?

_____

_____

EXERCISE 3

Part A

→ Circle the correct answer(s). In some cases, more than one answer is possible.

1. Which of the following statements is *false*? A thesis statement is

a) the expression of an essay writer's opinion on a topic.

b) analogous to theme.

c) placed at the end of the introductory paragraph.

d) synonymous with *preview statement*.

2. Which of the following is an example of a grabber appropriate to a literary analysis on perspective?

a) Smith and Wilhelm contend that "… literature allows us to try on perspectives other than our own and to test what comes from adopting those perspectives" (25).

b) A perspective may be defined as "a point of view" or "a way of looking at something."

c) No two people share the same perspective about everything and everyone.

3. Which of the following is a thesis statement?

a) The short story is a literary genre.

b) All Canadian college students should be required to take at least one literature course.

c) Should all Canadian college students be required to take at least one literature course?

4. A topic sentence
   a) is located at the end of each paragraph in the development.
   b) is located at the start of each paragraph in the development.
   c) is preceded by evidence.
   d) is followed by evidence.
   e) supports the thesis statement.
   f) is a controlling idea.

5. Indicate the type of evidence used in the following excerpt from a literary analysis on the importance of literature: "Scholes maintains that literature is only worthy of attention if it speaks to our concerns as human beings (24)."
   a) Statistics
   b) Expert opinion
   c) Example

6. A summary statement is
   a) identical in wording to the thesis statement.
   b) located at the start of the concluding paragraph.
   c) located at the end of the concluding paragraph.
   d) introduced by a transition term.

7. Indicate the type of clincher used in the following excerpt from a literary analysis on reading literature: "Reading opens up worlds of possibility, worlds that remain open long after the book is closed. Who then can deny its transformative power?"
   a) Connecting with the introduction
   b) Asking a rhetorical question
   c) Offering a suggestion

Part B

→ Answer each of the questions below about "'Happy Endings': A Didactic Work on Plot."

1. What type of grabber is used?

   _____

2. Copy out the preview statement.

   _____

   _____

   _____

   _____

3. List the transition terms that introduce each of the topic sentences.

   _____

4. What type of evidence is used in each of the developing paragraphs?

_____

5. Which transition term introduces the summary statement?

_____

6. Copy out the summary statement.

_____

_____

7. What type of clincher is used?

_____

Happy Endings

by Margaret Atwood

John and Mary meet.

What happens next?

If you want a happy ending, try A.

A. John and Mary fall in love and get married. They both have worthwhile and remunerative jobs which they find stimulating and challenging. They buy a charming house. Real estate values go up. Eventually, when they can afford live-in help, they have two children, to whom they are devoted. The children turn out well. John and Mary have a stimulating and challenging sex life and worthwhile friends. They go on fun vacations together. They retire. They both have hobbies which they find stimulating and challenging. Eventually they die. This is the end of the story.

B. Mary falls in love with John but John doesn't fall in love with Mary. He merely uses her body for selfish pleasure and ego gratification of a tepid kind. He comes to her apartment twice a week and she cooks him dinner, you'll notice that he doesn't even consider her worth the price of a dinner out, and after he's eaten the dinner he fucks her and after that he falls asleep, while she does the dishes so he won't think she's untidy, having all those dirty dishes lying around, and puts on fresh lipstick so she'll look good when he wakes up, but when he wakes up he doesn't even notice, he puts on his socks and his shorts and his pants and his shirt and his tie and his shoes, the reverse order from the one in which he took them off. He doesn't take off Mary's clothes, she takes them off herself, she acts as if she's dying for it every time, not because she likes sex exactly, she doesn't, but she wants John to think she does because if they do it often enough surely he'll get used to her, he'll come to depend on her and they will get married, but John goes out the door with hardly so much as a goodnight and three days later he turns up at six o'clock and they do the whole thing over again.

Mary gets run down. Crying is bad for your face, everyone knows that
30 and so does Mary but she can't stop. People at work notice. Her friends tell her John is a rat, a pig, a dog, he isn't good enough for her, but she can't believe it. Inside John, she thinks, is another John, who is much nicer. This other John will emerge like a butterfly from a cocoon, a Jack from a box, a pit from a prune, if the first John is only squeezed enough.

35 One evening John complains about the food. He has never complained about the food before. Mary is hurt.

Her friends tell her they've seen him in a restaurant with another woman, whose name is Madge. It's not even Madge that finally gets to Mary: it's the restaurant. John has never taken Mary to a restaurant. Mary collects all the
40 sleeping pills and aspirins she can find, and takes them and half a bottle of sherry. You can see what kind of a woman she is by the fact that it's not even whisky. She leaves a note for John. She hopes he'll discover her and get her to the hospital in time and repent and then they can get married, but this fails to happen and she dies.

45 John marries Madge and everything continues as in A.

C. John, who is an older man, falls in love with Mary, and Mary, who is only twenty-two, feels sorry for him because he's worried about his hair falling out. She sleeps with him even though she's not in love with him. She met him at work. She's in love with someone called James, who is twenty-two
50 also and not yet ready to settle down.

John on the contrary settled down long ago: this is what is bothering him. John has a steady respectable job and is getting ahead in his field, but Mary isn't impressed by him, she's impressed by James, who has a motor-cycle and a fabulous record collection. But James is often away on his
55 motorcycle, being free. Freedom isn't the same for girls, so in the meantime Mary spends Thursday evenings with John. Thursdays are the only days John can get away.

John is married to a woman called Madge and they have two children, a charming house which they bought just before the real estate values went
60 up, and hobbies which they find stimulating and challenging, when they have the time. John tells Mary how important she is to him, but of course he can't leave his wife because a commitment is a commitment. He goes on about this more than is necessary and Mary finds it boring, but older men can keep it up longer so on the whole she has a fairly good time.

65 One day James breezes in on his motorcycle with some top grade Califor-nia hybrid and James and Mary get higher than you'd believe possible and they climb into bed. Everything becomes very underwater, but along comes John, who has a key to Mary's apartment. He finds them stoned and entwined. He's hardly in any position to be jealous, considering Madge, but
70 nevertheless he's overcome with despair. Finally he's middle-aged, in two

years he'll be bald as an egg and he can't stand it. He purchases a handgun, saying he needs it for target practice—this is the thin part of the plot, but it can be dealt with later—and shoots the two of them and himself.

Madge, after a suitable period of mourning, marries an understanding man called Fred and everything continues as in A, but under different names.

D. Fred and Madge have no problems. They get along exceptionally well and are good at working out any little difficulties that may arise. But their charming house is by the seashore and one day a giant tidal wave approaches. Real estate values go down. The rest of the story is about what caused the tidal wave and how they escape from it. They do, though thousands drown. Some of the story is about how the thousands drown, but Fred and Madge are virtuous and lucky. Finally on high ground they clasp each other, wet and dripping and grateful, and continue as in A.

E. Yes, but Fred has a bad heart. The rest of the story is about how kind and understanding they both are until Fred dies. Then Madge devotes herself to charity work until the end of A. If you like, it can be "Madge," "cancer," "guilty and confused," and "bird watching."

F. If you think this is all too bourgeois, make John a revolutionary and Mary a counter-espionage agent and see how far that gets you. Remember, this is Canada. You'll still end up with A, though in between you may get a lustful brawling saga of passionate involvement, a chronicle of our times, sort of.

✥

You'll have to face it, the endings are the same however you slice it. Don't be deluded by any other endings, they're all fake, either deliberately fake, with malicious intent to deceive, or just motivated by excessive optimism if not by downright sentimentality.

The only authentic ending is the one provided here:

John and Mary die. John and Mary die. John and Mary die.

✥

So much for endings. Beginnings are always more fun. True connoisseurs, however, are known to favour the stretch in between, since it's the hardest to do anything with.

That's about all that can be said for plots, which anyway are just one thing after another, a what and a what and a what.

Now try How and Why.

(1287 words)

Source: Atwood, Margaret. *Murder in the Dark*. Toronto: New Canadian Library, 1997. 47–51. Print.

The Formal Analytical Speech

In the Present section of each unit in *Perspectives Plus*, one short and one long speaking activity are proposed: a small-group speaking activity and an individual formal analytical speech. In this appendix, you will learn about giving a formal analytical speech on a literary or cultural work.

Elements and Structure

The structure of a formal analytical speech is identical to that of a formal analytical essay: an introduction (with grabber and preview statement), a development (with transition terms, main ideas and evidence) and a conclusion (with summary statement and clincher) are all required (see pages 185–187). However, different grabber and clincher techniques, better suited to oral expression, are often used. While a formal analytical speech may be a self-created analysis or a secondary-source analysis, only a reader-response approach is recommended. (See page 184 for more information.) Contrary to the formal analytical essay, the first and second persons are freely used (*I, you, we, my, your, our,* etc.) as are contractions (*he's, they're, we're,* etc.). Like the formal analytical essay, the topic of a formal analytical speech should pass the 4-S test (see page 185).

Introduction

The opening line of a formal speech is the *grabber*. Grabber techniques suggested for oral expression include (but are not limited to) rhetorical questions (questions for which no answers are expected), provocative statements and short anecdotes. At the end of the introduction, a *preview statement* is required (see page 186).

Development

Typically, two or three main points are presented during a formal speech. Each main point should be introduced with an appropriate transition term (see page 186). Each main (or *controlling*) idea should be supported with evidence: statistics, an expert opinion or an example. Ideally, different types of evidence are used in the development. Should you be responding to more than one work, you may wish to focus exclusively on one work in each of the main points; for example, you could support your thesis by referring to a short story in your first main point, an oral story in your second main point and a memoir in your third main point.

Conclusion

The conclusion begins with an appropriate transition term followed by a brief summary statement. The conclusion ends with a clincher. Clincher techniques suggested for oral expression include (but are not limited to) connecting with the introduction and offering a suggestion (techniques also recommended for written expression) as well as demonstrating the importance of the thesis statement.

OUTLINE OF A FORMAL ANALYTICAL SPEECH	
Title	
Introduction	Grabber:
	Preview statement:
Development	First main (or controlling) idea and supporting evidence:
	Second main (or controlling) idea and supporting evidence:
	Third main (or controlling) idea and supporting evidence (if required):
Conclusion	Summary statement:
	Clincher:

Model Speech and Exercise

In this section, you will listen to a formal analytical speech about the main character in Carol Shields's "Mrs. Turner Cutting the Grass" (page 3). Before listening, read the questions below; as you are listening, answer each question in the space provided.

EXERCISE

1. What grabber technique is used? More than one answer is possible.

   _____

2. What is the preview statement? (Due to the length of the statement, a paraphrase will suffice.)

   _____
   _____
   _____
   _____
   _____

3. Which transition term introduces the first main (or controlling) idea? The second?

   _____

4. What type of evidence is used during the presentation?

   _____

5. Which transition term introduces the summary statement?

   _____

6. Which clincher technique is used? More than one clincher technique may be used.

   _____

7. Is the presentation a self-created or a secondary-source analysis?

   _____

COMPANION web+ LISTENING

The Transformative Power of Literature:
A Brief Reflection on Perspectives in Carol Shields's "Mrs. Turner Cutting the Grass"

by Brent Davis Reid

Researching, Referencing and Revising

In this appendix, we will examine the three Rs: researching, referencing and revising.

Researching

When writing a formal analytical essay or giving a formal analytical speech, you may have to conduct some research; this is particularly true when writing a secondary-source analysis of a literary work (see page 184).

With the rise of the Internet, research techniques have changed; before the Internet, students were sent to libraries to consult books, magazines, newspapers, academic journals, etc. Since the Internet, students have gone online to consult books, magazines, newspapers and academic journals—as well as web pages, blogs and wikis.

The advantages of researching on the Internet are obvious:

1. **Research can be conducted more quickly.**
   Research can be conducted at a time and in a place convenient to the researcher.
2. **Research can be conducted more efficiently.**
   Ask your parents and grandparents about using card catalogues to find research material. Long live the search engine!
3. **Sources consulted are current.**
   By the time some books are published, the content may be out of date.

The disadvantage of Internet research is perhaps less obvious: not everything read or heard online is necessarily true because not everyone writing online is necessarily credible. In pre-Internet days, it was the task of publishers and academics to determine the veracity of information and hence the credibility of the information providers. Today, this task falls more squarely on the shoulders of the researcher.

Evaluating Website Credibility

There are eight basic types of websites:[1]

1. Personal (vanity pages)
2. Promotional (sales)
3. Current events (newspapers, magazines, etc.)

---

1. Landsberger, Joe. "Evaluating Website Content." *Study Guides and Strategies*. Joe Landsberger, n.d. Web. 31 July 2008.

4. Informational (specific subjects)
5. Advocacy (propaganda)
6. Instructional (academics)
7. Registrational (product and course registrations)
8. Entertainment

Some of these types of sites are obviously more credible than others.

Consider the following five guidelines when evaluating the credibility of website content:[2]

QUESTIONS	WHERE TO LOOK FOR ANSWERS
Guideline 1: Authority a) Who is responsible for the content? b) Is the person qualified? c) What are his or her academic credentials?	Footer[3]
Guideline 2: Currency d) Are creation and editing dates indicated? e) Is the content up to date?	Footer, header,[4] dateline or wiki "history" pages
Guideline 3: Coverage f) What is the focus (main topic) of the site? g) Is there a clear outline? Is the site easy to navigate?	Footer, header, titles, subtitles and navigation menu
Guideline 4: Objectivity h) Is the website content biased? (E.g., Is a smokers' rights organization downplaying the dangers of second-hand smoke?)	Main content, hyperlinks, header, footer and URL (.gov, .com, .edu, etc.)
Guideline 5: Accuracy i) Are sources listed? j) Are sources varied and verifiable? k) Are sources reliable? l) Is the website content accurate?	Content (spelling, grammar and facts), bibliography, hyperlinks, header, footer and URLs cited (.gov, .com, .edu, etc.)

Refer to the Evaluation Sheet on the next page to help you evaluate website credibility when conducting research. Photocopy and complete one sheet for each website consulted.

---

2. Landsberger, Joe. "Evaluating Website Content." *Study Guides and Strategies*. Joe Landsberger, n.d. Web. 31 July 2008.
3. information placed at the bottom of a page, separated from the main text
4. information placed at the top of a page, separated from the main text

Evaluation Sheet

IDENTIFICATION
Your name
Name of website evaluated
URL of website evaluated
Type of website evaluated Circle one: personal / promotional / current events / informational / advocacy / instructional / registrational / entertainment

EVALUATION	
QUESTIONS	ANSWERS
a) Who is responsible for the content?	
b) Is the person qualified?	☐ Yes ☐ No
c) What are his/her academic credentials?	
d) Are creation and editing dates indicated?	☐ Yes ☐ No
e) Is the content up to date?	☐ Yes ☐ No
f) What is the focus (main topic) of the site?	
g) Is there a clear outline? / Is the site easy to navigate?	☐ Yes ☐ No
h) Is the website content biased?	☐ Yes ☐ No
i) Are sources listed?	☐ Yes ☐ No
j) Are sources varied and verifiable?	☐ Yes ☐ No
k) Are sources reliable?	☐ Yes ☐ No
l) Is the website content accurate?	☐ Yes ☐ No

In your opinion, is the content of the website credible? Why or why not?

_____

_____

_____

_____

Referencing

Any research referred to in an essay must be correctly cited.

When you quote (use somebody's exact words), paraphrase (rephrase somebody's words) or refer to another writer's work, you must reference the writer to avoid being accused of plagiarism.

There are many different citation styles. The style suggested in this textbook is based on the *MLA Handbook for Writers of Research Papers*, seventh edition.

Basically, a citation has two interrelated parts:

1. Parenthetical reference
2. List of works cited

The parenthetical reference is in the body of the essay, and the works-cited list appears at the end of the essay.

Parenthetical References

Parenthetical references are essential for quotations and paraphrases. Print sources (newspapers, books) and Internet sources are cited differently.

SOURCE	AUTHOR'S NAME IS MENTIONED IN THE REFERENCE	AUTHOR'S NAME IS NOT MENTIONED IN THE REFERENCE
Print	Parenthetical references should include the **page number**. *Wayson Choy establishes the setting of* The Jade Peony *in the very first sentence: "The old man first visited our house when I was five, in 1933" (5).*	Parenthetical references should include the **author's last name** and the **page number**. *The setting is established in the very first sentence of* The Jade Peony*: "The old man first visited our house when I was five, in 1933" (Choy 5).*
Internet	No parenthetical reference is required. *Claire Ramplin gives a favourable review of Wayson Choy's memoir* Not Yet, *adding that the memoir "... has cemented his position as one of his country's most beloved elders."*	Parenthetical references should include the **author's last name**. *Wayson Choy's memoir* Not Yet *"... has cemented his position as one of his country's most beloved elders" (Ramplin).*

Complete references to Choy and Ramplin must appear in the works-cited list. If the author of your quotation is cited in somebody else's work, put the abbreviation *qtd. in* ("quoted in") before the indirect source you quote. For example: (Smith, qtd. in Jones 25). In this case, a complete reference to Jones should appear in the works-cited list.

Remember: If an organization publishes an article, the organization is considered to be the author.

Works Cited

On a separate page at the end of your essay, you must list all the sources that you paraphrased or quoted. Follow these guidelines:

- The sources are in alphabetical order by last name (or by organization or title if no author has been identified).

- *Italicize* or <u>underline</u> all titles of complete works (newspapers, books, TV series, etc.).

- Use quotation marks for titles of works contained in another work (articles, book chapters, TV episodes, etc.).

- Capitalize all important words in a title.

- If using an Internet source, indicate the date of publication (using the form "Day Month Year"),[5] the medium (web) and the date accessed.

- All entries are double-spaced, and the second (third, fourth, etc.) lines of each entry are indented.

   The chart below lists common types of sources, accompanied by examples:

TYPE OF SOURCE	EXAMPLE
Book with One Author	Choy, Wayson. *The Jade Peony*. Vancouver: Douglas & McIntyre, 1995. Print.
Book with Two or Three Authors	Smith, Michael W. & Jeffrey D. Wilhelm. *Fresh Takes on Teaching Literary Elements*. Toronto: Scholastic, 2010. Print.
Anthology	Urquhart, Jane, ed. *The Penguin Book of Canadian Short Stories*. Toronto: Penguin Canada, 2007. Print.
Article in a Newspaper or Magazine	Careless, James. "Plugged In Anyway, So Why Not with a Book?" *Gazette* [Montreal] 28 Sept. 2011: GA3. Print.
Article on a Website	Ramplin, Claire. "Surviving Two Big Heart Attacks Made Wayson Choy a Firm Believer in Luck." *Sunday Times* [Perth]. The Sunday Times, 19 Sept. 2009. Web. 9 Nov. 2009.
Entire Website	*Literature*. Library and Archives Canada. 17 Nov. 2010. Web. 29 Sept. 2011.
Film	*The Awful Fate of Melpomenus Jones*. Dir. Gerald Potterton. NFB, 1983. DVD.

---

5. Write "n.d." if the publication date is not indicated.

Revising

Before submitting your writing for evaluation, you must revise your work. Revising requires that you carefully reread your work, improving your writing (editing) and isolating and correcting any errors you might have made (proofreading).

The Proofreading Process

When proofreading your work:

1. On a separate sheet of paper, make a list of the types of errors you commonly make. (It is easier to spot errors when you know what you are looking for!) Update your list regularly as you receive feedback from your instructor.

2. Read your work aloud (if the context permits), circling any parts you have trouble reading (difficulty reading may indicate a mistake) and any words that "look wrong."

3. Read your work again (silently or aloud)—this time from the end to the beginning—circling any words that look misspelled: this strategy is great for identifying spelling mistakes and spotting typos!

4. Reread your paper one final time (silently or aloud), completing the checklist below.

5. Rewrite your paragraph or essay, using reference materials (your common-error checklist, dictionaries and a grammar book) to help you correct any mistakes.[6]

Proofreading Checklist

Place a check mark beside each of the tasks completed.

TASKS	✓
1. All important words in the title of my essay are capitalized.	
2. Each sentence starts with a capital letter and ends with a period, a question mark or an exclamation mark.	
3. I have varied the types of sentences used: simple, compound and complex.	
4. All verbs are conjugated correctly.	
5. Pronouns agree with the nouns for which they stand.	
6. I have verified my spelling in a dictionary.	
7. I have verified my choice of vocabulary in a dictionary.	
8. I have paid special attention to verifying frequently misspelled or misused words.	

》 》 》

---

6. Wells, Jaclyn M. et al. "Proofreading Your Writing." *The Purdue OWL*. Purdue U Writing Lab, n.d. Web. 31 Dec. 2008.
Writing@CSU. "Editing and Proofreading Strategies." *Writing Guides*. Colorado State University, n.d. Web. 31 Dec. 2008.

TASKS	✓
9. I have verified all punctuation in a grammar book.	
10. The number of words used meets the minimum (and maximum) word counts.	
11. The base form of the verb is used after modal auxiliaries.	
12. All conditionals are correctly used.	
13. Regular and irregular nouns are correctly pluralized.	
14. All verbs used with non-count nouns are singular.	
15. Comparative and superlative adjective and adverb forms are correctly used.	
16. Adjectives and adverbs are placed in the correct order.	
17. There are no dangling or misplaced modifiers.	
18. There are no examples of faulty parallelism.	
19. There are no unnecessary shifts in tense or voice.	
20. My writing is double-spaced, and my handwriting (if the assignment is not completed on a computer) is legible.	

EXERCISE

→ Proofread the paragraph below, detecting and correcting any errors noted.

My opinion have been influenced by a variety of factors, the most important of wich are age and gender. As a older man in his 40's, I have come to realize that the world in witch I live is not the same as the one inhabited by my female friends. While my grey hair is "distinguished," there's is died. While I cannot sit alone in a playground, they can. (Admit it! A man siting alone in a playground elicits suspicion while a woman sitting alone in a playground elicits little more then a smile and a "Nice day, isn't it?") While we share the same time and the same place, we experience both from completly different perspectives.

Grammar and Style Guide

Preface

All words can be classified as one of eight parts of speech: noun, pronoun, verb, adjective, adverb, preposition, conjunction or interjection.

1. A noun names a person, place or thing: *mother*, *Canada*, *love*, *team*, …

2. A pronoun stands for or replaces a noun: *he*, *herself*, *everybody*, *this*, *theirs*, *who*, …

3. A verb expresses an action or a state: *walk*, *is*, …

4. An adjective describes a noun or pronoun: *new*, *blue*, *a*, *an*, *the*,[1] …

5. An adverb describes a verb, an adjective or another adverb: *brilliantly*, *fairly*, *quickly*, …

6. A preposition shows the relationship between a noun and other words: *on*, *under*, *up*, *through*, *in*, *with*, …

7. A conjunction connects words, phrases or clauses: *and*, *but*, *or*, *furthermore*, *however*, *otherwise*, *although*, *because*, *since*, *whether*, …

8. An interjection expresses strong emotion: *Great! Look out!* …

In this Grammar and Style Guide, you will examine the eight parts of speech and how they work together to form phrases, clauses and sentences. You will also examine rules of capitalization, punctuation, spelling and style. At the end of each of the twelve sections in this guide, you will be given a chance to evaluate how well you have mastered the notions presented by completing a Pinpoint exercise, which your teacher will correct with you. You can then work online to complete related exercises with automatic correction and instant feedback.

GRAMMAR TIP

A clause is a group of words that contains a subject and a verb: **She ate**. A phrase is a group of words that forms a unit of meaning in a sentence but that does not include a verb: *She ate* **at the restaurant**.

---

1. *A*, *an* and *the* are all articles; articles are classified as adjectives.

① Sentence Structure

A sentence is a word or a group of words that has a stated or implied subject, a verb and expresses a complete thought.

> *Go!*
> *Bob is leaving.*

A sentence may be affirmative, negative or interrogative.

> *She studies.*
> *She does not study.*
> *Does she study?*

In this section, we will examine types of sentences that people use when writing down their thoughts.

There are three basic types of sentences:

1. **Simple**
   Mr. Johnson is a teacher.

2. **Compound**
   Kevin is a student, and he works part-time.
   Mary is tired; however, she will finish the work.
   Edith is leaving; she is going home.

3. **Complex**
   Tell Charlie to call me when he gets up.
   Because he works hard, he does well in English.

Simple Sentences

Another term for a simple sentence is an *independent clause*.

A simple sentence has only one independent clause, typically comprising one subject and one verb.

Compound Sentences

A compound sentence has two (or more) independent clauses. There are three basic types.

TYPE	DESCRIPTION	EXAMPLE
1	Two (or more) independent clauses linked by a *coordinate conjunction*	Kent eats well, *and* he exercises.
2	Two (or more) independent clauses linked by an *adverbial conjunction*	I want you to leave; *moreover*, I want you to leave now!
3	Two (or more) independent clauses linked by a *semicolon*	I walk quickly; she walks slowly.
Note:	• The coordinate conjunction is preceded by a comma. • The adverbial conjunction is preceded by a semicolon and followed by a comma.	

There are seven coordinate conjunctions.

COORDINATE CONJUNCTION	FUNCTION	EXAMPLE
and	To add	Sally moved to Toronto, *and* she got a job.
but	To contrast	Jennifer got an A, *but* Anne got a B.
for	To introduce a reason	Christopher did well on his test, *for* he worked hard.
nor	To add an idea after a negative statement	He didn't laugh, *nor* did he cry.
or	To show an alternative	You can do the dishes, *or* you can take out the trash.
so	To show a result	He worked hard, *so* he made a lot of money.
yet	To introduce two opposing ideas	I slept well, *yet* I am still tired.

Note:
- *Nor* is followed directly by an auxiliary + subject + base form of the verb: *She doesn't work, nor **does she study***.
- As a coordinate conjunction, *for* means "because."
- The acronym *fanboys* is a useful mnemonic: **f**or, **a**nd, **n**or, **b**ut, **o**r, **y**et, **s**o.

There are many adverbial conjunctions. The following chart lists the more common ones:

ADVERBIAL CONJUNCTION	FUNCTION	EXAMPLES
accordingly as a result consequently hence therefore thus	To show a result	The instructions said to wash before using; *accordingly*, I put my new set of dishes in the dishwasher and turned it on. My gas gauge wasn't working properly; *as a result*, I ran out of gas on the way to the cottage. They arrived late for work every day last week; *consequently*, they were fired. Julie had a lot of alterations made to her wedding dress; *hence*, it cost twice the original price. Only residents are allowed to park in that lot; *therefore*, you must show your ID at the gate. Our bank account was overdrawn last month; *thus*, we had to pay a bank fee.
at the same time meanwhile	To show simultaneous actions	Please make the additions I have noted; *at the same time*, check the document for gender-specific vocabulary. Susan was rushing about; *meanwhile*, her husband was taking a nap.
for example for instance	To introduce an example	Strong earthquakes can actually move cities; *for example*, Concepción, Chile, was moved at least three metres in the February 2010 quake. Houseplants can remove chemical pollutants from the air; *for instance*, English ivy and rubber plants are very effective in cleaning the air in your house.

furthermore moreover	To add	Tina's parents bought her a car; *furthermore*, they paid for her studies. Students must register for the trip to Ecuador by Friday; *moreover*, a cheque for $500 must accompany their registration forms.
however nevertheless nonetheless	To contrast	Todd does well in school; *however*, he is not enjoying his studies. Derek didn't have time to study very much for his geography exam; *nevertheless*, he passed the mid-term. I can't do a complete revision of your document; *nonetheless*, I will check it for spelling mistakes.
indeed in fact	To emphasize	Jenny did well on her test; *indeed*, she received a perfect grade. Joan won the half-marathon last weekend; *in fact*, she set a new record.
likewise similarly	To show similarity	Drivers must wear seat belts; *likewise*, all passengers must buckle up. Teenage boys often perform worse than teenage girls on tests; *similarly*, teenage boys often behave worse than teenage girls at school.
otherwise	To show an alternative consequence	Arrive at work on time; *otherwise*, you will be fired.

Note:
- Coordinate and adverbial conjunctions can express similar functions: to add, to contrast, to show a result and to show an alternative.
- An adverbial conjunction can also be used as an adverb at the start of a sentence: **Nevertheless**, *he was fired.*

Complex Sentences

A complex sentence has two (or more) clauses, at least one of which is a dependent clause.

When a dependent clause precedes an independent clause, a comma separates the two clauses.

A dependent clause begins with a subordinate conjunction (or dependent marker) such as *because*: the idea expressed is incomplete. To complete the idea, an independent clause is required.

$\underbrace{\textit{Because she had run five miles,}}_{\text{dependent clause}} \underbrace{\textit{Shelly was exhausted.}}_{\text{independent clause}} \Big\}$ complex sentence

The following chart lists the more common subordinate conjunctions:

SUBORDINATE CONJUNCTIONS	FUNCTION	EXAMPLES
after before	To establish a sequence	*After* the police officer had stopped me last night, she asked me to take a Breathalyzer test. They had reviewed their notes *before* they went to class.

© ERPI • REPRODUCTION PROHIBITED

GRAMMAR AND STYLE GUIDE | **209**

SUBORDINATE CONJUNCTIONS	FUNCTION	EXAMPLES
although even if even though though	To present opposing ideas	*Although* she likes mathematics, she is not doing well in his course. *Even if* the condominium is expensive, she is going to have a home of her own. He accepted the invitation *even though* he will have to rent a tuxedo for the occasion. He came to the party *though* he was not invited.
as as though just as	To make a comparison	You will do *as* you are told. He behaved *as though* he didn't want to be there. *Just as* smoking is bad for your health, it is a very expensive habit.
as long as	To introduce a period of time	He will love her *as long as* he lives.
because	To give a reason	*Because* the teachers were on strike, classes were cancelled.
if unless	To set a condition	*If* it rains, she will stay home. *Unless* skateboarders want to run the risk of serious head injuries, they should wear helmets.
since when	To refer to a point in time	*Since* they got married, they have been fighting like cats and dogs. *When* we painted the pool, we repaired the broken tiles as well.
until	To introduce a specific time	He will work *until* it's time to leave.
where wherever	To introduce a place	He will go *where* she goes. Special agents are sent *wherever* people report UFO sightings.
whether	To introduce a choice	She does not seem to care *whether* she lives or dies.
while	To show simultaneous actions	They were in chemistry class *while* their friends were in French class.

Note: • Sentences containing relative clauses are also complex sentences as a relative clause is a dependent clause. Relative clauses are introduced by relative pronouns such as *who*, *whom*, *that*, *which* and *whose*.

*The student **who ran five miles** was exhausted.*

GRAMMAR TIP

A compound-complex sentence is a sentence with two or more independent clauses and one or more dependent clauses: *Unless you work hard, you will not get good grades, and you will not get into medical school.*

Types of Dependent Clauses

There are three types of dependent clauses.[2]

TYPE	FUNCTIONS	EXAMPLES
Adjective clause	• Modifies a noun or a pronoun • Answers the questions "Which one?" or "What kind?"	There's the book *that I wanted*! (The dependent clause "that I wanted" modifies the noun "book," answering the question "Which one?")
Adverb clause	• Modifies a verb, an adjective or another adverb • Answers the questions "When?" "Where?" "How?" "Why?" "To what extent?" or "Under what condition?"	John is smiling *because he is happy*. (The dependent clause "because he is happy" modifies the verb "is smiling," answering the question "Why?")
Noun clause	• Acts as a subject, a direct object, an object of the preposition or a subjective complement	*Whatever you say* is of little importance. (subject) They hoped *that they would win*. (direct object) I was thinking about *when we first met*. (object of the preposition) My hope is *that you will leave*. (subjective complement)

Note:
- Adjective clauses introduced by relative pronouns are also called *relative clauses*:
  *Where's the car **that she bought?***
- Noun clauses are singular:
  *When she gets home **is** her business.*
- A direct object follows a transitive verb in a sentence and answers the questions "What?" or "Whom?"
  He wrote the report. (What did he write? Answer: The report.)
  She took her sister to lunch. (Whom did she take to lunch? Answer: Her sister.)
- A subjective complement is connected to a subject by a linking verb. Common linking verbs include the following: *appear, be, become, feel, grow, look, remain, seem, smell, sound, stay* and *taste*.
  *He **looked** exhausted; now, he **looks** energized.* (*Exhausted* and *energized* are subjective complements.)

GRAMMAR TIP

Action verbs may be transitive or intransitive: a transitive verb is followed by a direct object whereas an intransitive verb is not.

He broke the window. (break = transitive)

She arrived. (arrive = intransitive)

---

2. Hefty, Marye, Sally Ortiz, and Sara Nelson. *Sentence Diagramming: A Step-by-Step Guide to Learning Grammar through Diagramming*. Toronto: Pearson Education, 2008. 45–67. Print.

Pinpoint

Part A

Join each pair of sentences by adding the conjunction indicated. Make any necessary changes to punctuation, capitalization and sentence order. Write your answers in the space provided. In some cases, more than one answer is possible.

1. You can cut the grass. You can wash the car. (CC – show an alternative)

_____

2. There had been an avalanche. The highway through the mountains was closed. (SC – give a reason)

_____

_____

3. He won the lottery. He quit his job. (CC – show a result)

_____

4. Geoff exercises three times a week. He has not lost any weight.
(AC – show a contrast)

_____

_____

5. Robin got an A. Ryland got a B. (CC – show a contrast)

_____

6. There was a serious accident on the highway. They missed their exam.
(AC – show a result)

_____

_____

7. My e-mail account was hacked yesterday. My computer was infected with a virus. (AC – add)

_____

_____

8. He lives two blocks from his office. He is often late for work.
(SC – present opposing ideas)

_____

_____

9. She doesn't eat red meat. She doesn't drink wine. (CC – add)

_____

_____

10. I am finding my chemistry course difficult. I nearly failed my last exam.
(AC – emphasize)

_____

_____

Part B

Indicate whether each of the clauses in italics is an independent clause or a dependent clause. If the clause is dependent, indicate the type of dependent clause: adjective, adverb or noun. The first one has been done for you as an example.

1. Where's the appetizer *that I ordered*?
   ☐ Independent clause ☑ Dependent clause

   Type of dependent clause:
   ☑ adjective clause ☐ adverb clause ☐ noun clause

2. Her most cherished dream is *that she will retire*.
   ☐ Independent clause ☐ Dependent clause

   Type of dependent clause:
   ☐ adjective clause ☐ adverb clause ☐ noun clause

3. *I enjoy walking my dogs* when the weather is fine.
   ☐ Independent clause ☐ Dependent clause

   Type of dependent clause:
   ☐ adjective clause ☐ adverb clause ☐ noun clause

4. I was dreaming of *where I will vacation*.
   ☐ Independent clause ☐ Dependent clause

   Type of dependent clause:
   ☐ adjective clause ☐ adverb clause ☐ noun clause

5. *I wanted to eat in*, but my girlfriend, who loves fine dining, wanted to eat out.
   ☐ Independent clause ☐ Dependent clause

   Type of dependent clause:
   ☐ adjective clause ☐ adverb clause ☐ noun clause

6. That's the man *who I met*.
   ☐ Independent clause ☐ Dependent clause

   Type of dependent clause:
   ☐ adjective clause ☐ adverb clause ☐ noun clause

7. The little boy is crying *because he is lost*.
   ☐ Independent clause ☐ Dependent clause

   Type of dependent clause:
   ☐ adjective clause ☐ adverb clause ☐ noun clause

8. They wished *that he would leave*.
   ☐ Independent clause ☐ Dependent clause

   Type of dependent clause:
   ☐ adjective clause ☐ adverb clause ☐ noun clause

9. *This exercise is interesting*; however, I find it difficult.

☐ Independent clause   ☐ Dependent clause

Type of dependent clause:

☐ adjective clause   ☐ adverb clause   ☐ noun clause

10. *Where she lives* is a mystery.

☐ Independent clause   ☐ Dependent clause

Type of dependent clause:

☐ adjective clause   ☐ adverb clause   ☐ noun clause

COMPANION web+

Now that you have pin-pointed your current level of understanding of sentence types, complete related exercises on the Companion Website for practice and instant feedback.

② Present, Past and Future Tenses

THE PRESENT

The Simple Present Tense

The simple present is used to express

GRAMMAR TIP

Affirmative, third-person-singular forms of verbs take an *s*; all other persons (*I, you, we, they*) do not.

- general or repeated actions;
  *Jackson **drives** his children to school **every** morning.*

- facts.
  *We **add** a day to February **every** leap year.*

KEY TERMS:
in the morning, every (afternoon, day, morning, year, etc.), often, on the weekend, in general, always, often, as a rule …

Examine the conjugation chart below:

AFFIRMATIVE	NEGATIVE	INTERROGATIVE (YES/NO QUESTION)
I eat.	I do not eat. (I don't eat.)	Do I eat?
You eat.	You do not eat. (You don't eat.)	Do you eat?
He/She/It eats.	He/She/It does not eat. (He/She/It doesn't eat.)	Does he/she/it eat?
We eat.	We do not eat. (We don't eat.)	Do we eat?
They eat.	They do not eat. (They don't eat.)	Do they eat?

Note: • In the negative and interrogative forms, the auxiliary *does* is used for the third-person singular and *do* is used for all other persons.

• In the negative and interrogative forms, only the auxiliary is conjugated.

• In the negative form, the contractions *don't* and *doesn't* are formed by substituting an apostrophe for the letter *o* and contracting two words into one.

- In the interrogative form, the auxiliary precedes the subject.
- To transform a yes/no question into an information question, place the question word before the auxiliary:

  Does he eat? ➡ **Why** *does he eat?*
  Do they eat? ➡ **Where** *do they eat?*

- Common question words for information questions include *who, what, where, when, why* and *how.* (See Chart A, page 284.)

SPELLING TIPS:

- Add *s* to most verbs in the third-person singular.
  answer ➡ *answers*

- If the verb ends in *ch, sh, s* or *x*, add *es*.
  catch ➡ *catches*   *wash* ➡ *washes*
  miss ➡ *misses*   *fix* ➡ *fixes*

- If the verb ends in *y*, change the *y* to *i* and add *es*.
  study ➡ *studies*

Pronunciation of Final *S*

There are three ways to pronounce the final *s*:

1. When the last sound of the verb is voiceless,[3] pronounce the final *s* as an /s/ sound: *eats, talks, walks …*

2. When the last sound of the verb is voiced, pronounce the final *s* as a /z/ sound: *lives, loves, moves …*

3. When the base form of the verb ends in *s, z, sh, ch, x, se, ge* or *ce*, pronounce the final *s* as an /iz/ sound: *kisses, fizzes, washes …*

GRAMMAR TIP

Like the verb *be*, the verb *have* is conjugated differently in the third-person singular: *he has, she has, it has.*

The Verb *Be*

The verb *be* is conjugated differently from all other verbs. Take a look at the following conjugation chart:

AFFIRMATIVE	NEGATIVE	INTERROGATIVE (YES/NO QUESTION)
I am here. (I'm here.)	I am not here. (I'm not here.)	Am I here?
You are here. (You're here.)	You are not here. (You're not here. / You aren't here.)	Are you here?
He/She/It is here. (He's/She's/It's here.)	He/She/It is not here. (He's/She's/It's not here. / He/She/It isn't here.)	Is he/she/it here?
We are here. (We're here.)	We are not here. (We're not here. / We aren't here.)	Are we here?
They are here. (They're here.)	They are not here. (They're not here. / They aren't here.)	Are they here?

3. A voiceless sound causes no vocal-cord vibration when pronounced whereas a voiced sound does.

Note:
- The first-person singular (*I*) and the third-person singular (*he*, *she* or *it*) have different conjugations from the other persons: *am* and *is* are used, not *are*.
- No auxiliary is required for the negative and interrogative forms.
- In the negative form, contractions can be formed in two ways for all persons but the first-person singular.
- In the interrogative form, the verb precedes the subject.
- To transform a yes/no question into an information question, place the question word before the verb:
  Is he here? ➡ **Why** *is he here?*

GRAMMAR TIP

Use contractions for spoken English and informal writing:
I'm home.

The Present Continuous Tense

The present continuous is used to express

- actions occurring now;
  *The mayor **is speaking** with reporters **right now**.*

- planned future actions.
  *We **are leaving** for Europe **next** Monday.*

KEY TERMS:
at the moment, in an hour, now, right now, at this very minute, in a couple of hours, tomorrow, next (Monday, month, week, etc.) …

The present continuous is composed of an auxiliary (*be* conjugated in the simple present, see above) and a present participle (verb + *ing*). Examine the conjugation chart below:

AFFIRMATIVE	NEGATIVE	INTERROGATIVE (YES/NO QUESTION)
I am eating. (I'm eating.)	I am not eating. (I'm not eating.)	Am I eating?
You are eating. (You're eating.)	You are not eating. (You're not eating. / You aren't eating.)	Are you eating?
He/She/It is eating. (He's/She's/It's eating.)	He/She/It is not eating. (He's/She's/It's not eating. / He/She/It isn't eating.)	Is he/she/it eating?
We are eating. (We're eating.)	We are not eating. (We're not eating. / We aren't eating.)	Are we eating?
They are eating. (They're eating.)	They are not eating. (They're not eating. / They aren't eating.)	Are they eating?

Note:
- In the negative form, contractions can be formed in two ways for all persons but the first-person singular.
- In the interrogative form, the auxiliary precedes the subject.
- To transform a yes/no question into an information question, place the question word before the auxiliary:
  Are they eating? ➡ **When** *are they eating?*
- Non-action verbs (stative verbs) such as *know* cannot be used in the continuous form:
  *I ~~am knowing~~ **know** you.* Other non-action verbs include *be, believe, belong, exist, forget, hate, hear, like, love, need, own, possess, prefer, remember, see* and *understand*.

SPELLING TIPS:

- Add *ing* to the base form of most verbs to form the present participle:
  visit ➡ *visiting*
- If the verb ends in *e*, remove the *e* before adding *ing*:
  place ➡ *placing*
- Some verbs ending with a consonant-vowel-consonant structure require that you double the last consonant before adding *ing*:
  jog ➡ *jogging*
- If the verb ends in *ie*, change the *ie* to *y* before adding *ing*:
  die ➡ *dying*

THE PAST

The Simple Past Tense

The simple past is used to express

- completed actions.
  *She **won** two gold medals **at the 2010 Olympics**.* (past tense of irregular verb *win*)
  *He **moved** to Ireland **three years ago**.* (past tense of regular verb *move*)

KEY TERMS:
last (month, night, weekend, year, etc.), yesterday, three years ago ...

Irregular Verbs

Irregular verbs have irregular past forms: *eat* ➡ *ate*. The only way to know the form is to memorize it—or refer to an irregular-verb chart such as the one on pages 285–286. Examine the conjugation chart below:

AFFIRMATIVE	NEGATIVE	INTERROGATIVE (YES/NO QUESTION)
I ate.	I did not eat. (I didn't eat.)	Did I eat?
You ate.	You did not eat. (You didn't eat.)	Did you eat?
He/She/It ate.	He/She/It did not eat. (He/She/It didn't eat.)	Did he/she/it eat?
We ate.	We did not eat. (We didn't eat.)	Did we eat?
They ate.	They did not eat. (They didn't eat.)	Did they eat?

Note:
- In the affirmative form, the verb conjugation is always the same.
- In the negative and interrogative forms, only the auxiliary is conjugated and it is always the same: *did*.
- A yes/no question is created by placing the auxiliary before the subject. To transform a yes/no question into an information question, place the question word before the auxiliary:
  Did you eat? ➡ ***What** did you eat?*
- Some verbs are both regular and irregular.
  The simple past of the verb *burn* can be either *burnt* (irregular) or *burned* (regular).
  The simple past of the verb *learn* can be either *learnt* (irregular) or *learned* (regular).

The verb *be* is conjugated differently from all other verbs. Take a look at the conjugation chart below:

AFFIRMATIVE	NEGATIVE	INTERROGATIVE (YES/NO QUESTION)
I was there.	I was not there. (I wasn't there.)	Was I there?
You were there.	You were not there. (You weren't there.)	Were you there?
He/She/It was there.	He/She/It was not there. (He/She/It wasn't there.)	Was he/she/it there?
We were there.	We were not there. (We weren't there.)	Were we there?
They were there.	They were not there. (They weren't there.)	Were they there?

Note:
- *Be* is an "irregular" irregular verb. There are two simple-past forms: *was* for the first- and third-person singular (I, he/she/it) and *were* for all other persons.
- No auxiliary is required for the negative and interrogative forms.
- A yes/no question is created by placing the verb before the subject. To transform a yes/no question into an information question, place the question word before the verb:
  Was he there? ➡ **Why** *was he there?*

Regular Verbs

Now let's turn our attention to the regular verbs. Examine the conjugation chart below:

AFFIRMATIVE	NEGATIVE	INTERROGATIVE (YES/NO QUESTION)
I asked.	I did not ask. (I didn't ask.)	Did I ask?
You asked.	You did not ask. (You didn't ask.)	Did you ask?
He/She/It asked.	He/She/It did not ask. (He/She/It didn't ask.)	Did he/she/it ask?
We asked.	We did not ask. (We didn't ask.)	Did we ask?
They asked.	They did not ask. (They didn't ask.)	Did they ask?

Note:
- In the affirmative form, the verb conjugation is always the same (ending with *ed*).
- In the negative and interrogative forms, only the auxiliary is conjugated—and it is always the same: *did*.
- A yes/no question is formed by placing the auxiliary before the subject. To transform a yes/no question into an information question, place the question word before the auxiliary:
  Did you ask? ➡ **What** *did you ask?*

SPELLING TIPS:

- Add *ed* to form the simple past of most regular verbs:
  visit ➡ *visited*

- If the regular verb ends in *e*, simply add a *d*:
  place ➡ *placed*

- Some verbs ending with a consonant-vowel-consonant structure require that you double the last consonant before adding *ed*:
  jog ➡ *jogged*

- If the regular verb ends in *y*, change the *y* to *i* before adding *ed*:
  study ➡ *studied*

Pronunciation of *ed*

While the endings of regular verbs are quite regular (*ed*), the pronunciation of these endings is not. There are three ways to pronounce the final *ed* endings of regular verbs:

1. When the last sound of the verb is voiceless, pronounce the final *ed* as a /t/ sound: *walked, talked, stopped* …

2. When the last sound of the verb is voiced, pronounce the final *ed* as a /d/ sound: *planned, exercised, moved* …

3. When the last letters of the verb are *t, te, d* or *de*, pronounce the final *ed* as an /id/ sound: *downloaded, landed, planted* …

GRAMMAR TIP

The past continuous is sometimes called the *past progressive*. Think about the terms *continuous* or *progressive* to remind yourself to use this tense for ongoing actions only.

The Past Continuous Tense

The past continuous is used to express

- actions in progress at a specific time in the past;
  *They **were waiting** for the bus **at 8 a.m.***

- interrupted actions;
  *He **was preparing** supper **when** the electricity went off.*

- simultaneous actions;
  ***While** he **was completing** the bibliography, she **was proofreading** the report.*

- background actions.
  *The crew **was preparing** the stage **at the same time as** the band **was practising**.*

KEY TERMS:
at 8 a.m., when, while, at noon, at midnight, at the same time as …

The past continuous is composed of an auxiliary (*be* conjugated in the simple past) and a present participle (verb + *ing*). Examine the conjugation chart below:

AFFIRMATIVE	NEGATIVE	INTERROGATIVE (YES/NO QUESTION)
I was eating.	I was not eating. (I wasn't eating.)	Was I eating?
You were eating.	You were not eating. (You weren't eating.)	Were you eating?
He/She/It was eating.	He/She/It was not eating. (He/She/It wasn't eating.)	Was he/she/it eating?
We were eating.	We were not eating. (We weren't eating.)	Were we eating?
They were eating.	They were not eating. (They weren't eating.)	Were they eating?

Note:
- The present participle is always the same—but remember that the verb *be* has two irregular forms: *was* and *were*.
- A yes/no question is created by placing the auxiliary before the subject. To transform a yes/no question into an information question, place the question word before the auxiliary:
  Was he eating? ➡ ***Why** was he eating?*

GRAMMAR TIP

Don't use the past continuous to express past habits; use the simple past instead:
*When I was a teenager, I ~~was jogging~~ **jogged** every day.*

THE FUTURE

Both *will* and *be going to* can be used to express

- opinions about the future;
  *I hope he **will** call **today**.*
  *I hope he **is going to** call **today**.*

- predictions.
  *It **will** snow **on the weekend**.*
  *It **is going to** snow **on the weekend**.*

In most situations, *will* and *be going to* are interchangeable when used to express opinions about the future or to make predictions.

Exception: When the predicted action is imminent (about to happen), the *be going to* form is used.
*Look at those dark clouds! It ~~will rain~~ **is going to** rain any second.*

However, in some situations, only *will* can be used; in others, only the *be going to* form can be used.

Will

In addition to expressing opinions about the future and making predictions, *will* is used to express

- willingness;
  (A kitchen timer is ringing.)
  Sue: *Barb, **will** you take the cookies out of the oven?*
  Barb: *Sure, I'**ll** do that.*

- promises.
  *She promises she **will** finish the marketing plan on time.*

KEY TERMS:
today, tomorrow, promise, next (month, week, weekend, year, etc.), soon, tonight …

Examine the conjugation chart below:

AFFIRMATIVE	NEGATIVE	INTERROGATIVE (YES/NO QUESTION)
I will eat. (I'll eat.)	I will not eat. (I'll not eat. / I won't eat.)	Will I eat?
You will eat. (You'll eat.)	You will not eat. (You'll not eat. / You won't eat.)	Will you eat?
He/She/It will eat. (He'll/She'll/It'll eat.)	He/She/It will not eat. (He'll/She'll/It'll not eat. / He/She/It won't eat.)	Will he/she/it eat?
We will eat. (We'll eat.)	We will not eat. (We'll not eat. / We won't eat.)	Will we eat?
They will eat. (They'll eat.)	They will not eat. (They'll not eat. / They won't eat.)	Will they eat?

Note:
- The auxiliary *will* is used for all persons.
- In the negative form, contractions can be formed in two ways.
- In the interrogative form, the auxiliary precedes the subject.
- In the first-person singular and plural, *shall* is sometimes used instead of *will* in the interrogative form:
  ***Shall** I eat? **Shall** we eat?*
- To transform a yes/no question into an information question, place the question word before the auxiliary:
  Will you eat? ➡ ***What** will you eat?*
- We use the contracted form of *will* with nouns and interrogative pronouns in spoken English: ***Bob'll** be on time. **What'll** he do?*
  Do not use this form in written English.

The *Be Going To* Form

In addition to expressing opinions about the future and making predictions, *be going to* is used to express

- prior plans;
  (Papers, receipts and a calculator are on the desk.)
  He **is going to** prepare his income tax return **this evening**.

  (Suitcases are packed and at the door.)
  Tomorrow morning, they **are going to** drive to PEI to visit their grandparents.

- imminent actions.
  *Hurry up! You **are going to** miss your flight! Don't you know what time it is?*

KEY TERMS:

in a minute, next (month, week, weekend, year, etc.), soon, tonight …

The *be going to* form consists of the present continuous tense of the verb *go* + the full infinitive.

   She is going to eat.

Examine *be going to* conjugations in the chart below:

AFFIRMATIVE	NEGATIVE	INTERROGATIVE (YES/NO QUESTION)
I am going to eat. (I'm going to eat.)	I am not going to eat. (I'm not going to eat.)	Am I going to eat?
You are going to eat. (You're going to eat.)	You are not going to eat. (You're not going to eat. / You aren't going to eat.)	Are you going to eat?
He/She/It is going to eat. (He's/She's/It's going to eat.)	He/She/It is not going to eat. (He's/She's/It's not going to eat. / He/She/It isn't going to eat.)	Is he/she/it going to eat?
We are going to eat. (We're going to eat.)	We are not going to eat. (We're not going to eat. / We aren't going to eat.)	Are we going to eat?
They are going to eat. (They're going to eat.)	They are not going to eat. (They're not going to eat. / They aren't going to eat.)	Are they going to eat?

Note: • To transform a yes/no question into an information question, place the question word before the auxiliary:

   Is he going to eat? ➡ **Where** *is he going to eat?*

Pinpoint

Part A

Use the correct forms of the verbs in parentheses, choosing the appropriate tense from the two suggested at the end of each question. Do not use the same tense twice in the same question.

1. The city (fill) _____ potholes today. Workers (fill) _____ more than 30,000 potholes every year. (simple present / present continuous)

2. She (understand) _____ why her business (lose) _____ money, but she can't do anything to stop the losses. (simple present / present continuous).

3. Is that music you (listen) _____ to? All I (hear) _____ is noise! (simple present / present continuous)

4. The DVD Depot (have) _____ a sale this weekend. The store (have) _____ a great selection of indie movies. (simple present / present continuous)

5. The cashiers (count) _____ the deposits when a gunman (enter) _____ the bank. (simple past / past continuous)

6. While I (wash) _____ the dishes last night, I (cut) _____ my finger on a knife. (simple past / past continuous)

7. I (pour)_____ coffee when the handle on the coffee pot (break) _____, splattering coffee everywhere. (simple past / past continuous)

8. _____ you (be) _____ quiet? You (wake) _____ the baby! (future with *will* / future with *be going to*)

9. I (open) _____ that door for you; I can see your arms are full of groceries. _____ you (make)_____ supper tonight? (future with *will* / future with *be going to*)

10. I (bring) _____ the salad if you will bring the dessert. I am sure we (have) _____ a fabulous meal! (future with *will* / future with *be going to*)

Part B

Fill in each blank with the correct form of the verb in parentheses, using one of the following tenses: simple present, present continuous, simple past, past continuous, future with *will* or *be going to*. Do not use contractions. In some cases, more than one answer is possible.

1. Gerry usually (take) _____ the bus to school, but it's really cold today, so his father (drive) _____ him.

2. The students (read) _____ three novels for their course last semester. They (tell) _____ their teacher that two would have been enough.

3. I (speak) _____ with my parents last night and (make) _____ plans for the holidays. They (pay) _____ _____ for my ticket so I can fly home.

4. New furniture (cost) _____ a lot of money. Can you afford to redecorate your office?

5. Ned (change) _____ in the locker room when the fire alarm (ring) _____ yesterday.

6. I (go) _____ to the store in a few minutes. Do you need anything?

7. The children (sleep) _____. Don't disturb them.

8. Suzanne (travel) _____ a lot for her job. Last week, she (teach) _____ a course in Halifax. Right now, she (give) _____ a seminar in Quebec City. Next week, she (lead) _____ a workshop in Whitehorse.

9. We (need) _____ more printer paper today. We have only a hundred sheets left.

10. I (get) _____ the manager if you want more information about refunds.

③ The Perfect Aspect

In the previous section, you examined the present, past and future tenses. Here, you will examine the perfect aspect of these tenses.

The perfect aspect is used for a past happening that is seen in relation to a later time or event.[4]

The present perfect is used to express the past as it relates to a present time or event.

> *This morning, I **have drunk** three cups of coffee.*

The past perfect is used to express the past as it relates to a past time or event. The past perfect shows a relationship between two past times or events, one of which is "more in the past" than the other.

> *By 10 o'clock this morning, I **had drunk** three cups of coffee.*

The future perfect is used to express the past relative to a future time or event. The future perfect shows a relationship between two future times or events, one of which is "less in the future" than the other.

> *By 10 o'clock tomorrow morning, I **will have drunk** three cups of coffee.*

All three perfect tenses—present, past and future—can be used in the continuous form: *I have been drinking*; *I had been drinking*; and *I will have been drinking*. The continuous form indicates the (limited) duration of an event and that the event may not be complete.

The Simple Present Perfect

The present perfect is used to express

- actions occurring at an indefinite time in the past;
  *She **has eaten** at that restaurant.*
  (We don't know *when* she ate there; we know just that she has eaten there.)

- actions occurring in an incomplete period of time;
  *I **have done** my homework **today**.*
  (*Today* is not finished.)

- incomplete actions (or actions beginning in the past and continuing in the present);
  *They **have been** in that restaurant **for** two hours (or **since** 8:00 p.m.).*
  (They arrived at the restaurant two hours ago, and they are still there now.)

- recent actions.
  *They **have just finished** eating.*
  (A recent action is a past action close in time to the present moment.)

KEY TERMS:
today, for, since, just, ever, never, yet, this week, this year, recently …

The present perfect is formed by conjugating *have* in the simple present and adding the past participle of the main verb. The past participle of regular verbs is the same as the simple-past form: *walk* ➡ *walked* ➡ *walked*. The past participle of irregular verbs varies (see Chart B, page 285): *eat* ➡ *ate* ➡ *eaten*.

GRAMMAR TIP

Use *for* with periods of time (*two hours*) and *since* with points in time (*8:00 p.m.*).

---

4. Leech, Geoffrey N. *Meaning and the English Verb.* New York: Longman, 1987. 35. Print.

Examine the conjugation chart below:

AFFIRMATIVE	NEGATIVE	INTERROGATIVE (YES/NO QUESTION)
I have eaten. (I've eaten.)	I have not eaten. (I've not eaten. / I haven't eaten.)	Have I eaten?
You have eaten. (You've eaten.)	You have not eaten. (You've not eaten. / You haven't eaten.)	Have you eaten?
He/She/It has eaten. (He's/She's/It's eaten.)	He/She/It has not eaten. (He's/She's/It's not eaten. / He/She/It hasn't eaten.)	Has he/she/it eaten?
We have eaten. (We've eaten.)	We have not eaten. (We've not eaten. / We haven't eaten.)	Have we eaten?
They have eaten. (They've eaten.)	They have not eaten. (They've not eaten. / They haven't eaten.)	Have they eaten?

Note:
- The auxiliary *has* is used for the third-person singular, and *have* is used for all other persons.
- In the negative form, contractions can be formed in two ways.
- In the interrogative form, the auxiliary precedes the subject.
- To transform a yes/no question into an information question, place the question word before the auxiliary:
  Have you eaten? ➡ **What** *have you eaten?*

Questions with *Ever* and *Yet*

Compare the following two questions and answers:

1. *Has Karen **ever** eaten at that restaurant?*
  ➡ *Yes, Karen has eaten at that restaurant.*
  ➡ *No, Karen has **never** eaten at that restaurant.*

2. *Has Karen eaten at that restaurant **yet**?*
  ➡ *Yes, Karen has eaten at that restaurant.*
  ➡ *No, Karen has not eaten at that restaurant **yet**.*

In the first question, the speaker does not know whether Karen has eaten at the restaurant.

In the second question, the speaker does not know whether Karen has eaten at the restaurant—but thinks she will eat there one day if she hasn't already done so.

GRAMMAR TIP
- The adverb *yet* is placed at the end of interrogative and negative sentences.
- *Ever* is placed before the past participle in interrogative sentences.
- *Never* is placed before the past participle in negative sentences.

Comparing the Simple Past and the Present Perfect

Examine the following two sentences:

Simple past: *I **did** my homework this morning.*
Present perfect: *I **have done** my homework this morning.*

Both of these sentences are correct—in the right contexts! The first sentence is correct *if it is no longer morning,* while the second sentence is correct *if it is still morning.*

Sometimes, students have difficulty knowing whether to use the simple past or the present perfect.

When unsure which tense to use, ask yourself the following questions:

1. Do I know when the action occurred?
2. Is the period of time in which the action is occurring finished?
3. Is the action finished?
4. Is the action in the distant past?

If the answer to any of these questions is "yes," use the simple past; otherwise, use the present perfect.

GRAMMAR TIP

Conversations about past events often begin in the present perfect but continue in the simple past.

Q: *Have you eaten at any good restaurants lately?*
A: *Yes, yesterday we **ate** at the new bistro on the corner.*

The Present Perfect Continuous

Like the simple present perfect, the present perfect continuous is used to express

*   actions occurring at an indefinite time in the past;
    *She **has been sleeping** poorly.*

*   actions occurring in an incomplete period of time;
    *They **have been studying** hard **this year**.*

*   incomplete actions (or actions beginning in the past and continuing in the present).
    *We **have been dancing for** hours.*

When there is no specific reference to time, the present perfect continuous expresses a recent action.

KEY TERMS:
this year, today, for, since, just, recently …

Unlike the simple present perfect, the present perfect continuous emphasizes the

*   duration of an action, answering the question "How long?";
    She has been sleeping poorly (for a couple of weeks now).

*   continuation of an action;
    They have been studying hard this year (as they always have).

*   temporariness of an action.
    We have been dancing for hours (and will need to stop soon).

The present perfect continuous is formed by conjugating *be* in the simple present perfect and adding the present participle of the verb (verb + *ing*). Examine the conjugation chart below:

AFFIRMATIVE	NEGATIVE	INTERROGATIVE (YES/NO QUESTION)
I have been eating. (I've been eating.)	I have not been eating. (I've not been eating. / I haven't been eating.)	Have I been eating?
You have been eating. (You've been eating.)	You have not been eating. (You've not been eating. / You haven't been eating.)	Have you been eating?
He/She/It has been eating. (He's/She's/It's been eating.)	He/She/It has not been eating. (He's/She's/It's not been eating. / He/She/It hasn't been eating.)	Has he/she/it been eating?
We have been eating. (We've been eating.)	We have not been eating. (We've not been eating. / We haven't been eating.)	Have we been eating?
They have been eating. (They've been eating.)	They have not been eating. (They've not been eating. / They haven't been eating.)	Have they been eating?

Note:
- The auxiliary *has* is used for the third-person singular, and *have* is used for all other persons.
- In the negative form, contractions can be formed in two ways.
- In the interrogative form, the auxiliary precedes the subject.
- Remember that non-action verbs (stative verbs) cannot be used in the continuous form: *I have* ~~been knowing~~ **known** *them for decades.*
- To transform a yes/no question into an information question, place the question word before the auxiliary:
  Have you been eating? ➡ *What have you been eating?*

The Simple Past Perfect

The simple past perfect is used to express

- an action that occurred before another past time or action.
  *Before he started breakfast, he **had made** a big pot of coffee.*
  *After she **had corrected** her students' exams, she entered the marks on her computer.*
  *When Stephanie arrived at the arena, the team **had finished** its practice.*

In the first two examples, the time sequence is clear; it is not necessary to use the past perfect except in formal writing. In these examples, the simple past may be used.
  *Before he started breakfast, he **made** a big pot of coffee.*
  *After she **corrected** her students' exams, she entered the marks on her computer.*

In the third example, the time sequence is unclear; it is therefore necessary to use the past perfect to indicate that the team finished its practice *before* Stephanie arrived. Changing the past perfect to the simple past would also change the meaning of the sentence, indicating that the team finished its practice *after* Stephanie arrived.

*When Stephanie arrived at the arena, the team **finished** its practice.*

The simple past perfect is formed by conjugating *have* in the simple past and adding the past participle. Examine the conjugation chart below:

AFFIRMATIVE	NEGATIVE	INTERROGATIVE (YES/NO QUESTION)
I had eaten. (I'd eaten.)	I had not eaten. (I'd not eaten. / I hadn't eaten.)	Had I eaten?
You had eaten. (You'd eaten.)	You had not eaten. (You'd not eaten. / You hadn't eaten.)	Had you eaten?
He/She/It had eaten. (He'd/She'd/It'd eaten.)	He/She/It had not eaten. (He'd/She'd/It'd not eaten. / He/She/It hadn't eaten.)	Had he/she/it eaten?
We had eaten. (We'd eaten.)	We had not eaten. (We'd not eaten. / We hadn't eaten.)	Had we eaten?
They had eaten. (They'd eaten.)	They had not eaten. (They'd not eaten. / They hadn't eaten.)	Had they eaten?

Note:
- The auxiliary *had* is used for all persons.
- In the negative form, contractions can be formed in two ways.
- In the interrogative form, the auxiliary precedes the subject.
- To transform a yes/no question into an information question, place the question word before the auxiliary:
  Had you eaten? ➡ ***What** had you eaten?*

The Past Perfect Continuous

The past perfect continuous is used to express
- an ongoing action that occurred before another past time or action.
  *It **had been snowing** heavily for two days when the police finally closed the roads.*

The past perfect continuous emphasizes the duration of the ongoing action and may indicate that the action is recent.
  *His hands were dirty because he **had been gardening**.*

The past perfect continuous is formed by conjugating *be* in the simple past perfect and adding the present participle of the verb (verb + *ing*). Examine the following conjugation chart:

AFFIRMATIVE	NEGATIVE	INTERROGATIVE (YES/NO QUESTION)
I had been eating. (I'd been eating.)	I had not been eating. (I'd not been eating. / I hadn't been eating.)	Had I been eating?

AFFIRMATIVE	NEGATIVE	INTERROGATIVE (YES/NO QUESTION)
You had been eating. (You'd been eating.)	You had not been eating. (You'd not been eating. / You hadn't been eating.)	Had you been eating?
He/She/It had been eating. (He'd/She'd/It'd been eating.)	He/She/It had not been eating. (He'd/She'd/It'd not been eating. / He/She/It hadn't been eating.)	Had he/she/it been eating?
We had been eating. (We'd been eating.)	We had not been eating. (We'd not been eating. / We hadn't been eating.)	Had we been eating?
They had been eating. (They'd been eating.)	They had not been eating. (They'd not been eating. / They hadn't been eating.)	Had they been eating?

Note:
- The auxiliary *had* is used for all persons.
- In the negative form, contractions can be formed in two ways.
- In the interrogative form, the auxiliary precedes the subject.
- Remember that non-action verbs (stative verbs) cannot be used in the continuous form: *I had ~~been knowing~~ **known** them for decades.*
- To transform a yes/no question into an information question, place the question word before the auxiliary: *Had you been eating?* ➡ ***What** had you been eating?*

The Simple Future Perfect

The simple future perfect is used to express

- an action that will be completed before another future time or action.
  ***By the time** we next see one another, I **will have graduated** college.*

The dependent clause refers to the future but uses the simple present, and not the future with *will*.
  ***Before** Steve ~~will return~~ **returns** home, he will have played golf in many different countries.*

KEY TERMS:
by the time, before, by next January …

The simple future perfect is formed by conjugating *have* in the simple future (future with *will*) and adding the past participle. Examine the following conjugation chart:

AFFIRMATIVE	NEGATIVE	INTERROGATIVE (YES/NO QUESTION)
I will have eaten. (I'll have eaten.)	I will not have eaten. (I'll not have eaten. / I won't have eaten.)	Will I have eaten?
You will have eaten. (You'll have eaten.)	You will not have eaten. (You'll not have eaten. / You won't have eaten.)	Will you have eaten?

He/She/It will have eaten. (He'll/She'll/It'll have eaten.)	He/She/It will not have eaten. (He'll/She'll/It'll not have eaten. / He/She/It won't have eaten.)	Will he/she/it have eaten?
We will have eaten. (We'll have eaten.)	We will not have eaten. (We'll not have eaten. / We won't have eaten.)	Will we have eaten?
They will have eaten. (They'll have eaten.)	They will not have eaten. (They'll not have eaten. / They won't have eaten.)	Will they have eaten?

Note:
- The auxiliary *will* is used for all persons.
- In the negative form, contractions can be formed in two ways.
- In the interrogative form, the auxiliary precedes the subject.
- To transform a yes/no question into an information question, place the question word before the auxiliary:
  Will you have eaten? ➡ ***What** will you have eaten?*

The Future Perfect Continuous

The future perfect continuous is used to express

- an ongoing action that will be completed before another future time or action.
  *By the time I finish college, I **will have been studying** for nearly fifteen years.*

The future perfect continuous emphasizes the duration of the ongoing action.
  *By next summer, I **will have been working** at my current job **for more than a decade**!*

KEY TERMS:
by the time …, by next summer, by 2055 …

The future perfect continuous is formed by conjugating *be* in the simple future perfect and adding the present participle of the verb (verb + *ing*). Examine the following conjugation chart:

AFFIRMATIVE	NEGATIVE	INTERROGATIVE (YES/NO QUESTION)
I will have been eating. (I'll have been eating.)	I will not have been eating. (I'll not have been eating. / I won't have been eating.)	Will I have been eating?
You will have been eating. (You'll have been eating.)	You will not have been eating. (You'll not have been eating. / You won't have been eating.)	Will you have been eating?
He/She/It will have been eating. (He'll/She'll/It'll have been eating.)	He/She/It will not have been eating. (He'll/She'll/It'll not have been eating. / He/She/It won't have been eating.)	Will he/she/it have been eating?

AFFIRMATIVE	NEGATIVE	INTERROGATIVE (YES/NO QUESTION)
We will have been eating. (We'll have been eating.)	We will not have been eating. (We'll not have been eating. / We won't have been eating.)	Will we have been eating?
They will have been eating. (They'll have been eating.)	They will not have been eating. (They'll not have been eating. / They won't have been eating.)	Will they have been eating?

Note:
• The auxiliary *will* is used for all persons.
• In the negative form, contractions can be formed in two ways.
• In the interrogative form, the auxiliary precedes the subject.
• Remember that non-action verbs (stative verbs) cannot be used in the continuous form: *I will have ~~been knowing~~ **known** them for decades.*
• To transform a yes/no question into an information question, place the question word before the auxiliary: *Will you have been eating?* ➡ ***What** will you have been eating?*

Pinpoint

Fill in each blank with the correct form of the verb in parentheses, using one of the following tenses: simple present perfect, present perfect continuous, simple past perfect, past perfect continuous, simple future perfect or future perfect continuous. Do not use contractions. In some cases, more than one answer is possible.

1. I want to travel to Portugal next year. My grandmother (be) _____ _____ there many times, and her favourite city is Lisbon. I (save) _____ money for two years now, and I (accumulated) _____ over $1500. By the time this semester is over, I (add) _____ another $800 to my savings.

2. Last summer, I decided to get a credit card. After I (compare) _____ _____ information from several banks, I chose the GIP Bank. It (serve) _____ me well since then.

3. I wanted to buy a car last year. I checked out deals on the Internet. I (look) _____ for a used Corvette for a couple of weeks when I found one at a good price. However, I (not, check) _____ _____ the fine print: the car needed a new motor!

4. Fraudsters (develop) _____ a lot of telephone and Internet scams. By the time you finish this exercise, people around the world (lose) _____ money.

5. Our family moved from Mexico to Canada back in July, and we (live) _____ here for five months. When the first snowstorm hit, we wondered whether we (make) _____ the right move.

6. I (run) _____ for the bus last Saturday evening when I tripped; I sprained an ankle and fractured a wrist.

7. Sheila (ski) _____ for many years now. She placed tenth in the last Winter Olympics and is hoping for a gold medal in the next Games.

8. My uncle drove off the road on the way home last night. It was no surprise. He (have) _____ too much to drink before he left the party.

9. Our sociology study group is talking to octogenarians for our project on aging. By the end of the month, we (conduct) _____ _____ interviews for twenty-five days, and we (speak) _____ with more than one hundred people over the age of eighty.

10. I (have) _____ a lot of trouble with my computer lately. I (check) _____ it for viruses several times this week, but I (find) _____ any.

4 Modals, Conditionals and Subjunctives

MODALS

In this section, you will examine ways of expressing different moods, various conditions, and hypothetical situations.

Modal auxiliaries, also known as *modals*, are special verbs used along with other verbs to express a particular *mood*.

*Alexandre Despatie **can** dive superbly.* (ability)
*The government **should** negotiate with its workers.* (advisability)

Modals can be used to express

- ability;
*She **can** cook well.*
*He **could** jog for miles when he was a teenager.* (past)

- advisability;
*He **should** apologize to her today.*
*She **should** have put gas in the car yesterday.* (past)

- obligation;
*You **must** be on time.*
*You **have to** be on time.* (informal)
*He **has got to** pass all his exams to stay on the hockey team.* (informal)
*You **had to** be on time.* (past)

- possibility;
*They **may** study tonight.*
*He **might** do his homework.*
*John **could** call tomorrow morning.*
*She **might** have lost her gloves at the arena last night.* (past)

- logical conclusion;
*Someone is at the door. Oh, that **must** be Harold.*
*It **must** have snowed in the mountains.* (past)

- preference.
*I **would rather** have steak than chicken.*
*I **would rather** have had steak.* (past)

The base form of the verb directly follows most modal auxiliaries. In such cases, the modal auxiliary is the same for all persons. To indicate past time with some auxiliaries, use *have* plus the past participle, as seen in the above examples.

GRAMMAR TIP

Have to and *have got to* are semi-modals used to express obligation:
I have to study and *I have got to study* both mean *I must study.* These forms are frequently used in spoken English.

Examine the chart below:

FUNCTION	MODAL AUXILIARY	AFFIRMATIVE	NEGATIVE	INTERROGATIVE (YES/NO QUESTION)
Ability	can	He can skate.	He cannot skate. (He can't skate.)	Can he skate?
Past	could	He could skate.	He could not skate. (He couldn't skate.)	Could he skate?
Advisability	should	She should pay.	She should not pay. (She shouldn't pay.)	Should she pay?
Past	should	She should have paid.	She should not have paid. (She shouldn't have paid.)	Should she have paid?
Obligation	must	I must pay my bills.		Must I pay my bills?
Informal	have to	I have to pay the fine.	I do not have to pay the fine. (I don't have to pay the fine.)	Do I have to pay the fine?
Past	had to	I had to pay the fine.	I did not have to pay the fine. (I didn't have to pay the fine.)	Did I have to pay the fine?
Possibility	may	It may be sunny.	It may not be sunny.	
	might	It might rain.	It might not rain.	Might it rain?
	could	It could snow.		Could it snow?
Past	may	She may have remembered.	She may not have remembered.	
	might	He might have had an accident.	He might not have had an accident.	
	could	He could have prevented the accident.		Could he have prevented the accident?
Logical conclusion	must	That must be Carole at the door.	That must not be Carole at the door. (That mustn't be Carole at the door.)	Must that be Carole at the door?
Past	must	He must have been sick.	He must not have been sick. (He mustn't have been sick.)	
Preference	would rather	They would rather eat pizza.	They would rather not eat pizza.	Would they rather eat pizza?

Note:
- *Could* can also be used to make suggestions: *You **could** study harder.* In this case, *could* takes on a function similar to *should* when used as a modal of advisability: *You **should** study harder.*
- Do not use *must not* to express a lack of obligation: *He ~~must not~~ **does not have to** speak.* Only *had to* can be used to express a past obligation.
- Do not use *may* in the interrogative form to express possibility: *~~May~~ **Might** (**Could**) he speak?*
- Do not use *could not* to express a lack of possibility: *He ~~could~~ **may** (**might**) **not** speak.*
- The contractions *mayn't* and *mightn't* are rarely used.
- *Have to* is a semi-modal and is conjugated, unlike pure modals:
  a) Present: In the negative and interrogative forms, the auxiliary *does* is used for the third-person singular, while *do* is used for all other persons: *They **do not have to** go. **Does** he **have to** leave?*
  b) Past: In the negative and interrogative forms, the auxiliary *did* is used for all persons: *We **did not have to** do the test. **Did** she **have to** pay the fine?*
- The semi-modals *have to* and *have got to* are also followed by the base form of the verb, but remember to conjugate them for he/she/it: *he has, she has, it has*.

I have to leave.	*I have got to leave.*
You have to leave.	*You have got to leave.*
*He/She/It **has to** leave.*	*He/She/It **has got to** leave.*
We have to leave.	*We have got to leave.*
They have to leave.	*They have got to leave.*

- In the interrogative form, the modal auxiliary or the auxiliary *do*, *does* or *did* precedes the subject.
- To transform a yes/no question into an information question, place the question word before the auxiliary:
  Should he apologize? ➡ ***Why** should he apologize?*

Modals may also be used to make and respond to polite requests.

REQUESTS WITH *I* OR *WE* AS THE SUBJECT	REQUESTS WITH *YOU* AS THE SUBJECT
May I (we) leave? Yes, you may. / No, you may not.	*Will* you show me how to do this? Yes, I will. / No, I will not.
Might I (we) be excused? Yes, you ~~might~~ **may**. / No, you ~~might~~ **may** not.	*Would* you explain this to me? Yes, I ~~would~~ **will**. / No, I ~~would~~ **will** not.
Could I (we) go? Yes, you ~~could~~ **may**. / No, you ~~could~~ **may** not.	*Could* you repeat that, please? Yes, I ~~could~~ **will**. / No, I ~~could~~ **will** not.

CONDITIONALS

A conditional sentence contains an "if-clause" and a "result clause." The most common conditionals can be classified as follows:

1. **Present real conditional**
    If Sonia listens to the teacher, she will get great marks.
    (Sonia will probably listen to her teacher, so great marks are to be expected.)

    The present real conditional is used to talk about real present/future situations, as the action in the if-clause is quite *probable*.

2. **Present unreal conditional**
    If John listened to the teacher, he would get great marks.
    (John will probably not listen to his teacher, so great marks are not to be expected.)

    The present unreal conditional is used to talk about unreal present/future situations, as the action in the if-clause is *improbable* or *imaginary*.

3. **Past unreal conditional**
    If Adam and Christine had listened to the teacher, they would have gotten great marks.
    (Adam and Christine did not listen to the teacher, so great marks were not obtained.)

    The past unreal conditional is used to talk about unreal past situations, as the action in the if-clause did not occur. The situation is purely *hypothetical*.

GRAMMAR TIP

Use the present real conditional for *probable* situations.
Use the present unreal conditional for *improbable* or *imaginary* situations.
Use the past unreal conditional for *hypothetical* situations.

Examine the chart below:

CONDITIONAL	IF-CLAUSE	RESULT CLAUSE
Present real	Simple present If he studies,	Subject + *will* + base form of the verb he will (he'll) succeed.
Present unreal	Simple past If he studied,	Subject + *would* + base form of the verb he would (he'd) succeed.
Past unreal	Past perfect If he had (he'd) studied,	Subject + *would have* + past participle he would (he'd) have succeeded.

Note:
- Never use the simple future in an if-clause:
  *If he ~~will study~~ **studies**, he will succeed.*
- Even though the simple past is used in the if-clause of the present unreal conditional, the situation being discussed is in the present/future.
- The negative form may be used in either—or both—clauses:
  *If he **does not study** hard, he **will not** succeed.*
  *If he **did not study** hard, his father would be upset.*
  *If he had studied hard, his father **would not** have been disappointed in him.*

To form interrogative sentences, invert the subject and the auxiliary in the result clause.

If he studies, he will succeed. ➡ *If he studies, **will he** succeed?*

If he studied, he would succeed. ➡ *If he studied, **would he** succeed?*

If he had studied, he would have succeeded. ➡ *If he had studied, **would he** have succeeded?*

> **GRAMMAR TIP**
>
> If you place the result clause before the if-clause, remove the comma:
> *If he studies, he will succeed.* ➡ *He will succeed if he studies.*

Conditionals with Modals

The result clause of a conditional can contain a modal. Refer to the chart below for examples:

CONDITIONAL	EXAMPLES WITH MODALS
Present real	• Result clause with *may, can, must* or *should*: If she is hungry, she *may* eat my lunch. (permission) If he burns supper, we *can* eat out. (possibility) If his stomach is gurgling, he *must* be hungry. (logical conclusion) If we are served well, we *should* leave a good tip. (advisability)
Present unreal	• Result clause with *could* or *might*: If she knew his name, she *could* call him. (present ability) If she asked him out, he *might* accept. (present possibility)
Past unreal	• Result clause with *could have* or *might have*: If she had known his name, she *could have* called him. (past ability) If she had asked him out, he *might have* accepted. (past possibility)
Note:	• Never use a modal in an if-clause: *If he ~~would study~~ **studied**, he would succeed.*

SUBJUNCTIVES

Examine the following two sentences:

1. If Jane *were* here, we could start the meeting.
2. It is important that Jane *be* on time.

The verbs in italics are written in the subjunctive.

The subjunctive is used to express a hypothetical situation (sentence 1) or to stress importance (sentence 2). *Were* is used to express hypothetical situations, and the base form of the verb is used to stress importance.

Refer to the chart on the following page for examples.

FUNCTION	EXPLANATION AND EXAMPLES
To express a hypothetical situation	• Use with *as if*, *if*, *suppose* and *wish*. She talks about her dog *as if* it *were* a child. *If* I *were* you, I would apologize. *Suppose* your father *were* here. What would you tell him? I *wish* the weather *were* nicer.
To stress importance	• Use in noun clauses (see page 211) that come after the following verbs and expressions: *advise* (that); *ask* (that); *demand* (that); *insist* (that); *it is important/necessary/essential/vital/imperative* (that); *propose* (that); *recommend* (that); *request* (that); and *suggest* (that). I *propose that* the proposition *not be* adopted. It is *vital that* she *call* me as soon as possible. She *requested that* he *leave*.

Note: • You may omit *that* from the noun clause:
I propose the proposition **not be** *adopted.*
• To avoid the subjunctive when stressing importance, use a gerund (see page 248) or *should*:
I propose **not adopting** *the proposition.*
I propose that the proposition **should not be** *adopted.*

Pinpoint

Part A

Use an appropriate modal or semi-modal auxiliary with each of the verbs in parentheses, modifying verb forms as required. Do not use contractions. In some cases, more than one answer is possible.

1. My MP3 player isn't working; my brother (forgot) _____

to recharge it.

2. The sky is clouding over. We (get) _____ some rain

this afternoon.

3. Riding a bike without a helmet is dangerous. You (wear) _____

_____ protective headgear every time you go for a ride.

4. I have an appointment on Delaney Street. _____ you

(tell) _____ me how to get there?

5. I drove into a ditch last night on the way home, but it wasn't my fault.

I (avoid, not) _____ a deer on the highway.

6. Someone is knocking at the door. It (be) _____ Steve;

he said he would drop by today.

7. I need some help. I (lift, not) _____ this heavy box.

8. He (renew) _____ his lease before the end of the month, or he will lose the apartment.

9. Dorothy did not go to work yesterday. She (sick) _____ _____ .

10. When Josh was in high school, he was in terrible shape. He (run, not) _____ more than a mile.

Part B

Complete each of the following conditional sentences, using the correct form of the verb in parentheses. Do not use contractions. In some cases, more than one answer is possible.

1. If my parents retire next year, they (sell) _____ their big house and buy a condo.

2. If he had been over sixty-five years of age, he (receive) _____ _____ a discount at the cinema.

3. If Margaret worked Friday, she (take) _____ the following Monday off.

4. If seniors (be) _____ valued for their contribution to society, they would have higher self-esteem.

5. Karl could have been living a life of luxury if he (lose, not) _____ _____ so much money in the stock-market crash.

6. They (sign) _____ the contract if the working conditions had been better.

7. If the storm hadn't damaged our boat, we (leave) _____ _____ the island.

8. If the weather (be) _____ good tomorrow, we can go water skiing.

9. You (got) _____ a better tip if you had been polite to the customers.

10. If Mike (be) _____ here, we could serve the birthday cake.

⑤ Passive Voice and Reported Speech

In this section, you will examine two different ways of expressing yourself: using the active or the passive voice and using direct (quoted) or reported (indirect) speech.

The Active and the Passive Voice

There are two voices in English: the active voice and the passive voice. When the subject is doing the action, the active voice is being used. When the subject is being acted upon, the passive voice is being used.

ACTIVE	PASSIVE
Carol Shields *wrote* the story.	The story *was written* by Carol Shields.
You *must submit* the assignment on time.	The assignment *must be submitted* on time.

In the active voice, the subject (Carol Shields / you) "acts": the subject is active.

In the passive voice, the subject (story/assignment) "is acted upon": the subject is passive.

In general, the passive voice is used when the performer of the action is
- unimportant;
  The lawn was mowed.
- unknown.
  The necklace has been stolen.

To make an active sentence passive:
1. Identify the verb tense of the active verb.
2. Conjugate *be* in the same tense as the active verb.
3. Add the past participle of the active verb.

*Andrew **is writing** the final report.* (active)
➡ *The final report **is being written** by Andrew.* (passive)

Note:
- The active verb is in the present continuous tense.
- *Be* in the present continuous tense = *is being*.
- The past participle of *write* = *written*.

The object of the active sentence ("the final report") becomes the subject in the passive sentence.

Look at the chart on the next page for examples of active and passive voices in different verb tenses and modal forms. Each example shows the affirmative, negative and interrogative forms.

GRAMMAR TIP

For passive-voice sentences containing modals, use the base form *be* followed by the past participle of the main verb: *They **must** do their work.* ➡ *Their work **must be done**.*

VERB TENSE/FORMS	ACTIVE VOICE	PASSIVE VOICE
Simple present	She *sends* a cheque every month.	A cheque *is sent* every month.
	He *does not (doesn't) send* a reply.	A reply *is not (isn't) sent*.
	Do they *discuss* the problem?	*Is* the problem *discussed*?
Present continuous	The thief *is hiding* the cash.	The cash *is being hidden*.
	The police *are not (aren't) arresting* the thief.	The thief *is not (isn't) being arrested*.
	Are the police *handcuffing* the thief?	*Is* the thief *being handcuffed*?
Simple past	We *took* the dog for a walk.	The dog *was taken* for a walk.
	We *did not (didn't) leash* the dog.	The dog *was not (wasn't) leashed*.
	Did they *feed* the dog?	*Was* the dog *fed*?
Past continuous	He *was doing* the homework.	The homework *was being done*.
	He *was not (wasn't) writing* a report.	A report *was not (wasn't) being written*.
	Was he *revising* the essay?	*Was* the essay *being revised*?
Present perfect	Steven *has paid* the bill.	The bill *has been paid*.
	The chef *has not (hasn't) made* lunch.	Lunch *has not (hasn't) been made*.
	Has someone *washed* the dishes?	*Have* the dishes *been washed*?
Past perfect	They *had paid* the bill before the due date.	The bill *had been paid* before the due date.
	They *had not (hadn't) painted* the house for years.	The house *had not (hadn't) been painted* for years.
	Had they cleaned the condo before they left?	*Had* the condo *been cleaned* before they left?
Future • With *will* • With *be going to*	They *will sell* the house. They *are going to sell* the house.	The house *will be sold*. The house *is going to be sold*.
	We *will not (won't) rent* the condo. We *are not (aren't) going to rent* the condo.	The condo *will not (won't) be rented*. The condo *is not (isn't) going to be rented*.
	Will he *give away* the money? *Is* he *going to give away* the money?	*Will* the money *be given away*? *Is* the money *going to be given away*?
Future perfect	They *will have returned* the books.	The books *will have been returned*.
	He *will not (won't) have done* the dishes.	The dishes *will not (won't) have been done*.
	Will they *have left* the door unlocked?	*Will* the door *have been left* unlocked?
Modals	He *might donate* some money.	Some money *might be donated*.
	She *could not (couldn't) answer* the question.	The question *could not (couldn't) be answered*.
	Must they *raise* a lot of money?	*Must* a lot of money *be raised*?

Modals (past)	She *might have paid* the bill.	The bill *might have been paid*.
	They *could not (couldn't) have recovered* the missing money.	The missing money *could not (couldn't) have been recovered*.
	Should he *have returned* the dog?	*Should* the dog *have been returned*?

Note:
- Form the passive with *be* and the past participle of the verb. (If you are unsure of the past participle of an irregular verb, refer to Chart B on pages 285–286.)
- In the passive interrogative form, the auxiliary precedes the subject.
- To transform a yes/no question into an information question, place the question word before the auxiliary:

  Was the dog fed? ➡ **When** *was the dog fed?*
- The passive voice may be used with *by* to stress the importance of the performer of the action: *The report was completed* **by** *Jason—not Andrew!*

GRAMMAR TIP

Only transitive verbs (verbs that take direct objects) can be used in the passive because the direct object becomes the subject of the passive sentence:

Sylvester walked to the store. ➡ ~~*The store was walked to by Sylvester.*~~

Direct (Quoted) and Reported (Indirect) Speech

You can directly relate (quote) or indirectly report someone's words:

Albert Einstein said, "The true sign of intelligence is not knowledge but imagination." (direct speech)

Albert Einstein said (that) the true sign of intelligence is not knowledge but imagination. (reported speech)

When reporting speech, you usually need to make changes to various parts of speech. Examine the following chart, paying particular attention to any underlined words; then read through the notes at the end of the chart.

DIRECT SPEECH	REPORTED SPEECH
1. He says, "I always <u>speak</u> Spanish with <u>my</u> girlfriend."	He says (that) <u>he</u> always <u>speaks</u> Spanish with <u>his</u> girlfriend.
2. Jerry said, "<u>I am</u> always tired."	Jerry said (that) <u>he was</u> always tired.
3. Estelle said, "<u>I am looking</u> for someone to work <u>my</u> Friday shift."	Estelle said (that) <u>she was looking</u> for someone to work <u>her</u> Friday shift.
4. The captain said, "The coach <u>cancelled</u> the afternoon practice."	The captain said (that) the coach <u>had cancelled</u> the afternoon practice.
5. The bystanders said, "<u>We were minding our</u> own business."	The bystanders said (that) <u>they had been minding their</u> own business.
6. Allan said, "<u>I have been</u> to Toronto."	Allan said (that) <u>he had been</u> to Toronto.
7. Harvey and Tanya said, "<u>We will make our</u> own supper <u>today</u>."	Harvey and Tanya said (that) <u>they would make their</u> own supper <u>yesterday</u>.
8. Corinne said, "Victoria <u>is</u> the capital of British Columbia."	Corinne said (that) Victoria <u>is</u> the capital of British Columbia.

© ERPI • REPRODUCTION PROHIBITED

DIRECT SPEECH	REPORTED SPEECH
9. She said, "I can drive you to the airport."	She said (that) she could drive me to the airport.
10. She said, "I must drive you to the airport."	She said (that) she had to drive me to the airport.
11. She asked, "When does the meeting start?"	She asked when the meeting started.
12. The instructions say, "Shake the container before opening."	The instructions say to shake the container before opening.

Note:
- When the introductory verb is in the present tense (*say/says*), do not change the tense used in the reported speech (see 1).
- When the introductory verb is in the past tense (*said, asked, replied, ...*), change the tense used in the reported speech by moving the tense *one step back into the past*. This is called *back-shifting*. See 2 through 7 for examples of back-shifting for the simple present, present continuous, simple past, past continuous, present perfect and simple future tenses respectively. Both the simple past and the present perfect are back-shifted to the past perfect (see 4 and 6).
- If a general truth is reported, do not change the tense used in the reported speech even if the introductory verb is in the past tense (see 8).
- Modals sometimes require a back-shift (see 9 and 10).
- In reported speech, you can often omit *that* after the verb *said*.
- Back-shift tenses when changing a direct question into an indirect question, and do not invert the subject and the auxiliary in an indirect question (see 11): *She asked when ~~did the meeting start~~ the meeting started*.
- When reporting instructions or orders, use an infinitive (see 12).
- Pronouns (references to people), adjectives and adverbs often need to be changed: *Bob said, "I am sailing away on my boat today."* Bob said that **he** was sailing away on **his** boat **yesterday**.

Pinpoint

Part A

Rewrite the following sentences in the passive voice. It is not necessary to repeat the subject. The first one has been done for you as an example.

1. The bank will process your loan request tomorrow.

   Your loan request will be processed tomorrow.

2. The authorities released the prisoner last Saturday.

   _____

3. Mark hadn't cleaned the oven in years.

   _____

4. Must you throw out the food?

   _____

5. She pays the phone bill by credit card.

   _____

6. The cleaner wasn't washing the floors at 9:00 p.m.

_____

7. Are they going to plow the roads tonight?

_____

8. Someone has deleted all my files.

_____

9. The students will have completed the tests by 10:00 a.m.

_____

10. Could Carter have stolen the money?

_____

Part B

Rewrite the following sentences using reported speech. Make required changes to verb tenses, pronouns, adjectives and adverbs. Maintain contracted forms. The first one has been done for you as an example.

1. Louise said, "I won't call you back."

Louise said (that) she wouldn't call you/me back.

2. Paul said, "I have never read such a clear report."

_____

3. The children said, "We wanted to go to camp this summer."

_____

4. George replied, "I am not interested in going to France."

_____

5. Melissa said, "My parents are coming for dinner."

_____

6. David answered, "Iqaluit is the capital of Nunavut."

_____

7. The police officer said, "Put your hands up!"

_____

8. Steve said, "I can fix the car."

_____

9. Mike said, "The teacher was sitting at her desk."

_____

10. The witness replied, "I have never seen this man in my life!"

_____

COMPANION **WEB+**

Now that you have pinpointed your current level of understanding of the active and passive voice, as well as direct and reported speech, complete related exercises on the Companion Website for practice and instant feedback.

⑥ Nouns and Pronouns

NOUNS

A noun is a word or a group of words that names people, places or things.

In this section we will consider kinds of nouns, plural noun forms, non-count nouns, possessive nouns and verbs as nouns.

Kinds of Nouns

There are four kinds of nouns:

1. Common (general)
   mother, father, baby …

2. Proper (specific)
   Canada, Montreal, Rufus Wainwright …

3. Abstract (things that are not concrete)
   love, hate, jealousy …

4. Collective (group)
   team, group, herd …

Plural Noun Forms

Refer to the following table for the rules concerning regular and irregular plurals:

RULE	EXAMPLES	
Most (regular) nouns: The plural is formed by simply adding *s*.	mother ➡ mothers	
Nouns that end in *ch, sh, s, x* or *o*: Add *es*.	match ➡ matches bush ➡ bushes bus ➡ buses	box ➡ boxes hero ➡ heroes
Nouns that end in *y*: a) If a vowel precedes the *y*, add *s*. b) If a consonant precedes the *y*, change the *y* to *i* and add *es*.	a) boy ➡ boys b) baby ➡ babies	
Most nouns ending in *f* or *fe*: Change the *f* or *fe* to *v* and add *es*.	half ➡ halves knife ➡ knives leaf ➡ leaves life ➡ lives loaf ➡ loaves	self ➡ selves shelf ➡ shelves thief ➡ thieves wife ➡ wives wolf ➡ wolves
Other nouns ending in *f* or *fe*: Simply add *s*. (Note: Some of these nouns have two plural forms.)	reef ➡ reefs carafe ➡ carafes scarf ➡ scarfs or scarves	

❯❯❯ ❯

Some nouns: The plural is formed with a vowel change.	fireman ➡ firemen foot ➡ feet goose ➡ geese man ➡ men	policeman ➡ policemen policewoman ➡ policewomen tooth ➡ teeth woman ➡ women
Some other nouns: The singular is the same as the plural.	aircraft ➡ aircraft craft[5] ➡ craft deer ➡ deer fish ➡ fish offspring ➡ offspring	salmon ➡ salmon series ➡ series sheep ➡ sheep species ➡ species trout ➡ trout
Certain nouns are always plural.	clothes eyeglasses goods pants pliers	police pyjamas scissors stairs surroundings
Many nouns of Greek or Latin origin form their plurals according to the rules of those languages.	ax*is* ➡ ax*es* bacteri*um* ➡ bacteri*a* bas*is* ➡ bas*es* cris*is* ➡ cris*es* dat*um* ➡ dat*a*	diagnos*is* ➡ diagnos*es* emphas*is* ➡ emphas*es* hypothes*is* ➡ hypothes*es* nucle*us* ➡ nucle*i* ov*um* ➡ ov*a*

Note: • Abbreviations, decades, letters and numbers can be pluralized: *RRSPs*, *1980s*, *7s*.
• The usual plural of *person* is *people*, not *persons*.
• The plural of *child* is *children*.
• The correct pronunciation of *women* is/wimmin/.
• Sometimes nouns that look plural are actually singular: *AIDS*, *billiards*, *news*.

Non-Count Nouns

Nouns that have a plural form are called *count* nouns.

Some nouns do not have a plural form: they are called *non-count* (or *mass*) nouns because they cannot be counted.

The chart below summarizes common non-count nouns:

KIND OF NON-COUNT NOUN	EXAMPLES
Abstract	advice, information, life, love, music
Academic subjects	chemistry, eugenics, history, mathematics, physics
Categories	clothing, food, furniture, homework, money
No separate parts	coffee, meat, milk, soup, water
Parts too small to count	grass, hair, salt, sand, sugar

5. vessel (boat, ship or airplane)

Non-count nouns are not preceded by *a* or *an*. However, they may be preceded by expressions of quantity, such as *a bottle of, a bowl of, a cup of, a great deal of, a lot of, a piece of, a little, any, lots of, most, much, no, plenty of* and *some*.

> They drank ~~a~~ **some coffee**.
> Did she give you ~~an~~ **any advice**?
> He does not have ~~a~~ **much clothing**.

Non-count nouns always take a singular verb.

> My homework ~~are~~ **is** done.

Use *there is* with non-count nouns and singular count nouns.

> **There is** some mail.
> **There is** a letter.

Use *there are* with plural count nouns.

> **There are** two letters.

Possessive Nouns

Nouns referring to people, places, animals and time can be "possessors":

> *Mr. Anderson's car, Montreal's stadium, the dogs' bones, Tuesday's class, …*

To indicate possession:

- Add *'s* to singular nouns and to plural nouns not ending in *s*.
  woman's work   people's lives

- Add an apostrophe only (') to plural nouns ending in *s*.
  two boys' bikes

Verbs as Nouns

A *verbal* is a word—derived from a verb—that functions as a noun, an adjective or an adverb. When functioning as a noun, there are two types of verbals: gerunds and infinitives. Examine the chart below:

TYPE	EXAMPLES
Gerund	Subject: *Reading* is interesting. Direct object: I enjoy *reading*. Object of a preposition: That armchair is great for *reading*. Subjective complement: My favourite pastime is *reading*.
Infinitive	Subject: *To eat* is divine. Direct object: I like *to eat*. Subjective complement: My hobby is *to eat*.

Note: • Gerunds can be subjects, direct objects, objects of a preposition or subjective complements.
 • Infinitives can be subjects, direct objects or subjective complements.
 • An infinitive cannot be an object of a preposition: *They talked about* ~~to ski~~ **skiing**.
 • When acting as subjects, gerunds and infinitives are singular.
 • The gerund always ends in *ing*.
 • The infinitive is the base form of the verb, preceded by *to*.
 • For information on verbs that function as adjectives and adverbs, see page 258.

Gerunds

Gerunds are always used after certain verbs.

*Kevin enjoys ~~to paint~~ **painting**.*

The chart below provides a list of some common verbs that are always followed by gerunds:

COMMON VERBS FOLLOWED BY GERUNDS				
admit	can't see	enjoy	miss	resent
advise	complete	finish	practise	resist
anticipate	consider	imagine	quit	risk
appreciate	deny	keep	recall	suggest
avoid	discuss	mention	recommend	tolerate
can't help	dislike	mind	regret	understand

Infinitives

Infinitives are always used after certain verbs.

*Jane hopes ~~spending~~ **to spend** her summer vacation in South America.*

The chart below provides a list of some common verbs that are always followed by infinitives:

COMMON VERBS FOLLOWED BY INFINITIVES				
agree	consent	happen	mean	promise
appear	decide	hesitate	need	refuse
arrange	demand	hope	offer	seem
ask	deserve	intend	plan	threaten
choose	expect	learn	prepare	wait
claim	fail	manage	pretend	want

Some verbs may be followed by either a gerund or an infinitive, often with little or no change in meaning.

*It **started to rain** at midnight.*
*It **started raining** at midnight.*

Additional examples of such verbs include *begin*, *like*, *love*, *prefer*, *can't stand*, *continue* and *hate*.

Some verbs may be followed by either a gerund or an infinitive, but the meaning changes.

*I **forgot to lock** the door. (I didn't lock the door.)*
*I **forgot locking** the door. (I locked the door, but I forgot that I had locked it.)*

Additional examples of such verbs include *remember*, *try* and *stop*.

A pronoun is a word that stands for or replaces a noun.
Sam filmed the recital. ➡ *He filmed the recital.*

Pronouns are important: without them, sentences would be repetitive and hard to understand. Compare the following:
Kevin gave Susan a letter Kevin had written, and Susan read the letter.
*Kevin gave Susan a letter **he** had written, and **she** read it.*

There are many different types of pronouns:

- Personal
  *He bought a new cellphone, but **he** does not know how to use **it**.*
- Reflexive
  *She made **herself** something to eat.*
- Indefinite
  ***Everybody** complained about the homework.*
- Demonstrative
  ***This** is my textbook.*
- Possessive
  *Whose car did you take? We took **theirs**.*
- Relative
  *That is the person **who** drove the car.*

Personal Pronouns

A personal pronoun may be singular or plural and act as a subject or object.

	PERSON	SUBJECT	OBJECT	EXAMPLE
Singular	**First**	I	me	*I told Todd to give me the keys.*
	Second	you	you	*You were late even though the teacher had asked you to be on time.*
	Third	he/she/it	him/her/it	*She gave him some money.*
Plural	**First**	we	us	*We insist that the money be given to us.*
	Second	you	you	*You failed the exam, but the teacher will give each of you a makeup exam.*
	Third	they	them	*They want the teacher to give them an extension.*

Note:
- *You* and *it* have the same subject and object forms.
- Use *it* to refer to a thing or an animal.
- Use *they* to refer to people, things or animals.

Reflexive Pronouns

A reflexive pronoun refers to the doer.

GRAMMAR TIP

Theirself, *theirselves* and *hisself* are not part of standard English.

	PERSON	SUBJECT	EXAMPLE
Singular	**First**	myself	I gave *myself* a treat.
	Second	yourself	You must behave *yourself*.
	Third	himself/herself/itself	He asked *himself* whether she loved him.
Plural	**First**	ourselves	We need to discipline *ourselves* to do our homework.
	Second	yourselves	You should discipline *yourselves* to work harder.
	Third	themselves	They invited *themselves* over for dinner.

Note:
- The subject and the object are the same person.
- The second-person singular is *yourself*, and the second-person plural is *yourselves*.
- A reflexive pronoun can be used to emphasize a noun or a pronoun: *Karen **herself** made the cake.*

Indefinite Pronouns

An indefinite pronoun does not refer to a specific person or thing. Some indefinite pronouns are singular, some are plural, and some are both.

INDEFINITE PRONOUN	SINGULAR	PLURAL	INDEFINITE PRONOUN	SINGULAR	PLURAL
anybody	X		somebody	X	
anyone	X		someone	X	
each	X		both		X
either	X		few		X
everybody	X		many		X
everyone	X		several		X
everything	X		all	X	X
neither	X		any	X	X
no one	X		most	X	X
nobody	X		none	X	X
one	X		some	X	X

Note:
- In formal English, make sure your pronouns agree in number: *Everybody should do ~~their~~ **his/her** homework.*
- For *all*, *any*, *most*, *none* and *some*, use a singular verb if you want the subject to answer the question "How much?" and use a plural verb if you want the subject to answer the question "How many?" ***How much** of the room **was** painted? **None was** painted.* ***How many** of the rooms **were** painted? **None were** painted.*

Demonstrative Pronouns

Demonstrative pronouns point to a person or a thing, and they may be singular or plural.

	NEAR	FAR	EXAMPLES
Singular	this	that	*This* is my shirt. *That* is yours.
Plural	these	those	*These* are my books. *Those* are yours.

Note:
- Typically, *this* and *these* refer to what is near and *that* and *those* to what is far.
- The pronouns *this*, *that*, *these* and *those* may also be used as adjectives: **This shirt** *is new.* **Those shirts** *are old.*

Possessive Pronouns

Possessive pronouns (and possessive adjectives) indicate ownership.

	PERSON	POSSESSIVE ADJECTIVE	POSSESSIVE PRONOUN	EXAMPLES
Singular	**First**	my	mine	Whose car is it? It's *my* car. It's *mine*.
	Second	your	yours	Whose shirts are they? They're *your* shirts. They're *yours*.
	Third	his/her/its	his/hers/its	Whose office is it? It's *her* office. It's *hers*.
Plural	**First**	our	ours	Whose books are they? They're *our* books. They're *ours*.
	Second	your	yours	Whose classroom is it? It's *your* classroom. It's *yours*.
	Third	their	theirs	Whose keys are they? They're *their* keys. They're *theirs*.

Note:
- Do not confuse the contraction of "it is" (*it's*) with the possessive pronoun *its*:
  It's time for *its* meal.
- Do not confuse the contraction of "they are" (*they're*) with the possessive adjective *their* or the adverb *there*:
  They're looking for *their* keys over *there*!
- For the third-person singular, the possessive adjective and the possessive pronoun are identical for *his* and *its*.

Relative Pronouns

Relative pronouns introduce relative clauses—dependent clauses that modify nouns and pronouns.

USE	RELATIVE PRONOUNS			EXAMPLES
	SUBJECTIVE	**OBJECTIVE**	**POSSESSIVE**	
People	who (that)	whom/ who (that)	whose	There is the man *who* (*that*) stole her purse. The man *whom* (*who, that*) I saw is over there. There is the woman *whose* purse was stolen. Anyone *who* says that is a liar!
Things	that	that	whose	That is the book *that* caused such uproar. Where is the book *that* I lent you? Here is the book *whose* cover is torn. Take anything *that* you want.

Note:
- In informal English, *that* is often used to refer to both people and things.
- *Which* is used instead of *that* when relating non-essential information about things:
  *The documentary, **which** lasted ninety minutes, won an award.*
- *Whom* is primarily used in formal English.
- The relative pronouns *whom*, *who* and *that* can be omitted when they are objects of verbs in relative clauses:
  *The teacher (**whom**/**who**/**that**) I wanted to meet was unavailable.*
- When *who* and *that* are used as subjects, make sure that the verb that follows agrees with the noun or pronoun being modified:
  *Look at the students who ~~is~~ **are** waiting in line.*
  *A book that ~~have~~ **has** a red sticker is on sale.*
- Do not confuse *whose* with *who's*, which is the contraction of "who is":
  *Where is the student ~~whose~~ **who's** supposed to do her presentation?*

Pinpoint

Part A

Write the correct form of each noun in parentheses.

1. We have three small sons. The (boys) _____ toys are all over the house.

2. Scientists have suggested several (hypothesis) _____ to explain why stars disappear.

3. We'll need more (raspberry) _____ for the pie.

4. Did you recall (feed) _____ the cat before you left this morning?

5. (Wolf) _____ can't help (chase) _____ (sheep) _____.

Part B

Complete each sentence by circling the correct word in parentheses.

1. I need (an / some) advice about purchasing a used car. Could you help me?

2. There (is / are) some food in the cupboard.

3. News about the accidents (is / are) incomplete at the moment.

4. The Beatles became famous in the (1960's / 1960s).

5. The police (is / are) investigating the robbery.

Part C

Circle the correct pronoun(s) for each sentence. Use formal English. In some cases, more than one answer is possible.

1. Would anyone who needs more time please raise (his / her / their) hand?

2. The teacher and the students all have dictionaries. (Her / Hers) is on her desk and (their / theirs) are in the cupboard.

3. You need to contact the supervisor (which / who) signed the evaluation.

4. We finally found (ourselves / ourself) a table in the busy restaurant.

5. Travellers (who's / whose) luggage is not identified must obtain a name tag from the guide.

7 Adjectives and Adverbs

Adjectives describe nouns or pronouns.
*Vicki has a **new** car; it is **blue**.*

Adverbs describe verbs, adjectives or other adverbs.
*Vicki drives her **brilliantly** blue car **fairly quickly**.*

There are many different types of adjectives and adverbs.

In this section, we will focus our attention on the following:

1. Adjectives of quality

2. Adverbs of manner

3. Verbs as adjectives and adverbs

Adjectives of Quality

Adjectives of quality indicate "which kind" of noun or pronoun and may be divided into two broad categories:

1. Opinion
   nice, intelligent, beautiful, horrible, delicious, …

2. Fact
   big, new, flat, orange, Canadian, …

A fact adjective precedes the noun it modifies.
*He bought a **new** car.*

Opinion adjectives precede fact adjectives.
*He married ~~a Canadian intelligent~~ an **intelligent Canadian** doctor.*

Simple, Comparative and Superlative Adjective Forms

Most adjectives of quality have three forms: simple, comparative and superlative.

The comparative form is used to compare two people or things.
*Joe is **shorter than** Jason.*

The superlative form is used to compare three or more people or things.
*Joe weighs 140 pounds, Jason weighs 150 pounds and Erick weighs 160 pounds. Of the three, Erick is **the heaviest**.*

Many comparatives and superlatives are formed by adding *er* and *est* endings to the adjective. Other adjectives do not take endings; instead, the words *more* or *most* are placed in front of them.

Refer to the chart below for the rules to apply when forming the comparative and superlative:

ADJECTIVES	SIMPLE	COMPARATIVE	SUPERLATIVE
One-syllable adjectives: Simply add *er* or *est*.	short	shorter (than)	(the) shortest
One-syllable adjectives ending with consonant-vowel-consonant: Double the last consonant before adding *er* or *est*.	hot	hotter (than)	(the) hottest
One-syllable adjectives ending in *e*: Simply add *r* or *st*.	blue	bluer (than)	(the) bluest
Two-syllable adjectives ending with consonant-*y*: Change the *y* to *i* before adding *er* or *est*.	heavy pretty	heavier (than) prettier (than)	(the) heaviest (the) prettiest
Other two-syllable adjectives: Place *more* or *most* before the adjective.	splendid	more splendid (than)	(the) most splendid
Three-or-more-syllable adjectives: Place *more* or *most* before the adjective.	elegant	more elegant (than)	(the) most elegant
Common irregular adjectives: Memorize forms.	good bad little a lot	better (than) worse (than) less (than) more (than)	(the) best (the) worst (the) least (the) most

Note:
- The following one-syllable adjectives use the *more* and *most* forms: *bored* and *tired*. For example: *more tired* and *most tired*.
- The following two-syllable adjectives use the *er* and *est* forms as well as the *more* and *most* forms: *simple, common, handsome, quiet, gentle, narrow, clever, friendly* and *angry*. For example: *handsomer* or *more handsome* and *handsomest* or *most handsome*.
- Only adjectives of quality that are **not absolute** can be used in the comparative or the superlative forms: *Mary's essay was* ~~more perfect~~ **better than** *Steve's.*

Adverbs of Manner

Adverbs of manner indicate how something happens.

SPELLING TIPS: FORMING ADVERBS

- Many adverbs of manner are formed by simply adding *ly* to the corresponding adjectives:
  nice ➡ *nicely*
  intelligent ➡ *intelligently*
  enormous ➡ *enormously*

- If the adjective ends with consonant-*y*, change the final *y* to an *i* before adding *ly*:
  merry ➡ *merrily*

- If the adjective ends with consonant-*le*, drop the *e* before adding *y*:
  *am**ple*** ➡ *am**ply***
- If the adjective ends in *ic*, add *ally*:
  *bas**ic*** ➡ *bas**ically***
- The adjectives *true*, *due* and *whole* drop the final *e* before adding *ly*:
  true ➡ *tru**ly***
  due ➡ *du**ly***
  whole ➡ *whol**ly***
- Some adjectives of quality and adverbs of manner have the same form:
  hard ➡ *hard*
  fast ➡ *fast*
  kindly ➡ *kindly*

Position of Adverbs of Manner

The chart below provides an overview of some basic rules:

CONTEXT	EXAMPLE
If there is no direct object, the adverb of manner usually goes **after** the verb.	He answered *carefully*.
If there is a direct object and it is long, the adverb of manner usually goes **after** the object.	He answered the questions *carefully*.
If there is a direct object and it is long, the adverb of manner usually goes **before** the verb.	He *carefully* answered the questions that the officers asked him.

Note: • To provide emphasis, adverbs of manner that usually go after the verb or direct object can be placed before the verb:
  He **carefully** answered.
  He **carefully** answered the questions.

GRAMMAR TIP

With the exception of the verb *be*, adverbs of frequency such as *never*, *rarely*, *sometimes*, *often*, *usually* and *always* are placed before the main verb in an affirmative sentence: *He **usually arrives** early. He **is usually** early.*

Simple, Comparative and Superlative Adverb Forms

Most adverbs of manner have three forms: simple, comparative and superlative.

ADVERBS	SIMPLE	COMPARATIVE	SUPERLATIVE
One-syllable adverbs	fast	faster (than)	(the) fastest
Adverbs ending in *ly*	bravely	more bravely (than)	(the) most bravely
Common irregular adverbs	well badly	better (than) worse (than)	(the) best (the) worst

Comparisons of Equality

Use the structure "as … as" with adjectives and adverbs to make comparisons of equality.

*His son is **as tall as** he is.*
*His mother drives **as quickly as** he does.*

Verbs as Adjectives and Adverbs

A *verbal* is a word—derived from a verb—that functions as a noun, an adjective or an adverb. When functioning as an adjective or adverb, there are two types of verbals: participles and infinitives. Examine the chart below:

TYPE	FUNCTION	EXAMPLES
Participle	Adjective	Present participle: *losing* team
		Present-participle phrase: The team *losing the game* is the home team.
		Past participle: *buried* treasure
		Past-participle phrase: The treasure *buried in the backyard* belongs to the previous owner.
Infinitive	Adjective	The list of food *to buy* for the party is on the kitchen counter.
	Adverb	They went *to buy* the food for the party.

Note: • The present participle ends in *ing*.
• For spelling tips on forming the present participle, see page 217.
• The past participle ends in *d*, *ed*, *t* or *en*.
• For spelling tips on forming the past participle of regular verbs, see page 219; for the past participles of common irregular verbs, see Chart B on pages 285–286.
• The infinitive is the base form of the verb, preceded by *to*.
• For information on verbs as nouns, see page 248.

GRAMMAR TIP

Do not confuse a present-participle phrase (which acts as an adjective) with a gerund phrase (which acts as a noun):

***Grinning from ear to ear**, the little boy ran into his mother's arms.* "Grinning from ear to ear" is a participle phrase that modifies the noun "boy."

***Laughing out loud** is good for the soul.* "Laughing out loud" is a gerund phrase that acts as the subject of the sentence.

When a participle phrase introduces a main clause, separate the phrase from the clause with a comma: *Wanting to share the good news, John called his parents.*

When a participle phrase concludes a main clause and describes the word that immediately precedes the phrase, do not separate the phrase from the clause with a comma: *Did you see the treasure buried in the backyard?*

When a participle phrase concludes a main clause and describes a word that does not immediately precede the phrase, separate the phrase from the clause with a comma: *Stephanie worked hard, taking only an occasional break.*

For information on misplaced or dangling modifiers, see page 269.

Pinpoint

Part A

The sentences below contain errors related to adjectives and adverbs. Underline these errors, and write the corrections in the space provided. In some cases, more than one answer is possible.

1. We enjoyed a Chinese delicious meal last night. _____

2. Let's leave. This is the worse movie I have ever seen. _____

3. Be careful! The security guard told us specificly not to open this door.

   _____

4. Jean's eyes are more green than her twin's. _____

5. Mona jogs more often than her brother, and she is fiter than he.

   _____

6. I was truely amazed by the findings presented in the report. _____

7. My step-brother drives fast his car. _____

8. I think Highway 33 was built more recent than Highway 35. _____

9. Of all the players, Oliver skates the better. _____

10. You'll have to work fastly to finish by 5:00 p.m. _____

Part B

Fill in each blank, using the present or past participle of the verb in parentheses. Watch your spelling!

1. Do you like (smoke) _____ salmon?

2. (Speed) _____ along a slippery road, Carla lost control of her car.

3. He is nothing but a (lie) _____ coward!

4. It is, as they say, a (do) _____ deal.

5. It's the fastest (race) _____ car on the circuit.

6. The china doll, (break) _____ during the fight, could not be repaired.

7. The little boy (sit) _____ on the sidelines is my son.

8. The money was safe, (hide) _____ beneath the floorboards.

9. The Titanic was a ship (build) _____ to amaze, and amaze it did.

10. What were his (die) _____ words?

8 Articles and Prepositions

The articles *a*, *an* and *the* are used with nouns, often to single out members (or instances) of the classes named by the nouns.

> *For lunch, he ate **a** banana and **an** orange.*
> *I want **the** blue book, not **the** red book.*

As you work through this section, you may need to refer to section six (page 246) and review singular and plural nouns and count and non-count nouns.

Articles

There are two kinds of articles: indefinite (*a* and *an*) and definite (*the*). In general, indefinite articles are used with generic singular count nouns while definite articles are used with specific singular and plural nouns and specific count and non-count nouns.

> *Has anyone seen **a** robin this spring?* (generic)
> *Has anyone seen **the** robin with **the** broken wing?* (specific)

Examine the chart below:

INDEFINITE	DEFINITE
1. I want to take *a* course next term.	3. *The* book we are reading in our philosophy class is boring.
2. I'm looking for *an* apartment near the college.	4. Where did you put *the* newspapers that were on the table?
	5. Please pass me *the* meat.
	6. She lives in *the* United States, close to *the* Pacific Ocean.

Note:
- When deciding whether to use *a* or *an*, pronounce the word first. If the word begins with a vowel sound (and not simply the vowel *a*, *e*, *i*, *o* or *u*), use *an*; if the word begins with a consonant sound (and not simply a consonant such as *b*, *c*, *d*, ...), use *a*. Be careful with words starting with *e*, *h* or *u* as well as abbreviations such as RCMP (Royal Canadian Mounted Police)—for example, *an escape* **but** *a European vacation; a hotel* **but** *an honour; an umbrella* **but** *a university; a recreational vehicle* **but** *an RV* (1 and 2).
- Use *the* with specific singular count nouns (3).
- Use *the* with specific plural count nouns (4).
- Use *the* with specific non-count nouns (5).
- Use *the* with oceans, seas and rivers, as well as with countries in the plural (6).

Do not use indefinite articles before

- plural count nouns;
  I sometimes eat ~~a~~ oranges for breakfast.
- non-count nouns.
  I always eat ~~a~~ cereal for breakfast.

Do not use definite articles before

- generic singular count nouns;
  *In general, I prefer reading ~~the~~ **a** book to watching ~~the~~ **a** movie.*
- generic plural count nouns;
  Everyone knows that ~~the~~ teenagers under sixteen are not allowed to drive cars.
- generic non-count nouns;
  Some believe that ~~the~~ meat is a necessary part of a healthy diet.
- names of cities, provinces, states or singular countries;
  ~~The~~ Ontario is the most populated province in ~~the~~ Canada.
- meals.
  I'm going grocery shopping; what do you want for ~~the~~ breakfast, ~~the~~ lunch and ~~the~~ supper?

Prepositions

Prepositions are used to show a relationship between a noun and other words.
  *The swim team is practising **in** the pool **after** school.* (The preposition "in" shows a relationship of place, and the preposition "after" shows a relationship of time.)

Prepositions can show a relationship by answering the following questions:

1. Where? (static)
   *The dishes **on** the counter are clean; those **in** the sink are dirty.*

2. Where? (movement)
   *He jumped **off** the dock and **into** the water.*

3. When?
   *I wake up **at** noon **on** weekends.*

4. How?
   *We went **by** car and they went **on** foot.*

Here are some common single- and multi-word prepositions:

QUESTION	PREPOSITIONS
Where? (static)	above, against, along, among, around, at, behind, below, beneath, beside, between, by, in, in front of, inside, near, next to, on, on top of, outside, over, to the left of, to the right of, under, underneath, within
Where? (movement)	across, along, around, away from, down, from, into, off, onto, out of, over, past, through, toward, under, up
When?	after, at, before, by, in, on
How?	by, in, like, on, with

Prepositional Phrases

When used in a sentence, prepositions are found only as part of a prepositional phrase, consisting of a preposition, its object and any modifiers. The object of a preposition must always be a noun or a pronoun. Consider the following examples (taken from the example sentences on the previous page); the prepositions are single-underlined and the objects, double-underlined.

GRAMMAR TIP

Prepositional phrases that indicate "where" precede those that indicate "when":
*The newspaper will be left **at** your front door **before** dawn.*

1. on the counter
2. into the water
3. at noon
4. by car

Prepositional phrases act as modifiers, modifying either nouns or verbs. When prepositional phrases modify nouns, they are called *adjectival* prepositional phrases; when they modify verbs, they are called *adverbial* prepositional phrases. Prepositional phrases between the subject and the verb do not normally affect agreement.

> *The students (in the back row) ~~has~~ **have** not been paying attention.*

See the last note at the bottom of the chart on page 271 for the exception to this rule.

Pinpoint

Part A

Circle the correct article in parentheses. A *0* indicates no article is required.

1. My daughter is looking for (a / an) used motorcycle. (A / The) motorcycle has to be in (a / 0) good condition and economical on (the / 0) gas.

2. I have been waiting here for (a / an) hour! I wonder if (a / the) bus route has been changed.

3. Alex is studying wildlife in (the / 0) Falkland Islands. The islands are in (the / 0) South Atlantic Ocean. In (a / an) attempt to reclaim this territory, (the / 0) Argentina invaded (the / 0) Falklands in 1982. This attempt was unsuccessful.

4. Investing in (a / an) RRSP is (a / 0) good idea for workers who do not have (a / an) employee pension plan.

5. Do you have (a / an) BA or (a / an) MA? We need someone with (a / an) university degree. For this job, you must have (a / the) degree in (the / 0) psychology.

Part B

Fill in the blanks with the correct prepositions. In some cases, more than one answer is possible. Refer to the chart at the bottom of page 261 for examples of common prepositions.

1. As I was walking _____ a path through the park, I heard a noise _____ me. I turned _____ and came face to face with a bear.

2. We were sailing _____ the St. Lawrence River _____ October. We were heading _____ the marina when we saw an animal swimming _____ the boat. When we looked closely, we saw it was a seal.

3. You can see the doctor this morning, any time _____ noon. When you come _____ the office, go _____ the side door and wait in the hall.

4. My twin brother swims _____ a fish, but I swim _____ a rock. He actually swam _____ the English Channel last year. He went _____ England _____ France.

5. You need to arrive for your job interview _____ 10:45. _____ the interview, you have a questionnaire to answer. Then, the interview starts _____ 11:00 sharp. If you pass the first interview, there will be a second one _____ the afternoon, _____ lunch.

Part C

Circle the prepositional phrases in each of the sentences below. Then, underline the preposition and double underline the object of the preposition. Copy out the subject and the verb. The first one has been done for you as an example.

1. You are the nicest person (in the <u>world</u>)!

   Subject: ____you____   Verb: ____are____

2. I left my keys beside the coffee maker.

   Subject: _____   Verb: _____

3. Each of the students is late.

   Subject: _____   Verb: _____

4. The twenty-dollar bill between the pages of that book is mine.

   Subject: _____   Verb: _____

5. Calvin went by car to the hockey game.

   Subject: _____   Verb: _____

6. People from her generation don't discuss things like that.

   Subject: _____   Verb: _____

COMPANION
web+

Now that you have pin-pointed your current level of understanding of articles and prepositions, complete related exercises on the Companion Website for practice and instant feedback.

⑨ Capitalization and Punctuation

Capital letters and punctuation marks make words, groups of words (phrases) and sentences (clauses) easier to understand. Capital letters distinguish the meaning of words such as *AIDS* from *aids*, and they signal the start of new sentences. Punctuation marks separate words into groups, clarifying sentence meaning; for example:

Woman, without her man, is nothing.
Woman: without her, man is nothing.

In this section, you will examine when and how to capitalize words and punctuate sentences.

Capitalization

The following chart indicates when to use capital letters and provides examples of correct usage:

USE	EXAMPLES
The first word of a sentence	*Interest* rates have declined over the past year.
The first-person singular	Mark asked if *I* could help him, and *I* said *I* could.
Direct quotations of complete sentences	Her lawyer said, "*You* will win your case." "*Please* give John my message," said Evelyn.
The first word of each item in a numbered or bulleted list	You will need these items for your art project: • *Coloured* pencils • *Graph* paper • *Scissors*
Job and courtesy titles, first and last names	Have you met *Dr.* and *Mrs. Abernathy*? Our next contestant is *Ms. Michelle Potter*. *Captain Edward John Smith* was the captain of a famous ship.
All important words in a title	Sky Wilson wrote the trilogy composed of *The Dome*, *Under the Dome* and *When the Dome Breaks*. Have you read *To Live or to Die*?
Holidays, weekdays, months	*Labour Day* falls on the first *Monday* in *September*.
Countries, languages, nationalities, races and religions	In three days, I am leaving for *Cuba*, where the people speak *Spanish*. Many *Cubans* are *Christians* or *Santerians*. The *Santeria* religion was introduced to *Cuba* by *African* slaves.
Specific place names and vehicles	According to people living in *Toronto*, *Yonge Street* is the longest street in the world. Who was the captain of the *Titanic*? I believe it was Edward John Smith.
Acronyms and abbreviations	*AIDS* is caused by *HIV*, a virus that attacks the human immune system. *UNESCO* is a *UN* organization that deals with education, social and natural science, culture and communication.

> **Note:**
> - Always capitalize the first and last words of titles; do not capitalize articles, prepositions or the conjunctions *and*, *as*, *but*, *if*, *nor* or *or* unless they appear as the first or last word of a title.
> - Some acronyms that have entered the language as words are not written in capital letters:
>   *You can rent **scuba** (**s**elf-**c**ontained **u**nderwater **b**reathing **a**pparatus) diving equipment at the beach.*
>   *You can have **laser** (**l**ight **a**mplification by **s**timulated **e**mission of **r**adiation) treatments to remove unwanted tattoos.*

Punctuation

The following chart indicates when to use various punctuation marks and provides examples of correct usage:

PUNCTUATION	USE	EXAMPLES
Period	After a sentence	Don't speak on your cellphone while driving.
	With an abbreviation	The meeting will finish at 4:30 p.m. You must declare cats, dogs, birds, etc., when you cross the border.
Question mark	After a direct question	Would you like to go to a movie this evening?
	After a question tag	You have seen *Avatar*, haven't you?
Exclamation mark	To express strong emotion	Look out for that falling rock!
Comma	Between independent clauses joined by a coordinate conjunction	Jorge speaks Spanish, but he can't write it very well. I was having money problems, so I sold my car.
	After a dependent clause	If you need assistance, go to the Customer Service Department. Whenever it rains, our roof leaks.
	In a series	I put mushrooms, onion and red pepper in my omelette.
	Between coordinate adjectives	We can expect hot, humid, sticky weather at the end of July.
	After introductory words	Initially, Cindy wanted a big dog, but she changed her mind and bought a miniature poodle.
	After an introductory phrase	First of all, we need to organize our work. Every once in a while, you need to "defrag" your computer.
	Before a direct quotation	She asked, "Where do our fears come from?" As the saying goes, "All is fair in love and war."
	Between two consecutive numbers	In 2008, 162 heart transplants were performed in Canada.
Semicolon	Between independent clauses	Jane found a summer job; her friend Kelly didn't find one.

PUNCTUATION	USE	EXAMPLES
Colon	Before a list	Bring the following for the camping trip: a tent, a sleeping bag and warm clothes.
	After "note"	Note: Applications must be received before March 15. Note: Postdated cheques will not be accepted.
	Between hours and minutes	The flight leaves at 8:23 p.m. The 11:30 train is late.
Quotation marks (double)	For a direct quotation shorter than four lines	"Up with your hands," he shouted. The sign reads, "Do not touch. Wet paint."
	For the title of a work contained in another work (article, book chapter, TV episode, etc.)	Did you read the article "Life after Death" in *Newsmonth*? Do you watch *The Mentalist*? Did you see "Red Hair and Silver Tape"?
Quotation marks (single)	For a quote within a quote	The husband said, "My wife said, 'I did it.'"
Apostrophe	With a contraction	He doesn't know if he'll return or not. Jason can't swim.
	With a possessive noun	The Wilsons' house is up for sale. Have you seen Sheila's new car and her husband's new motorcycle?
Parentheses	With a reference to a page, unit, appendix, etc., or to add a clarification or personal thought	You should review the BNA Act (Chapter 5) before the exam. A good red wine (my personal favourite) is Norman Hardie's Pinot Noir.
Hyphen	To join a prefix to some words	Self-esteem is important for happiness and success. My math teacher is my sister's ex-boyfriend.
	To join two or more words to create a compound word	Use an up-to-date dictionary to check spelling. My neighbour has an eight-foot fence around his property.
	When writing numbers as words	Cheques will be deposited on the twenty-fifth of the month. Seventy-six poems were submitted for the poetry prize.

Note:
- In a website address, the period is called a "dot."
- In decimal numbers, the period is called a "point": *thirty-three **point** five* (33.5).
- Adjectives are coordinate when they modify the same noun equally, can be used in any order and can be written with *and* between them:
  *We are having a **warm**, **dry** spring.*
- For comma usage with participle phrases, see page 258.
- For a quotation longer than three lines, do not use quotation marks; rather, single space and indent the quoted material, leaving a line space above and below the quotation.
- For more information on possessive nouns, see page 248.

Pinpoint

Rewrite each sentence, adding capital letters and punctuation marks as required.

1. the witness said the taxi driver asked where to

_____

_____

2. our son in law speaks portuguese and a little english

_____

_____

3. the shining is such a scary book

_____

_____

4. costumes inc hasnt changed its address on its website

_____

_____

5. which organization has its headquarters in geneva

_____

_____

6. you can contact mr lombardi if you want an italian translation of the contract

_____

_____

7. steve didnt remember his wifes birthday but he did buy her chocolates for valentines day

_____

_____

8. the secretaries offices are being renovated next week new furniture has been ordered it will arrive tomorrow

_____

_____

_____

9. mr and mrs smiths cottage was destroyed by fire on may 15 2010 arson is suspected the police have no leads

_____

_____

_____

_____

COMPANION
web+

Now that you have pin-pointed your current level of understanding of capitalization and punctuation, complete related exercises on the Companion Website for practice and instant feedback.

⑩ Common Sentence Errors

Before submitting a writing assignment for evaluation, you should revise your work. An important part of revising is proofreading, a process in which you isolate and correct any errors you might have made. In this section, you will examine some of the more common types of sentence errors in order to assist you in the proofreading process. (For more information on proofreading, see Appendix C, page 203.)

Run-On Sentences

If you have two (or more) independent clauses, they must be joined by a comma followed by a coordinate conjunction, a semicolon followed by an adverbial conjunction or a semicolon (see page 207).

A run-on sentence error is committed when you omit the required punctuation or conjunction between two independent clauses.

There are two basic types of run-on sentences.

TYPE OF ERROR	EXAMPLE
Fused sentence	Ken wanted an SUV his wife wanted a convertible.
Comma splice	Ken wanted an SUV, his wife wanted a convertible.

Note: • Fused sentences and comma splices can be corrected by creating two simple sentences, one compound sentence or one complex sentence:
Ken wanted an SUV. His wife wanted a convertible.
(two simple sentences)
Ken wanted an SUV, but his wife wanted a convertible.
(compound sentence)
Ken wanted an SUV; however, his wife wanted a convertible.
(compound sentence)
Ken wanted an SUV; his wife wanted a convertible.
(compound sentence)
Although Ken wanted an SUV, his wife wanted a convertible.
(complex sentence)

Sentence Fragments

A sentence must have a subject and a verb and must express a complete thought (see page 207). A sentence fragment error occurs when you omit a subject, a verb and/or a complete thought.
In the garage. There is a racoon.

"In the garage" has neither a subject nor a verb but is followed by a period; as such, it constitutes a sentence fragment.

One possible correction would be:
There is a racoon in the garage.

The following is an example of a sentence fragment resulting from the expression of an incomplete thought.

Because she tripped a player. She was given a two-minute penalty.

"Because she tripped a player" is a dependent clause and as such, the thought expressed is incomplete (see page 209).

One possible correction would be:

Because she tripped a player, she was given a two-minute penalty.

(For more information on sentence structure, see section one, page 207.)

Misplaced or Dangling Modifiers

A modifier is a word or group of words that describes, explains or limits another word or group of words. Errors occur when the modifier is misplaced (not close enough to the word or group of words it describes, explains or limits) or dangling (does not describe, explain or limit any word or group of words in the sentence).

Examine the chart below:

TYPE OF ERROR	EXAMPLES AND CORRECTIONS
Misplaced modifier (word)	We can't complete the homework assigned by our math teacher *quickly*. (The modifier "quickly" modifies the verb "complete," not the verb "assigned.") • Correct by moving the modifier closer to the word it modifies: We can't *quickly* complete the homework assigned by our math teacher.

Misplaced modifier (phrase or clause)	*Being completely blind*, Aunt Mary read the newspaper to Uncle Fred. (The phrase "being completely blind" wrongly modifies the subject of the sentence, "Aunt Mary," since an adjective phrase placed at the beginning of a sentence modifies the subject of the sentence.)
	• Correct by changing the subject of the sentence:
	  Being completely blind, *Uncle Fred* had Aunt Mary read him the newspaper.
	• Correct by changing the modifier into a dependent clause:
	  Because he was blind, Aunt Mary read the newspaper to Uncle Fred.
	
	They wrote graffiti on the wall *that was offensive*. (The relative clause "that was offensive" wrongly modifies the noun "wall.")
	• Correct by moving the modifier closer to the word it modifies:
	  They wrote graffiti *that was offensive* on the wall.

Dangling modifier	*Having studied hard*, the test was easy. (The adjective phrase "having studied hard" should modify a person or a group of people, but neither is mentioned.) • Correct by changing the modifier into a dependent clause: *Because I had studied hard*, the test was easy.

Note: • Place limiting modifiers such as *almost, barely, hardly, just, merely, nearly, only, quickly, rarely, scarcely* and *slowly* right before the words they modify:
I ~~barely~~ *had enough time to finish.* ➡ *I had **barely** enough time to finish.*
("Barely" modifies the adjective "enough.")
  • For more information on the position of adverbs of manner, see page 257.

Faulty Parallelism

Items in a series should be written in the same grammatical form: they should respect parallelism. Faulty parallelism occurs when the items are of different forms.

*Campers like swimming, canoeing and **to hike**.*

"Swimming" and "canoeing" are both gerunds while "to hike" is an infinitive. (For more information on gerunds and infinitives, see page 248.) To correct errors in parallelism, give each of the items the same form.

*Campers like swimming, canoeing and **hiking**.*

(For more examples of non-parallel construction, see page 281.)

Subject-Verb Agreement Errors

Subjects and verbs need to agree; in other words, a singular subject takes a singular verb, and a plural subject takes a plural verb. When a subject and a verb don't agree, an error occurs.

*Each of the employees ~~have~~ **has** a private office.*

In the following chart, you will find ten basic rules of subject-verb agreement:

RULE	EXAMPLES
1. When two subjects are connected by *and*, use a plural verb.	His mother *and* her mother *are* here.
2. When two subjects separated by *and* refer to the same person or thing, use a singular verb.	Bacon *and* eggs *is* my favourite meal.
3. When the subject is *neither* or *either*, use a singular verb.	*Either is* right. *Neither is* right.
4. When two singular subjects are connected by *or, nor, either … or,* or *neither … nor*, use a singular verb.	His mother *or* her mother *is* invited. His mother is not invited, *nor is* her mother invited. *Either* his mother *or* her mother *is* invited. *Neither* his mother *nor* her mother *is* invited.
5. When a singular subject is connected to a plural subject by *or, nor, either … or,* or *neither … nor*, use the verb form for the subject that is nearer the verb.	His mother *or her parents are* invited. (Her parents *or his mother is* invited.) His mother is not invited, *nor are her parents* invited. (Her parents are not invited, *nor is his mother*.) *Either* his mother *or her parents are* invited. (*Either* her parents *or his mother is* invited.) *Neither* his mother *nor her parents are* invited. (*Neither* her parents *nor his mother is* invited.)
6. When a singular subject is separated from the verb by an expression such as *along with, as well as* or *together with*, use a singular verb.	Your curriculum vitae, *along with* a letter of introduction, *is* required. Good medical care, *as well as* a positive attitude, *is* the key. The driver, *together with* the passenger, *was* injured in the accident.

7. When sentences start with *there* or *here*, the subject follows the verb.	*There are* the *receipts*! *Here is* the *calculator*.
8. When the subject is an amount of money or a period of time, use a singular verb.	*Twenty dollars is* not too much to ask. *The 1960s is* an interesting decade to study.
9. When using a collective or group noun (see page 246), use a singular verb when the members are acting as a unit and a plural verb when the members are acting as individuals.	The *team is* great! The *team* (members) *need* to work together better.
10. When *the number* is the subject, use a singular verb; when *a number* is the subject, use a plural verb.	*The number* of people waiting in line *is* incredible! *A number* of people *are* waiting in line.

Note:
- Some nouns are always singular, some are always plural, and some have identical singular and plural forms: the noun *news* is singular; the noun *scissors* is plural; and the noun *fish* is the same in the singular and in the plural. (For more examples, see page 247.)
- Non-count nouns are always singular: *coffee, grass, clothing, advice, chemistry*, etc. (For more examples, see page 247.)
- Some indefinite pronouns are always singular, some are always plural, and some can be either singular or plural depending on their context: the pronoun *each* is singular, the pronoun *both* is plural, and the pronoun *all* can be either singular or plural. (For more examples and a detailed explanation, see page 251.)
- Prepositional phrases between the subject and the verb do not affect agreement unless the subject is a word that indicates portions, such as percentages or fractions:
  The dishes on the counter ~~is~~ are clean.
  Fifty percent of the floor is washed.
  Fifty percent of the floors are washed.

Pronoun-Antecedent Agreement Errors

A pronoun must agree in number with the noun it replaces and refer directly and correctly back to one noun.

There are three basic types of pronoun-antecedent agreement errors.

TYPE OF ERROR	EXAMPLES AND CORRECTIONS
Agreement (number, gender, person)	Where was the 2007 World Series? *They* were in Boston. (The noun "series" is singular.) • Correction: Where was the 2007 World Series? *It* was in Boston.
	A student should complete *his* homework. (Not all students are male.) • Correction: A student should complete *his or her* homework.
	Some readers enjoy adventure stories such as "Roger Woodward and Niagara Falls." *You* like being on the edge of *your* seat! (Do not shift from the first or the third person to the second person.) • Correction: Some readers enjoy adventure stories such as "Roger Woodward and Niagara Falls." *They* like being on the edge of *their* seats!

TYPE OF ERROR	EXAMPLES AND CORRECTIONS
Indefinite reference	Susan does not like to study with Carol because *she* is always tired. (The pronoun "she" could refer to Carol or Susan.) • Correction: Susan does not like to study with Carol because *Carol* is always tired. The teacher gave the wrong answer. *This* confused the students. (The pronoun "this" does not refer to anything definite.) • Correction: The teacher gave the wrong answer. *His error* confused the students.
Wrong reference	The teacher took out the plagiarized assignments, showed them to the two students and put them in an envelope. (The second pronoun "them" wrongly refers to the plural noun "students," with somewhat bizarre implications.) • Correction: The teacher took out the plagiarized assignments, showed them to the students and put *the assignments* in an envelope.

Note: • To avoid awkward structures, such as "his or her" in the second example of agreement errors, use the plural: **Students** *should complete* **their** *homework* **assignments**.

Verb-Tense and Voice Shifts

Be consistent in your writing, avoiding unnecessary shifts in tense and voice.

> *In winter, birds **eat** the seeds that I **bought**.* (verb-tense shift)
> *The lights **were turned off**, and he **locked** the door.* (voice shift)

In the first example, "eat" is in the simple present tense and "bought" is in the simple past tense. In the second example, "were turned off" is in the passive voice and "locked" is in the active voice. To correct these errors, make sure the tenses and the voices are the same.

> *In winter, birds **eat** the seeds that I **buy**.*
> *He **turned off** the lights, and he **locked** the door.*

(For more information on the active and the passive voice, see section five, page 241.)

Pinpoint

Part A

Rewrite each of the following sentences, correcting run-on sentences, sentence fragments, misplaced or dangling modifiers, faulty parallelism, and verb-tense and voice shifts. In some cases, more than one answer is possible.

1. Having trained every day, the marathon went well.

   _____

2. I was tired out it was difficult for me to finish the race.

   _____

3. On weekends, we order food, open a bottle of wine and watched old movies.

   _____

4. Please wash the dishes. As soon as you clear the table.

_____

5. She asked the teenager to babysit her newborn who lives next door.

_____

6. The organizing committee decorated the cafeteria and a band was hired.

_____

7. They realized the danger of neglecting car maintenance quickly.

_____

Part B

Underline the correct form of the verb in parentheses.

1. Each of the children (was having / were having) fun.

2. His positive attitude, along with his volunteer work, (was / were) appreciated by all.

3. Neither his father nor his friends (know / knows).

4. A number of students (is / are) working full-time jobs while going to college.

5. The number of students who work full-time jobs while going to college (is / are) astounding.

Part C

Rewrite each of the following sentences, correcting pronoun-antecedent errors. In some cases, more than one answer is possible.

1. Angelo enjoys working with Carla and Sandra even though she has a reputation for being difficult.

_____

_____

2. I completed exercises A and B. It was hard.

_____

3. Laura is a good writer, which she does often.

_____

4. Have you heard the news? Yes, they're awful!

_____

5. The teacher corrected tests, dined with colleagues and put them in her briefcase.

_____

_____

Now that you have pin-pointed your current level of understanding of common sentence errors, complete related exercises on the Companion Website for practice and instant feedback.

⑪ Commonly Misspelled and Misused Words

Commonly misspelled and misused words are often referred to as "sentence spoilers." Being aware of the words most likely to spoil sentences will keep you from spoiling your own!

Fifty Commonly Misspelled Words

CORRECT SPELLING	COMMON MISSPELLING	CORRECT SPELLING	COMMON MISSPELLING
acceptable	*acceptible*	immediately	*immediatly*
achieve	*acheive*	independent	*independant*
acknowledge	*acknowlege*	knowledge	*knowlege*
acquire	*aquire*	leisure	*liesure*
argument	*arguement*	licence/license	*lisence*
awful	*awfull*	marriage	*marrige*
basically	*basicly*	mischievous	*mischievious*
beautiful	*beautifull*	misspell	*mispell*
beginning	*begining*	necessary	*neccessary*
believe	*beleive*	occasionally	*occasionaly*
calendar	*calender*	occurred	*occured*
careful	*carefull*	personally	*personaly*
coming	*comming*	practical	*practicle*
committed	*comitted*	precede	*preceed*
completely	*completly*	preferred	*prefered*
definitely	*definately*	privilege	*privelege*
disappear	*disapear*	proceed	*procede*
embarrass	*embarass*	really	*realy*
exaggerate	*exagerate*	referred	*refered*
existence	*existance*	separate	*seperate*
familiar	*familier*	successful	*successfull*
forty	*fourty*	truly	*truely*
friend	*freind*	until	*untill*
grateful	*gratefull*	usually	*usualy*
hypocrisy	*hypocricy*	which	*wich*

❯ ❯ ❯

> Note:
> - Some words end in *ible*, and others in *able*: admiss**ible**, depend**able**. If you remove *able* from a word, you are left with a complete word; however, if you remove *ible* from a word, you are not left with a complete word. Exceptions to this rule include *accessible*, *contemptible*, *digestible*, *flexible* and *suggestible*.
> - When unsure whether to write *ie* or *ei*, remember the following rhyme: *i* before *e* except after *c*, or when sounding like /ay/, as in *neighbour* or *weigh*—for example: ach**ie**ve, c**ei**ling, b**ei**ge. Exceptions to this rule include *either*, *neither*, *foreign*, *height*, *leisure*, *protein*, *their*, *weird* and *seize*.

For more information on spelling exceptions, see the tips and charts on page 215 (third-person singular forms of the simple present), page 217 (present participles), page 219 (simple-past forms of regular verbs), pages 246–247 (plural nouns), page 256 (comparative and superlative forms of adjectives) and pages 256–257 (adverbs).

GRAMMAR TIP

Some American and Canadian spellings differ: compare *neighbor, traveled, center, theater* and *color* (American) to *neighbour, travelled, centre, theatre* and *colour* (Canadian—or British). When writing a text, use one system or the other—not both! When in doubt, use a dictionary!

Fifty Commonly Misused Words

MISUSED WORDS	EXPLANATION AND EXAMPLE
accept/except	*Accept* is a verb meaning "take or receive." *Except* is a preposition meaning "excluding": He could *accept* anything—*except* that!
advise/advice	*Advise* is a verb meaning "give an opinion." *Advice* is a noun meaning "an opinion": I *advise* you to ask someone else for *advice*.
affect/effect	*Affect* is a verb meaning "act on or produce a change in." *Effect* is a noun meaning "an outcome, a consequence or a result": The hurricane *affected* many people; the worst *effects* were felt by those living on the coast.
allot / a lot	*Allot* is a verb meaning "distribute." The noun *lot*, when preceded by *a*, means "a large number": After the disaster, the government *allotted* money to *a lot* of people. (*A lot* is never written as one word: ~~alot~~.)
choose/chose	*Choose* is a verb meaning "select." *Choose* is the base form of the verb, and *chose* is the simple-past form and the past participle: Which shirt did you *choose*? I *chose* the blue one.
coarse/course	*Coarse* is an adjective meaning "rough or unrefined." *Course* is a noun meaning "a series of lessons": My manners were *coarse*, so I took a *course* in etiquette.
compliment/ complement	*Compliment* is a noun meaning "a polite expression of admiration." *Complement* is a verb meaning "make perfect or complete": May I give you a *compliment*? Your blouse *complements* your skirt beautifully.

MISUSED WORDS	EXPLANATION AND EXAMPLE
conscious/conscience	*Conscious* is an adjective meaning "aware." *Conscience* is a noun meaning "the part of your mind that tells you whether your actions are right or wrong": Are you *conscious* that you have no *conscience*?
elicit/illicit	*Elicit* is a verb meaning "draw out." *Illicit* is an adjective meaning "unlawful" or "morally unacceptable": Were the police investigators able to *elicit* a confession from the suspect about his *illicit* behaviour?
further/farther	*Further* is an adjective meaning "additional." *Farther* is an adverb meaning "at or to a greater distance": The police made no *further* comments after informing the public that the victim's body was found *farther* from the murder site than had been anticipated.
its/it's	*Its* is a possessive adjective, and *it's* is the contracted form of "it is": *Its* location has been withheld because *it's* too dangerous to give out such information at this time.
lead/led	*Lead*, which rhymes with *heed*, is a verb meaning "guide." *Lead* is the base form of the verb, and *led*, which rhymes with *head*, is the simple-past form and the past participle: Did he *lead* the expedition? No, she *led* the expedition. (*Lead* rhyming with *head* is a noun meaning "a bluish-grey metal.")
lose/loose	*Lose* is a verb meaning "be deprived of." *Loose* is an adjective meaning "not tight": Did you *lose* the wheel because it was *loose*?
past/passed	*Past* is an adjective meaning "finished," an adverb meaning "by" and a noun meaning "at a time before the present." *Passed* is the simple-past form and the past participle of the verb *pass*, meaning "go by" or "successfully complete": As we walked *past* the school, we *passed* a teacher. (*Past* is not a verb.)
peace/piece	*Peace* is a noun meaning "harmony." *Piece* is a noun meaning "a part or an amount of something" or "a single item," or a verb meaning "assemble": They sat in *peace*, sharing a *piece* of bread, some cheese and a bottle of wine.
principal/principle	*Principal* is an adjective meaning "most important" or a noun meaning "person in charge of a school." *Principle* is a noun meaning "belief," "moral rules" or "basic idea": The *principal* reason she was hired was because she has remained true to her *principles*.
quite/quiet	*Quite* is an adverb meaning "relatively" or "really." *Quiet* is an adjective meaning "with little sound" or a noun meaning "the absence of sound": He can be *quite quiet* when necessary.
right/write	*Right* is an adjective meaning "in accordance with what is good" or "correct." *Write* is a verb meaning "form letters or numbers with a pen or pencil": You were *right* to *write* that letter.
their/there (also *they're*)	*Their* is a possessive adjective. *There* is an adverb meaning "at that place." (*They're* is the contracted form of "they are."): *Their* car is over *there*!
then/than	*Then* is an adverb meaning "at that time." *Than* is a conjunction used after a comparative: What happened *then*? He said he was better *than* she!

through/threw	*Through* is a preposition or an adverb meaning "in at one end and out the other" or an adjective meaning "finished." *Threw* is the simple-past form and the past participle of *throw*, meaning "propel something through the air": He was *through* after he *threw* the book *through* the window.
to/too (also *two*)	*To* is a preposition. *Too* is an adverb meaning "also": I can walk *to* school, *too*. (*Two* is a number.)
whether/weather	*Whether* is a conjunction used to discuss choice or uncertainty. *Weather* is a noun meaning "the temperature and other climatic conditions": They're not sure *whether* they like the *weather*.
who's/whose	*Who's* is the contracted form of "who is." *Whose* is a pronoun: *Who's* the person *whose* house burned down?
you're/your	*You're* is the contracted form of "you are." *Your* is a possessive adjective: *You're* lying about *your* whereabouts, aren't you?

Note: • Other common errors include the following:
   She could ~~of~~ **have** written.
   They were ~~suppose~~ **supposed** to leave.
   We ~~use~~ **used** to study.
   I didn't want to go, ~~anyways~~ **anyway**!
   I need to ~~lay~~ **lie** down for ten minutes.

Pinpoint

Each of the following sentences contains at least one misspelled or misused word. Underline the word(s) and write the correction(s) in the space provided.

1. Accept for Ronda, everyone was their on time.

   _____

2. Did you see that? She past right by without saying "hello."

   _____

3. He could of told her that he use to date her best friend!

   _____

4. I choose to take a grammar coarse last session because I want to improve my writting.

   _____

5. I truely beleive that reading literature can change a person's life for the better.

   _____

6. Its time to leave; are you comming?

   _____

7. Their going to be late if they don't check there watches.

_____

8. Wich author has effected you the most?

_____

9. Would you please stop talking? I need some piece and quite.

_____

10. Wow! And than what did he say?

_____

web+

Now that you have pin-pointed your current level of understanding of commonly misspelled and misused words, complete related exercises on the Companion Website for practice and instant feedback.

12 Writing Style

Good writing style is never out of fashion!

The Elements of Style by William Strunk, Jr., was first published in 1920, and since its publication, it has been a much-appreciated reference book for writers wanting to improve *how* they express *what* they express.

In this section, we will focus on seven tenets adapted from *The Elements of Style*:[6]

1. Use the active voice.
2. Be positive.
3. Be specific, definite and concrete.
4. Be concise.
5. Vary sentence type.
6. Respect parallel construction.
7. Keep related words together.

Use the Active Voice

Compare the following two sentences:
*I will always **love** you.* (active)
*You will always **be loved** by me.* (passive)

The active sentence is bolder and more direct. And if you remove "by me" from the passive sentence, it becomes indefinite.

Nonetheless, the passive voice has its place and should be used when the performer of the action is unimportant or unknown.
The dishes were done. (performer unimportant)
The child was kidnapped. (performer unknown)

(For more information on using the passive voice and on making an active sentence passive, see page 241.)

---

6. Strunk, William Jr. *The Elements of Style*. New York: Dover Publications, 2006. 19–29. Print.

Be Positive

In your writing, "use the word *not* as a means of denial or an antithesis, never as a means of evasion" (Strunk 21).

*The world is **not** flat.* (denial)
*I will marry him; I will **not** marry you.* (antithesis)
*They did **not** think you were very nice.* (evasion)
- Correction: *They thought you were mean.*

Readers prefer being told "what is" as opposed to "what isn't." As a result, it is better to reframe a negative as a positive. Consider the following examples:

NEGATIVE	POSITIVE REFRAMING
not be bright/intelligent	be dull/unintelligent
not be handsome/pretty	be unattractive
not be hungry	be full
not be nice	be unkind
not be outgoing	be shy
not agree	disagree
not believe	doubt
not enjoy	dislike/detest/loathe
not feel well	feel unwell
not honest	dishonest
not important	unimportant
not like	dislike
not love	hate / have no feeling for
not pay attention to	ignore
not remember	forget

If you must use a negative, try using *never* instead of *not* for a stronger sentence.
*I will ~~not~~ **never** forgive you!* (Strunk 22)

Be Specific, Definite and Concrete

To capture and hold the reader's attention, "prefer the specific to the general, the definite to the vague, the concrete to the abstract" (Strunk 22). Consider the following examples:

GENERAL/VAGUE/ABSTRACT	SPECIFIC/DEFINITE/CONCRETE
Her conversation was boring.	She spoke of subjects of little interest to anyone but herself: her button collection and her passion for polyester clothing.
It was a beautiful evening.	The evening was warm and the sky, lit by a thousand glittering stars.
I would just like to take this opportunity to offer you my gratitude for assisting me in my job search.	Thank you for helping me write up my resumé.

Be Concise

When revising, omit any unnecessary words and sentences.

*He didn't go to work ~~due to the fact that~~ **because** he was sick. ~~He wasn't feeling well at all, so he couldn't go.~~*

Many common and unnecessarily wordy expressions can be made concise. Consider the following examples:

WORDY EXPRESSION	CONCISE EXPRESSION
a large number of	many
a majority of	most
at the present time	now
at this point in time	at this point
due to the fact that	because
during the time that	while
has the ability to	can
has the opportunity to	can
in a strange way	strangely
in order to	to
in some cases	sometimes
in the event that	if
in the near future	soon
it is probable that	probably
it would appear that	apparently
she is a woman who	she
the question as to whether	whether
there is no doubt but that	no doubt / doubtless
this is a topic that is	this topic is
with regard to	regarding

The relative pronouns *whom*, *who* and *that* often can be omitted when they are objects of verbs in relative clauses.

*The car (**that**) I wanted to buy has been sold.*

(For more information on relative pronouns, see page 253.)

Structures such as "who is" and "which is" are often unnecessary.

*Your book report, (**which is**) due this Friday, must be double-spaced.*

A complex idea expressed in a series of independent clauses (sentences) often can be reduced to one sentence. Consider the examples on the next page:

COMPLEX IDEA	SINGLE SENTENCE
"My Husband's Jump" is a great story. It was written by Jessica Grant. She is a Canadian writer.	"My Husband's Jump," by Canadian writer Jessica Grant, is a great story.
They forgot their books. They didn't do their homework. They will probably fail the test. The test is next Monday.	Because they forgot their books and didn't do their homework, they will probably fail the test next Monday.

Vary Sentence Type

There are three basic types of sentence structure: simple, compound and complex.

A paragraph is weak when it contains only one type of sentence.

Consider the following paragraph:

> "The Woman Who Talked to Horses" is an interesting story, *and* I enjoyed it very much. A racehorse owner is having difficulty with his horses, *so* he consults a woman who claims she can talk to them. The man and the woman discuss the horses, *but* they cannot agree on a price. The man dislikes the woman, *and* the woman dislikes the man. She decides not to help him, *so* he is left on his own to solve his problem.

The paragraph is a series of five compound sentences: two independent clauses joined by a coordinate conjunction (*and*, *so*, *but*). To improve paragraphs of this type, rewrite them using a variety of sentence types.

(For more information on sentence structure, see pages 207–211.)

Respect Parallel Construction

Expressions of similar content and function should be expressed in similar form: they should respect the principle of parallel construction (Strunk 26). Consider the following example:

NON-PARALLEL CONSTRUCTION	PARALLEL CONSTRUCTION
As a child, I was the centre of my parents' world; now, my parents are central to me.	As a child, I was the centre of my parents' world; now, they are the centre of mine.

Parallel construction is required when using *correlative conjunctions*—pairs of words that are used to link words together. Examples of correlative conjunctions include the following: *as … as, both … and, either … or, neither … nor, not only … but also, whether … or*, and *first, … second, … third, …*

Consider the following examples of correlative conjunctions:

NON-PARALLEL CONSTRUCTION	PARALLEL CONSTRUCTION
My essay isn't *as good as* the essay you wrote.	My essay isn't *as good as* your essay.
Both the young *and* old people will enjoy the performance.	*Both* the young *and* the old will enjoy the performance.
You may have *either* a cup of coffee *or* tea.	You may have *either* a cup of coffee *or* a cup of tea.
I want *neither* a piece of steak *nor* fish.	I want *neither* steak *nor* fish.
He is *not only* nice *but also* looks good.	He is *not only* nice *but also* handsome.
She doesn't know *whether* to hate *or* love him.	She doesn't know *whether* to hate him *or* to love him.
First, you stole the money; *second*, you are a liar.	*First*, you stole the money; *second*, you told a lie.

(For more information on correcting faulty parallelism, see page 270.)

Keep Related Words Together

In a sentence, a subject should not be separated from the main verb by a phrase or clause that can be placed at the beginning.
*The teacher, **in the first course**, distributed the course plan.* ➡ ***In the first course**, the teacher distributed the course plan.*

A relative pronoun should come immediately after its antecedent.
*They completed the **homework** on the short story **that** their teacher assigned.* ➡ *They completed the **homework that** their teacher assigned on the short story.*
*This is **Kevin**, a friend of my brother's, **who** won an Olympic medal.* ➡ *This is **Kevin**, **who** won an Olympic medal. He is a friend of my brother's.*

Modifiers should be placed next to the words they modify.
*We **only** have **ten** minutes.* ➡ *We have **only ten** minutes.*
*The prime minister will hold a **press conference** later this morning, to which only a few reporters have been invited, **to respond to allegations of wrongdoing**.* ➡ *Later this morning, the prime minister will hold a **press conference to respond to allegations of wrongdoing**. Only a few reporters have been invited.*

Pinpoint

Each of the sentences below violates one of the seven tenets of good writing style: 1) use the active voice; 2) be positive; 3) be specific, definite and concrete; 4) be concise; 5) vary sentence type; 6) respect parallel construction; and 7) keep related words together. For each sentence, indicate the number of the tenet violated and suggest a correction in the space provided.

1. First, you should apologize; second, leave.

Tenet: _____   Correction: _____

2. He does not feel well.

Tenet: _____   Correction: _____

3. He is respected by her.

Tenet: _____   Correction: _____

4. He's retiring in the near future.

Tenet: _____   Correction: _____

5. I don't believe you are telling me the truth.

Tenet: _____   Correction: _____

6. My father and mother, every weekend, go golfing.

Tenet: _____   Correction: _____

7. My teacher isn't as demanding as the teacher you have.

Tenet: _____   Correction: _____

8. She's short.

Tenet: _____   Correction: _____

9. The professor is a man who likes to read novels.

Tenet: _____   Correction: _____

10. This is a difficult exercise because there are many possible answers to each question. My writing style needs work since I have never studied this topic before. I will do all the exercises even though it will take me a lot of time to complete them.

Tenet: _____   Correction: _____

_____

_____

_____

COMPANION
web+

Now that you have pin-pointed your current level of understanding of the tenets of writing style, complete related exercises on the Companion Website for practice and instant feedback.

Chart Ⓐ Common Information Question Words

INFORMATION QUESTION WORDS	EXAMPLES
Who	*Who* did Mary ask to the prom? Mary asked *Jason*. *Who* saw Jason at the prom? *Jason's brother* saw him.
What	*What* do you want for lunch? I want *chicken*. *What* was happening out there? *Two men were fighting*.
Where	*Where* do they live? They live *in Ottawa*.
When	*When* do you leave for South America? We leave *at the end of the month*.
Why	*Why* do you study so often? Because *I want to get good marks*.
Whose	*Whose book* is that? That's *Anna's book*.
Which	*Which* shirt will you buy? I will buy *the brown shirt*, not the green shirt.
How	*How* does she get such good marks? *She studies every day*.
How far	*How far* is Montreal from Toronto? It is *about 600 km*.
How much/many	*How much* money do you have with you? I have *about twenty dollars*. *How many* books did he buy? He bought *eleven books*.
How long	*How long* is the movie? It is *about two hours*.
How often	*How often* do you go to the supermarket? *About once a week*.

Note:
- *Who* and *what* can be used as subjects or objects:
  Who did you see? (object) *Who* saw you? (subject)
  What do you want? (object) *What* is that? (subject)
- *Whom* is used as an object in formal English:
  Whom did you see?
- *How much* is used with uncountable nouns and *how many* is used with countable nouns:
  How much coffee is left? (Coffee, a liquid, is uncountable.)
  How many cups of coffee have you had today? (Cups are countable.)

Chart B Common Irregular Verbs

The following verb chart lists 100 common irregular verbs:

BASE FORM	SIMPLE PAST	PAST PARTICIPLE	BASE FORM	SIMPLE PAST	PAST PARTICIPLE
be	was, were	been	find	found	found
become	became	become	fit	fit	fit
begin	began	begun	fly	flew	flown
bend	bent	bent	forbid	forbade	forbidden
bet	bet	bet	forget	forgot	forgotten
bite	bit	bitten	forgive	forgave	forgiven
bleed	bled	bled	freeze	froze	frozen
blow	blew	blown	get	got	gotten
break	broke	broken	give	gave	given
bring	brought	brought	go	went	gone
build	built	built	grow	grew	grown
burst	burst	burst	hang	hung	hung
buy	bought	bought	have	had	had
catch	caught	caught	hear	heard	heard
choose	chose	chosen	hide	hid	hidden
come	came	come	hit	hit	hit
cost	cost	cost	hold	held	held
cut	cut	cut	hurt	hurt	hurt
deal	dealt	dealt	keep	kept	kept
dig	dug	dug	know	knew	known
do	did	done	lay	laid	laid
draw	drew	drawn	lead	led	led
drink	drank	drunk	leave	left	left
drive	drove	driven	lend	lent	lent
eat	ate	eaten	let	let	let
fall	fell	fallen	lie	lay	lain
feed	fed	fed	light	lit	lit
feel	felt	felt	lose	lost	lost
fight	fought	fought	make	made	made

BASE FORM	SIMPLE PAST	PAST PARTICIPLE	BASE FORM	SIMPLE PAST	PAST PARTICIPLE
mean	meant	meant	sleep	slept	slept
meet	met	met	slide	slid	slid
pay	paid	paid	speak	spoke	spoken
put	put	put	spend	spent	spent
quit	quit	quit	stand	stood	stood
read	read	read	steal	stole	stolen
ride	rode	ridden	swim	swam	swum
ring	rang	rung	swing	swung	swung
rise	rose	risen	take	took	taken
run	ran	run	teach	taught	taught
say	said	said	tear	tore	torn
see	saw	seen	tell	told	told
seek	sought	sought	think	thought	thought
sell	sold	sold	throw	threw	thrown
send	sent	sent	understand	understood	understood
shake	shook	shaken	wake	woke	woken
shoot	shot	shot	wear	wore	worn
show	showed	shown	win	won	won
shut	shut	shut	wind	wound	wound
sing	sang	sung	withdraw	withdrew	withdrawn
sit	sat	sat	write	wrote	written